Students Won't Be Quiet

Students Won't Be Quiet

Edited by

Satarupa Chakraborty

Pindiga Ambedkar

LeftWord

First published in October 2022
Digital print edition December 2022

LeftWord Books
2254/2A, Shadi Khampur
New Ranjit Nagar
New Delhi 110008
INDIA

LeftWord Books and Vaam Prakashan are imprints of
Naya Rasta Publishers Pvt. Ltd.

leftword.com

ISBN 978-81-953546-3-4 (paperback)
978-93-92018-02-2 (e-book)

Visit website

Contents

STRUGGLES AGAINST AUTHORITARIANISM

STRUGGLES FOR EDUCATION AS A RIGHT

STRUGGLES AGAINST NEO-LIBERAL ASSAULTS ON EDUCATION

Introduction

Satarupa Chakraborty

> No oppressive order could permit the oppressed to begin to question: Why?
>
> Paulo Freire, *Pedagogy of the Oppressed*, 1968

A democracy dies when critical voices are absent. We, in India, are in danger of a silent democracy. Either we let the rulers suffocate our voices or we get the courage to stand up, raise questions, and fight back. *Students Won't Be Quiet* is a book that documents the stories of how students across the country have fought to define our idea of India.

PART 1. THE HOPE OF STRUGGLE

Across the world, democracy is in peril. Systematic attacks have silenced one section of the population after another, with social minorities often the first to be muzzled. The core of this assault has been the attack on critical thought and on the institutions that promote reason. That is why institutions of higher education have been at the centre of the assault by the cruel ruling class.

Higher education in modern society has a dual function: to train professionals to reproduce the system, and advance its goals and promote the ideals of the system. Some of these ideals sit uneasily in the system, ideas of equality – for instance – are uncomfortable in a system that widens the gap between classes. It is because universities transmit society's values that they become a repository of the critical intellectual, whether amongst the teaching faculty or amongst the students. Due to this dual function of higher education, Indian universities and colleges continue to promote critical thinking and many teaching faculty members and students guard the boundaries of reason, dissent, and innovation when these are challenged.

Students Won't Be Quiet is a testimony to our times that reflects: (a) the nature of the State's assaults on the country's critical voices and (b) the way young people are resisting them. It contains the voices of thousands of students, their aspirations, and their struggles. It records some historic student movements, which began with issues at the local level but became national issues. Each of the struggles documented in this book is fought on two levels, simultaneously separate yet integrated – they raise the immediate demands of the students, and they fight to keep Indian democracy alive. At the heart of these struggles is the fight to defend the inheritance of the freedom movement and of the early decades of nation-building: democracy, pluralism, secularism, and socialism.

The attack on higher education runs along two axes: (1)the assault on public education with promotion and implementation of privatization in higher education; and (2) the assault on reason and secularism as demonstrated by the promotion of narrow ideas of religious identity and forms of superstition. The first axe has hung over Indian higher education since the period of liberalization began in 1991; the second axe became substantially heavier when the Bharatiya Janata Party (BJP) took power in 2014, and they pushed both the privatization and communalization of education.

This book primarily focuses on the period from 2014 until 2019, during the first term of Prime Minister Narendra Modi-led government. This is a particularly important era because it was then that we saw an overall attack on a range of social groups in India, when opposition to any attack by the ruling party and its allies was stifled. The attack on students is not isolated but part of this large-scale attack on sections of Indian society.

Beginning in 1947, the idea of India has been part of a profound struggle between classes and regions of India. The fight was over whether to advance the country to socialism and deepen secularism or to remain in the grip of the capitalist system with a modest kind of pluralism. Struggles to advance socialism and secularism faced harsh repression, especially during the Emergency in 1975-1977. Since 2014, it feels like we have gone back to a time when we need to fight not to advance the process towards socialism and for genuine secularism, but to defend the Constitution and establish our rights as Indians against the idea of Hindu Rashtra.

Students are not immune from the strains and stresses in society. The conditions of social life have a direct bearing on a student's life. If a majority of the population is heavily exploited, if millions of Indians are hungry and poor, if millions of Indians are deprived of their fundamental rights and dignity, then this context impacts these students, who are the children of these Indians. The existential crisis of rural India and the systematic attacks on the socially marginalized sections set the stage for our social crises. Can students really focus on their studies amid such crises? Every social crisis has an inevitable impact on students.

The students' movement has been historically responding to issues that impact society. The history of the Indian student movement is rooted in the freedom struggle and can be traced back more than 190 years.[1] In 1828, Vivan Derozio, a young

[1] While India's students' movement has made extensive contribution to society and set an example of a resilient fight for decades, there is a dearth of literature on the history of the same. I am fortunate to have come across a publication by the Central Executive Committee of the SFI which produced a remarkable text in 1993, which in a way preserved the legacy and history of the students' struggles in India. The historical details of the events in this piece are drawn primarily from that text. See Tapas Basu, *Probing Into the History of Indian Student Movement* (New Delhi: S.F.I. Central Executive Committee, 1993).

professor at the erstwhile Hindu College at Calcutta (now the Presidency University, Kolkata), along with a group of students, formed the Academic Association. The association focused on spreading scientific consciousness and democratic ideas amongst the people, vociferously attacking superstition, obscurantism, and even the actions of the ruling class through its newspaper *Parthenon,* established in 1829. The association and its newspaper faced attacks from the ruling class, and the group's activities could not be sustained for long. However, with the spread of modern educational institutions adding to the volume of the educated students and youth, various study circles, debating societies, and associations emerged during the nineteenth century, which gradually gave rise to several political activities and an active political culture amongst the students and youth. These societies and associations focused on a range of issues, beginning with confronting British oppression, to spreading consciousness amongst various classes of the masses and advancing scientific temper, to opposing the zamindari (landlordism) system, to developing a sense of protecting the Mother Tongue amongst the people, to creating forums for the open exchange of thoughts and knowledge, and to preparing the educated sections of the people to understanding the idea of nationalism as well as the need to participate in the national liberation movement. Through the several associations, India's educated sections began to reflect on the contemporary challenges in the arena of politics. By the time the Students' Association or the Indian Association was formed in 1875, the conditions were laid for them to deeply influence the student-youth. The association became a common platform for all the students across India to unite. Later, by participating in several movements, the students played a crucial role in the struggles for India's freedom.

Militant student activism was prevalent in both the Swadeshi movement and the boycott movement. In 1905, the students vehemently opposed the partitioning of Bengal. They organized massive strikes in schools and colleges across Bengal. These agitations could not stop the partition, but they channelled the students' anger towards a more passionate and collective movement for the country's freedom.

The student uprisings during the Swadeshi movement laid the foundation for the united and organized students' movement in India. Later, during World War I, students' activities also took shape in Madras and Bombay. The Home-rule movement, demanding local self-government in 1914, encouraged thousands of students to take part in the movement. Later, in 1919, there were student uprisings in Punjab against the Rowlatt Act. In 1920, amid the non-cooperation movement, the students' activities spread across northern India, particularly in Aligarh, Meerut, Banaras, and Allahabad. India's student movement took on a national character as students across provinces began to participate in political activities.

Between 1920 and 1935, the students' activities accelerated. During this period, two cases significantly impacted the building of left-leaning organizations: the Meerut Conspiracy case, which ended with penalizing a range of working-class leaders, and the Lahore Conspiracy Case, which ended with the execution of Bhagat Singh and his comrades.

After the death of Bhagat Singh and others, and with the increasing problems in the social, political, and economic spheres, students' activities intensified with the emergence and spread of various revolutionary organizations across regions. The period between the late 1920s and early 1930s saw remarkable events. The formation of the Young Communist League in 1928-1930 and the All India Students' Federation (AISF) in 1936 were the results of a national upsurge with a large section of the student-youth leaning towards Marxism and socialism. It was from AISF that India's first leaders were born.

While the ruling class, through its political formations, tries to instil fear in the people, struggles of one kind or another inspire us to reject fear for hope. The farmers' movement, the strikes by workers, the movement of oppressed castes and oppressed minorities, the protests by women for dignity and rights, these spectacular struggles have been inspirational. The struggles of the students, and of others, have saved a generation of young people from being imprisoned by hopelessness and cynicism. It is not so dangerous to lose one or two battles, but it is dangerous if young people live with a sense of fear and defeat, and if they cannot speak the truth to power. These struggles are not only essential for today, but they are also central to shaping our future.

These struggles inflict a series of costs on those who wage them. There is the time lost for studies and many academic years lost; many students sacrificed their academic dreams and aspirations. There are the harsh penalties of physical pain from beatings, tear gas, and jail time; there is the ultimate cost when lives are lost in the struggle. These struggles were not simple.

Students have not been mere recipients of oppression; they have been active players in building resistance to it. A robust and revolutionary character has been built in these struggles, harnessed, and elaborated by the organizational forms of the students' unions and the student organizations. This character produces its own revolutionary theory out of the direct experiences of the conditions of society and the fight to defend the right of students to advance social goals.

Our past struggles, which remain alive in the present, lay the foundation for our future. Students participated actively in freeing India from British imperialism. They played a leading role in deepening democracy in the decades of free India. Now, we are fighting to assert the supremacy of our Constitution and for the fundamental rights of all Indians in our country.

PART 2: THE ASSAULTS ON HIGHER EDUCATION AND CONSTITUTION

Since 1991, higher education in India began to face pressure of privatization of education more directly. This was accompanied by the toxicity of communalism pushed by the Hindutva politics. Both these assaults were attacks on our constitution. With the BJP gaining strength in the parliament in 2014 these assaults deepened. There are fresh attacks on the Indian constitution since then, and the authoritarian State is trampling upon all voices of resistance. This situation is causing great distress for the students and youth of India. These assaults on the basic ethos of our constitution are due to the fact that the RSS-BJP never believed in the progressive transformative agenda of the constitution.

Privatization of Education

The push for privatization began during the 1980s when neoliberalism or liberalization appeared on the agenda in India. The National Education Policy, proposed in 1986, sought to shift publicly financed higher education to a donation-driven model with cuts in State subsidies for education. In 1994, the World Trade Organization (WTO) and the General Agreement on Trade in Services (GATS)-led reforms attempted to privatize education globally. These reforms were met with strong resistance in most parts of the world. In India, *A Policy Framework for Reforms in Education*, often dubbed as the 'Birla-Ambani report of 2000', encouraged by the BJP government, suggested an increase in fees to generate profit from higher education as well as a ban on political activities on campus. The report drew substantial criticism and resistance, which meant that the government could not implement it. Both the BJP and the Indian National Congress (INC) tried to meet their promises to the World Bank. Though the INC, during both of the United Progressive Alliance (UPA) governments (2004-2008 and 2008-2014), could not implement it due to pressure from the Left (in parliament by the Left parties and on the streets by the students and teachers).

The BJP-led National Democratic Alliance governments (NDA) (1999-2004, 2014-2019, 2019-), however, drove this agenda with the passage of the *Model Act for all Universities* (MAU, 2003) and the National Education Policy (NEP, 2020). MAU argued for creating a uniform framework for universities, flexibility for the administration, and responsiveness to the changing conditions of the labour market, while the NEP (2020) called for full-scale privatization of education.[2] The BJP-led government wants to create a cohort of students who will be divorced from the socio-economic reality of their own country. Due to the many fissures in the country, of diversity in a positive way and hierarchy in a negative way, this has proved very difficult for the government. If the government were to succeed in shrinking the pool of those who attend higher education, those left out would become a politically conscious section that would challenge the status quo. Both the diversity and hierarchy and the threat of further alienation prevent wholesale privatization.

Subversion of Constitution

The BJP-led government has pushed an agenda to undermine the secular fabric of the country. This agenda has been mirrored in educational institutions, with Hindutva intellectuals driving an educational policy favouring a narrow interpretation of Indian history and Indian society. Over the past few years, we have experienced this in a magnified way through the abrogation of Article 370 of the Constitution and through the drive to adopt Citizenship (Amendment) Act, 2019 (CAA). Both the abrogation and CAA brought together the campus struggles against the communalization of education.

The BJP revoked Article 370 in 2019 and subordinated Kashmir

[2] Vijender Sharma, 'UPA's Agenda of Academic 'Reforms' Facilitating Trade in Higher Education,' *Social Scientist*, 38, No. 9/12 (2010): pp. 91-127.

to the Central government.[3] This built upon decades of alienation inside Kashmir. Kashmiri students have found it challenging to lead their everyday lives, let alone study. Aqib Yusuf, a law student at University of Kashmir and a student activist, explained the situation:

> Students feel that they are in jail rather than in an educational institution. Students' organizations are entirely banned here. It becomes tough for the students to raise their concerns. Imagine a student getting caught by the armed forces while going to attend a class under the pretext of stone-pelting by the extremists! The irregular system, as well as constant conflict, pushed many students into depression as well as other mental health issues. Due to the internet gag in the aftermath of the abrogation of Article 370, communications blackouts rendered the student community helpless, isolated, and wayward. The students who did not live at home could not communicate with their families. There were deaths at home, and students who lived on or near campus did not know about them for days. Due to the internet gag [order] post 5 August 2019, I couldn't download the required study material or watch the online videos. After twenty-five days, I reached Srinagar somehow, and from there, I went to Delhi. The communication blackout continued for almost eight months. I had to find a way to continue my studies. As the internet is part and parcel of today's learning, I needed access to materials that I could not access in Kashmir. Depriving people of their right to information has proven to be destructive. What is further alarming is how communications' blackouts have taken a heavy toll on the mental health of the student community. It

3 Laxmi Murthy and Geeta Seshu, 'Silence in the Valley: Kashmiri Media After the Abrogation of Article 370,' *Economic and Political Weekly*, 54, No. 43, (2019), https://www.epw.in/engage/article/silence-valley-kashmiri-media-after-abrogation.

is hard to estimate the number of affected people in a society where talking about mental health has traditionally not been encouraged. But the frustration amongst the Kashmiri youth today has undoubtedly increased. Besides, there are no jobs for the youth in the government sector. On the other hand, the conflict does not allow them to set up their own business or participate in other business undertakings. This kind of pressure pushes them to pick up guns or die by suicide.

After the abrogation of Article 370, the BJP government pushed through CAA, which undermined the secular foundation of Indian nationality. The first protests against CAA, the National Register of Citizens (NRC), and the National Population Register (NPR) came from students mainly at the Aligarh Muslim University (AMU) and Jamia Millia Islamia (JMI), both schools with predominantly Muslim populations. On 15 December 2019, the State cracked down on the JMI protests.[4] This shook all of us because we had never experienced or even seen such a brutal crackdown. Simeen Anjum, a fine arts student at JMI, told me about her experiences on the campus during that period:

> It was just another protest for us. We had all gathered for a protest march against the Citizenship Amendment Bill. I remember being at the back of the crowd, hearing loud shots, and then suddenly everyone was running back to the campus. My friend and I initially took shelter in a corner, trying to make sense of what was happening. We were horrified and confused. We ran inside the campus, went immediately to the campus canteen, and tried to call other friends to figure out what had gone wrong and what we should do. In the moments following, we saw more students running inside the campus towards the buildings and policemen shooting smoke guns

[4] Nehal Ahmed, *Nothing Will Be Forgotten: From Jamia to Shaheen Bagh*, (New Delhi: LeftWord Books, 2022).

> and beating up anyone they could get their hands on. The visual in itself was horrifying. I couldn't believe what I was witnessing. It seemed like a scene from a violent movie, except it was happening in front of me in my place of education. To escape the situation, I ran with my friend, and we climbed over the boundary wall to get out. While we managed to find shelter in the neighbouring colony of the campus, the whole night was filled with SOS calls from friends trapped in different places on campus and pleas to be rescued and taken to hospitals. I remember feeling numb and cold. Amid all the disturbing visuals and calls for help, I remember that my mind was constantly going back to a picture of a close friend. He was hit on his head by the police. He was stuck in the hostel with other students, bleeding and requiring medical attention, but could not leave as the police were still attacking students. The police baton charged the students indiscriminately. They shouted communal slurs while they beat them.

The campus became a war zone. Students were treated as enemies, as 'anti-national', in the words of the ruling party.

From the protests by JMI students emerged the great Shaheen Bagh agitation – a protest that was an exemplary movement of our time. The BJP did not leave a single stone unturned in dividing the people of India through the instigation of religious sentiments. However, such attempts faced massive counter-protests from the students. The solidarity from the entire students' community, except Akhil Bharatiya Vidyarthi Parishad (ABVP) – the student wing of the Rashtriya Swayamsevak Sangh (RSS), particularly after the attack on JMI students, was remarkable. These protests carry the story of pain and hope.

So, if a student is not affected by these conditions, it means that they adapted to the requirements of neoliberal capitalism that seeks to produce only consumers and not critical intellectuals. Indian students, by and large, defied this conditioning.

This book demonstrates the wide range of issues around which the students were fighting, from combating neoliberal capitalism, to fighting caste and gender-based discrimination and violence, to safeguarding democracy, to opposing political appointments at institutions, and to vigorously countering the Hindu right-wing's attack on the universities. Students showed great strength and compassion. Inspired by critical slogans, they came out onto the streets frequently; they defied the orders of the rulers by taking several risks. They are never quiet. Thus, they became 'troublemakers' in the eyes of the ruling class. History, however, is a witness to the fact that the 'troublemakers' are, in fact, nation builders.

Troublemakers or anti-nationals?

I recall the students' protests in 2015. The Jawaharlal Nehru Students' Union (JNUSU) called for a protest at the central office of the University Grants Commission (UGC) in New Delhi. The protest demanded immediate withdrawal of the UGC's decision to scrap the research fellowship (the UGC non-National Eligibility Test (NET) fellowship). Students from various universities, such as Delhi University (DU), JMI, and AMU, joined the call. In response to the authoritarian attitude of the Ministry of Education (MoE, formerly the Ministry of Human Resource Development (MHRD)) and the UGC, the students started a round-the-clock sit-in protest at the gate of UGC headquarters, which became the 'Occupy UGC' movement. The ninety-day-long movement in Delhi lit a fire in students' unions nationwide. They, along with progressive organizations, held protests outside the state offices of the UGC across the country. The students knew that without a fellowship a large number of research scholars would be forced to leave higher education; higher education would become an exclusive preserve of the rich. The agitation demanded the expansion of the fellowships to state-level universities and an increase in the fellowship amount. On the seventeenth day of the protest, students marched to the MHRD office at Shastri Bhawan. Smriti Irani, the then HRD minister, was forced to leave her office and answer the students. The protest drew public support. A bank employee whose office was located near the protest site saw the students at Occupy UGC. He talked to us and then told us that he had a son who wanted to go to a university and earn a PhD. The father became a strong supporter of the movement. The decision to scrap the non-NET fellowship was reversed in the face of the large-scale protest. It was a significant victory for the students. The government was on the backfoot.

Around this time, on 14 December 2015, Prime Minister Narendra Modi went to the World Trade Organization meeting in Nairobi. Students from various cities came to New Delhi and launched a week-long agitation to resist the agreement to include education under GATS. This agitation, and the fight for non-NET fellowships, ignited the discourse on the need for public funding of higher education and the need to prevent the commodification of education.

Unable to overpower the students and change the discourse, the government reverted to propaganda, pushing the Hindutva agenda, and shifting the debate from public funds for higher education to saffron 'nationalism'. Mob violence became their currency. This shift occurred alongside a general deepening of communal rhetoric and practice by BJP and its allies against Muslims, Dalits, and other social minorities. Mob-lynchings were carried out against those who were 'accused' of possessing or consuming beef. Minorities were targetted with accusations of 'love jihad' (Muslim men and Hindu women involved in interreligious relationships). The framework suggested that Hindutva was the true nationalism, and everything else – especially the secularism pushed by the students – was anti-national. During those protests, the BJP championed the narrative that it was the only force that genuinely represented India, and therefore, anyone who criticized BJP became an anti-Indian. The students who protested the various policies of BJP had to face the brunt of this aggressive Hindutva nationalism. The students knew that if the RSS-BJP propaganda of one culture, one tradition, responsible for the mob violence, was normalized in our society, it would have marked the death of plurality, diversity, tolerance, and hence – the end of democracy.

The government's discourse to delegitimize the students' protests was potent: students were troublemakers, anti-national, and were wasting the money of tax-paying citizens with their antics. This discourse attempted to break up the public support for the students through an attempt to paint public institutions as breeding grounds for anti-nationals, which wasted public resources. Many student activists were arrested on trumped-up charges of sedition. They argued that students were supposed to study and not protest. There was a concerted effort to depoliticize the campuses through intimidation.

The deliberate campaign had a deeper meaning; it was and remains today a class assault that the government launched against the students. The Constitution mandates that the government create publicly funded institutions to accommodate students from a range of socio-economic backgrounds. This mandate forces the campuses to become diverse, which in turn germinates struggles to expand democracy further. Diversity and democracy on a university campus challenge the capitalist social order and the authoritarian political dispensation. If the ruling class can defame student protest and paint student activists as 'anti-national' and 'seditious', it would be easy for them to erode the democratic ethos of the country. It is against this anti-democratic rule that the students will not be quiet.

PART 3: VECTORS OF STRUGGLE

Around the protests against privatization and communalization of education, three main vectors of struggle developed on campuses in the period after 2014: fights against caste, fights against patriarchy, and fights against irrationality.

Students Against Caste

The Constitution tasks Indian governments with the abolishment of caste discrimination. Over the years, the State has opted for affirmative action and positive discrimination policies to enable the representation of Scheduled Castes (SCs) and Scheduled Tribes (STs) in educational institutions and in government employment. These policies were put in place to undermine centuries of discrimination and humiliation.

Education is typically seen as a powerful instrument to address inequalities and indignities in modern society. That is why movements in colonial India demanded schools for oppressed castes and girls to overcome the denial of education to marginalized sections of society. Although decreed by law, the reservation policy has not been effectively implemented. In his essay, Subhankar Chakraborty looks at the data from the country's premier science and technology institutions, only to find systematic caste-based bias. For years, non-fulfilment of the reservation policy was repeated in the country's best institutions of higher learning and research, making India's higher educational institutions a place only for the social elites. The author exposes the politics of 'candidates – not found suitable' a politics that ensures non-implementation of the reservation policy within academic institutions, and thus maintains the chain of caste bias at all levels.

The caste-bias in the society is manifested in open discrimination in higher educational institutions across India. This bias and its effects were more visible during the anti-reservation movement after the Mandal Commission Report was announced as accepted in the parliament in 1990.[5] Payal Tadvi, Rohith Vemula,

[5] There have been a series of protests on the implementation of reservation policy in students' admission to higher educational institutions for decades. During the 1980s and later in 2006 debates picked up around the Mandal Commission Report to implement 27 per cent reservations for the Other

and many more were victims of 'institutional murder' as they faced discrimination on campuses, whose administrations exacerbated the hierarchies of oppression. Bal Mukund Bharati, a Dalit student in Uttar Pradesh, heard remarks such as: 'How can Chamars become doctors? You have only come here because of quotas. You cannot go ahead'. Bharati was the first Dalit student from his village to attend university; through a gruelling entrance examination, he was the first to reach the All-India Institute of Medical Sciences (AIIMS). He died by suicide in 2010.[6] Payal Tadvi, Rohith Vemula, and Bal Mukund Bharati died in institutions that had moved toward privatization and communalization, institutions that had begun to shape themselves in the image of the dominant castes and the wealthy, and that had started to treat students from oppressed castes and from working-class and peasant families as interlopers, as outsiders.

Students have struggled against the caste-ridden campus environment for decades. In addition, there was renewed interest in the works of Dr B.R. Ambedkar and other such political and social reformers. This interest led students to find ways to counter

Backward Classes (OBCs) in employment and higher education. Around the same time, the anti-reservation student protests also witnessed a great force in opposing the already mandated reservation for SCs and STs. The RSS took an open position against the reservation policy. The members of the BJP and the soft-Hindu section of the INC advocated the caste Hindu positions and supported the preservation of upper-caste dominance in education and employment sector. This anti-reservation agitation gained some currency amongst the aspiring students-youth from the forward caste groups. The agitation against reservation thoroughly neglected the historical, social, cultural, and economic deprivation as well as marginalization, which held the centuries-old caste system continuously perpetuating various forms of oppression. However, the Left at that time took an important position, and it raised the demand for a proportional increase of seats in students' admission. The Left emphatically supported the reservation for the SCs and STs, and extended nuanced support for OBCs Reservations. See: Prakash Karat, 'Protect Unity With Social Justice,' Commuist Party of India (Marxist), https://cpim.org/content/obc-reservations.

6 D. Karthikeyan, 'Suicide By Dalit Students in 4 Years,' *The Hindu*, 5 September 2011, https://www.thehindu.com/news/cities/Madurai/suicide-by-dalit-students- in-4-years/article2425965.ece. e

the dominant caste hegemony on campuses and to struggle for the rights of marginalized students. In this context, the UGC provided funds to set up institutes to study social exclusion in India. A new discourse on caste oppression arrived on university campuses by the 2000s.

The approach of the ruling class is not to grant equal access and social status to everyone. They want to manipulate sections of the marginalized communities to come into the fold of the Hindu religion to establish a majoritarian block of Hindus where the dominant caste governs. Privatization of education denies the right of equal access and violates the reservation policy, thus, ensuring the hegemony of the social elites in the institutions. The period between 2014 and 2019, nevertheless, is worth observing as the attacks intensified on two levels: (a) by attempts to make education accessible for the few and (b) by the aggressive projection of the Hindu right ideology upon institutions and provisions that had made some advances towards the social justice project.

It was clear to students that the attack on fellowships and the increase in fees were directly linked to pushing out students from poorer backgrounds, typically from oppressed caste communities. In 2016, a UGC gazette introduced massive seat reductions in the research courses at universities, which would have undermined the entire reservation policy. It also replaced the progressive admission policy in universities like Jawaharlal Nehru University (JNU), where important measures were adopted to address socio-economic and regional deprivation.

Awareness of the direction of government policy at public universities shaped the protests. The students' movement around social justice was imbued with fresh energy after 2016. Through political and legal battles, the students fought tooth and nail against UGC gazette changes. The Students' Federation of India (SFI) petition against the 2016 UGC gazette in the Delhi High Court secured a massive victory in favour of the students where the provisions of the UGC gazette were pronounced as 'arbitrary and unconstitutional' by the court.[7] We saw joint actions by the Left and democratic organizations on the streets, including Ambedkarite organizations. The University of Hyderabad (UoH) was at the centre of setting such an example not only with the joint political movements but also by forging electoral alliances. Three young scholars and activists from UoH, Kuldeep Singh Nagi, Zuhail K.P., and Suddhabrata Deb Roy, explained this perspective in their joint essay in this book.

The January 2016 institutional murder of Rohith Vemula, a Research Scholar at UoH, anguished the student community across the country. Consequently, the 'Justice for Rohith Vemula' campaign took shape and facilitated joint movements against corporate-Hindutva politics. The term 'institutional murder' surfaced with great force for the first time. The movement demanded a 'Rohith Act' to be institutionalized within institutions of higher learning to check discrimination.

Student organizations raise issues of caste discrimination, oppression, etc., on campuses. Where students' unions were not possible, students formed study circles to engage with the Dalit-Adivasi literature and sharpen their understanding. University administrations, notably those with closer BJP ties, have tried to shut down these study circles. The key example is the attack on the Ambedkar-Periyar Study Circle (APSC) at the Indian Institute of Technology Madras (IIT-M). The new anti-caste discourse on campuses has moved us away from shame and hopelessness to activism. Dontha Prashanth's voice reflects this; before he became part of the Ambedkarite movement, he used to be hesitant to raise his voice confidently on the issues of caste oppression. As he became an Ambedkar Students' Association (ASA) activist, it changed. He reflected the worry that under conditions of continuous subjugation and precarity, there was less ability for an

[7] *Students Federation of India & Ors. vs Union Of India & Ors.*, Judgement pronounced by Delhi High Court on 1 October 2018. https://indiankanoon.org/doc/22644304/

individual in vulnerable conditions to keep the fight constant.

Institutional murders have become commonplace. Each of these deaths is caused by structural inequality and the heartlessness of the powerful. It is this structural inequality that the progressive and democratic students are fighting, i.e., a struggle for total annihilation of caste. Sheetal Sathe's poem for Rohith Vemula offers a sense of the harshness and the hope:

> Brahmanism is being fostered even at the doorstep of education and in the house of knowledge.
>
> Rohith is gone, a Dalit is gone, this Democracy is dying . . .
>
> . . . With our full strength, with our full courage, we will continue this struggle
>
> (We) will annihilate the Caste, (we) will burry Manu, (we) will finish this supremacy
>
> Dalits joined, Students joined to keep this democracy alive . . . [8]

Students Against Patriarchy

During my student days at the UoH and then at JNU, I experienced a considerable cultural shock. I watched young, independent, assertive women argue vociferously; I watched them wear clothes of their choice and study a range of subjects. I watched them study all night long at the library, having discussions in the dorms or tea shops until late into the night, spending time with male friends, and raising loud slogans at rallies. These experiences cannot be generalized. However, those were new to me, new to the kind of girl I had been and to the woman I was supposed to become. Life on university campuses gives women like me the opportunity to experience equality and strive to bring equality into the world.

On 31 July 2013, an incident at JNU, during the admissions

[8] Translation from the original Marathi song by Tushar Kamble and edited by Ravi Kadam.

process, shocked the university community. A male student from the School of Languages, Literature, and Cultural Studies attacked his classmate with sharp weapons for refusing to accept his 'love'. He then drank poison and killed himself. Fortunately, the woman, after a long, painful battle, survived. I joined JNU that day. By dinner time, the entire campus was agitated. The student activists from the Left organizations went door-to-door in all hostels across the campus. They engaged with the students on the deterioration of democratic and gender-just values; they collected mass signatures in support of holding a University General Body Meeting (UGBM) about the missing rigour on campus regarding gender sensitization drives that had been frequent before. All night, the UGBM debated issues: patriarchy, sexism, women's security, and the growing insensitivity on the campus, and adopted resolutions on escalating the gender sensitization drives and struggles for gender justice. The campus channelled the anger into a collective concern to bring back the public discourse on gender through programs, campaigns, and a plan of action for the Gender Sensitization Committee Against Sexual Harassment (GSCASH).

In fact, JNU was the first university to have GSCASH. After a prolonged struggle by the students, aided by the Supreme Court's Vishaka Judgment and with support from a section of teaching faculty, GSCASH was formally created in 1999. It adopted its constitution and evolved into a tremendously effective body, which even became a model institution for higher educational institutions across India. The mandate for GSCASH was not only for it to operate as a redressal cell but, at the very core of it, had the objective of gender sensitization, instilling a sense of equality in the minds of the entire university community.

The first sensitization program by GSCASH that I attended opened my eyes; it broke apart many beliefs that I had proudly carried until then and educated me about the basics of patriarchy and what constitutes sexual harassment. In the absence of gender discourse in most of our family conversations or at our colleges and peer groups, we never learned the basic principles of equality. We learned nothing about questions of consent, rights, or sexism. No one taught us about the objectification of women's bodies, about how stalking is not an expression of love, and what it means for a woman to be under the control and protection of a man in society. With the exposure to the GSCASH sensitization program, I became educated like the hundreds of men and women who had the opportunity to study in a university like ours.

This, however, does not mean that everything is perfect in such universities. When an incident of this nature, such as the 31 July incident, occurs in a university that has supported a great degree of progressive thinking and sensitization for decades, it points out deeper problems. These are the times when politically charged campuses like JNU paused for a while and reflected on how deep the roots of patriarchy are and how well we can battle them! With many forms of patriarchy existing and operating in all spheres of capitalist society, gender sensitization is never a thing that is achieved once and for all; it is a process that needs sincere efforts in continuing to flag the tendencies of patriarchy within our society and continuing to confront it by imparting rigorous education on breaking the patriarchal social order.

Through the voices of this book's contributors, whether it is Mineshi Mishra's account from Banaras Hindu University (BHU), or Sangita Das' report from Assam, or the struggle by Kavya M. and Vidya T. Appukkuttan from Pondicherry University (PU), or Gitosri Sarkar's narration from Jadavpur University (JU), a clear fact emerges that patriarchy in the larger society has a strong influence upon institutions of higher education and learning. From the students' accounts across various campuses, it is evident that in Indian universities, multiple forms of gender discrimination, patriarchal violence, and endorsement of feudal values are practised without much debate. For instance, it emerges from the contributors' accounts that there is active reinforcement of patriarchy by imposing a particular dress code for women, hostel curfew timings, or a specific 'code of conduct' put in place on most Indian campuses. There are also several instances of sexual harassment (some surface, some do not) where girls and women are subjected to patriarchal violence from classmates, professors, partners, or even strangers. This violence receives active or passive support from the administration in most cases. Whenever anyone raises a voice against the patriarchal assaults, instead of acting on the complaints and providing a safe space for the victims/ complainants, the authorities blame them, accusing them of bringing disrepute to the institution and tarnishing its name. This attitude reflects how the authorities, in higher educational institutions, reinforce the feudal and patriarchal mindset that seeks to control women and deny them a voice.

With the extreme right-wing assuming power, gender rights received a fresh attack. While constituting GSCASH across institutions became a national demand over time, the right-wing administrations left no stone unturned in dismantling GSCASH at the few universities, like JNU and UoH, where it existed. As a result, an accused sexual predator, such as JNU professor Atul Johri, against whom eight women students had filed complaints (which was clubbed in a single First Information Report (FIR)), enjoyed impunity, and was promoted to higher positions[9] Due to such insensitive actions by the authority, the democratic space on campus shrunk, and women began to feel unsafe and imprisoned. If an administration indulges hyper-masculine attitudes and condones various forms of patriarchal norms and behaviour by men, such actions simply deny women equal rights to the space for studying. In this book, we hear of voices of women who have faced similar kind of gender-based violence. Whether in a

[9] Anand Mohan J. and Aranya Shankar, 'Sexual harassment allegations against JNU professor: Eight complaints but one FIR, police face protests in Atul Johri case,' *The Indian Express*, 20 March 2018, https://indianexpress.com/article/cities/delhi/sexual-harassment-allegations-against-jnu-professor-eight-complaints-but-one-fir-police-face-protests-in-atul-kumar-johri-case-5103870/.

small state college in Assam or on the prestigious BHU campus premises, the gender divide and discrimination in public spaces is increasingly deepened, stereotypical understanding rules, misogynistic attitudes are frequent, and the infantilization of women is common. When these go unchallenged, they lead to the manifestation of gender-based violence.

Within a highly unequal power structure, we find only a few examples of larger resistance against discrimination and patriarchal assault, but even these few instances are powerful. A girl, or a woman, is expected to remain silent even when there is an incident of sexual harassment. Defying this expectation, whenever a victim or a survivor of patriarchal violence attempts to confront it, that confrontation immediately invites character assassination and moral policing, as evidenced in this book. In the cases of sexual harassment, the onus of horrible violence often falls on the shoulders of the victim or the survivor. The moral code of our society is so profoundly bankrupt that it never imagines a woman in a role to confront societal norms. 'Silent' and a 'soft-spoken nature' are benchmarks attributed to 'good' girls or women, thus assuming that an outspoken or rebellious woman is never a 'good girl/woman'. They are often called names such as 'prostitutes' or even certified as characterless and arrogant as they confront feudal and patriarchal morality.

A movement for gender rights and justice by women potentially poses a threat to those insecure about the caesura of their power. Therefore, they attempt to defame such a movement.

During the hype of Narendra Modi and the BJP's '*Beti Bachao, Beti Padhao*' (Save the daughter, Educate the daughter) campaign, the BHU women directly confronted the farcical campaign. Their counter slogan was '*Bachegi Beti, Tabhi Toh Padhegi Beti*' (Only when a daughter is safe, she'll be able to study). They led the movement against patriarchal assaults, holding the system accountable for perpetually giving space to and shielding sexual harassers. Similarly, when Shubh Laxmi from Assam came out in public, narrating the horrific experiences she endured, it was discomforting for the ruling party and the patriarchs. It brought to light the regular occurrences of sexual harassment incidents in the state and gave women confidence, knowing they were not alone. It also made a statement that silence can only ensure deteriorating and harsher conditions for women. Therefore, even if the fight is hard, it is worth fighting. When young women, such as Gitorsri of JU and a hundred other students, refused to accept their Gold Medals or degrees as a protest against gender-based violence at the convocation ceremony and thus advanced the struggle for gender justice, it gave courage and strength to everyone, reigniting hope and faith that our collective resistance will change our society. Jishnu E.N.'s report on Kavya's and Vidya's struggle at PU, from campus to courtroom, is evidence that a movement for gender justice not only brings a gender discourse to the campus, but also strengthens other democratic struggles and voices on campus. PU is now one such campus that is leading many vital battles.

Through continuous individual and collective struggles, women are holding patriarchy by its collar every day. The more we create space for such struggles on our campuses, the more democratic and forward-looking our society can become. If our universities fail to instil a sense of equality through institutional measures and democratic actions, then it defeats the purpose of the existence of an institution of higher education. The women of India refuse to let universities and institutions defeat the idea of gender justice, and the idea of an institution of higher learning.

Students Against Unreason

Struggles for reason, science, and critical thought shape India's modern period. Evidence of educated youths confronting obscurantism and irrationality can be found during colonial rule. There is now a strange combination at work: embracing technological advancements that celebrate capitalism alongside promoting non-science, mythical thinking, and obscurantism.

There was a time when India was led by Prime Minister Jawaharlal Nehru, who called science a way of life; now, we have a Prime Minister who publicly hails non-scientific beliefs and irrational positions. The outrageousness of the anti-science views (like drinking urine) pushed by the government during the pandemic was only a more exaggerated version of what has been going on since 2014. Part of the anti-science thrust has been the attempt to change the syllabi of higher educational institutions to replace facts with myths, to rehabilitate traitors, and to undermine social reformers. The resistance to the assault on scientific temper is not only needed to safeguard science but also to safeguard society.

Such assaults on the ideological plane are now combined with the physical assaults by the Hindutva mob, the hooligans, the ABVP, and the institutional authorities. In the recent past, such attacks were thwarted by the collective effort of the students and teachers at various universities. By February-March 2016, JNU was the epicentre of many of these attacks. In March, a discussion on 'The Life and Writings of Bhagat Singh' to mark Bhagat Singh's martyrdom day was organized by a student group at DU. When retired JNU Professor Chaman Lal, one of the most distinguished scholars on Bhagat Singh, was invited to speak, ABVP activists disrupted the event.[10] In August 2016, Amnesty International India organized an event titled *Broken Families,* based on their report *Denied: Failures in accountability for human rights violations by security force personnel in Jammu and Kashmir,* published in July 2015; this report documented the human rights violations in Jammu and Kashmir.[11] ABVP leadership attacked the organizers with a police complaint, accusing them with sedition.

[10] Harshita Murarka, 'Ramjas Not Alone, ABVP Has a Legacy of Violence and Vandalism,' *The Quint*, 23 February 2017, https://www.thequint.com/news/politics/delhi-university-ramjas-college-not-alone-abvp-has-history-of-violence-like-rohith-vemula-jnu- kanhaiya-kumar.

[11] Amnesty International India responds to sedition allegations,' Amnesty International, 16 August 2016, https://www.amnestyusa.org/press-releases/amnesty-international-india-responds-to-sedition-allegations/.

In September 2016, an event to honour Mahasweta Devi, after she passed away, was organized by the students and teachers at Central University of Haryana. Their presentation of Devi's critically acclaimed play *Draupadi* was attacked by ABVP members who called the organizers anti-national.[12] At Ramjas College DU, a seminar was attacked by the Hindutva mob led by ABVP, narrated in detail by one of our contributors, Vikas Bhadauria. DU is a classic example of the direct impact of neoliberal policies, both in terms of an assault on the structure of an inclusive education as well as pushing students more towards individualism, and thus distancing them from larger social realities. This provides spaces for the right-wing organizations to show their strength whereas the progressive students' movement face a challenge. Vikas's account narrates some of these aspects in this book.

In contrast, the campuses which historically lacked student activism until recently are showing new possibilities with the emergence of progressive student organizations. Abhinav Surya's article on the attack on the study circle at IIT-M provides a historical account on the advent of alternative politics on a conservative campus. Surya describes the emergence of APSC and their struggles as the result of the dialectical process 'between IIT-M's history of perpetuating conservatism and the rising new currents for change'.

In another chapter, Subin Dennis describes the attack on JNU and the robust response that gained national attention, where every conscious and rational citizen extended their unconditional solidarity for the well-known 'Stand with JNU' movement. The targeting of JNU in 2016 was part of the larger scheme of the RSS-BJP, that aimed to dismount democratic and inclusive institutions which produced critical thinking. JNU as a public university,

[12] Express News Service, 'Play staged by students of Central Univerity of Haryana sparks row, ABVP calls it seditious,' *The Indian Express*, 29 September 2016, https://indianexpress.com/article/india/india-news-india/haryana-university-play-mahasweta-devi-row-sedition-abvp-3055222/.

known for its unique character – offers diversity in research, non-conventional, critical approach to teaching and learning, a culture of mutual coexistence, and encouraged debate and dissent within the institution. It stood out, and became one of the best universities in the country due to these factors. The other important aspect is that, being one of the best universities in India, JNU is accessible to all. This was possible due to the vibrant student movement that fought for every student's rights and it continues to struggle for preserving the idea of a public university, which can produce critical intellectuals. The author makes it clear in his article that through the 'Shut Down JNU' campaign the RSS and its outfits ran the agenda to destroy a model public university, which was built by the struggles, contribution and sacrifice of generations of progressive people.

The common threads that join all these events at various campuses are: (a) the Hindutva assaults, which used an Indian soldier as a symbol of nationalism to simultaneously channel the nationalist sentiment of a larger section of the people, while propagating falsehoods that the students were anti-soldier, and hence, anti-national, and thus seeking to project the RSS and its affiliates as the only nationalist forces; and (b) the attacks on debate and dialogue on the campuses, because debate and dialogue produce critical thinking and 'argumentative' students. Therefore, the RSS was hellbent on creating a class of individuals who would care less about society and its peoples or their fundamental human rights. The attacks were organized so that the Hindutva right-wing could take control of the campuses once they were depoliticized.

The progressive students, however, did not succumb to such attacks. Across the country, at various universities and institutes, students held seminars, cultural events, movie screenings, and open classes. A remarkable development in this period was the academic and political solidarity that was built amongst the students, the teachers, and in a few instances, drew solidarity even from staff members and associations.

The second attack on the higher educational institutions was through corrupt, incompetent, and political appointments of institutional administrators. Vacancies were filled by bypassing all the decision-making bodies of the universities and eliminating the scrutiny of the candidates' knowledge and credits in the subject to ensure that RSS represented the teaching faculty collective of the institutions. This tendency began with the recruitment of the institutional head in the Film and Television Institute of India (FTII) in Pune. The brave resistance by the students is documented in the book through the thoughtful narration of Ameya Vivek Gore.

At the core of every attack is neoliberalism; it is, at times, invisible but always present with immense force to sharpen the attacks. Kadigalla Bhaskar describes the struggle for the Welfare Hostels in the united Andhra Pradesh (from a slightly earlier period), highlighting not only what the students' movement could achieve but also what makes education for the depressed castes and oppressed classes possible. In this book, we also have the jointly authored article by Sandeep Mahato, Gaurav Gharde, and Aravindhan Natarajan from the Tata Institute of Social Sciences (TISS). They exposed how the Modi-led government's reduction of fellowship funds directly hit the poor and marginalized students. They wrote about the historic students' protest at TISS Mumbai demanding fellowships.

We have some publicly funded universities in our country that survived due to the relentless struggles. JNU was defamed as 'anti-national' in 2016; it took much effort from the students, teachers, and pro-constitution and secular-minded people to defend the idea of a university and what a university means for a nation. Many struggles were fought between 2014 and 2019, and they continue. But 2019 was again remarkable when JNU stood up against the fee hike, and its students stated loudly – 'Not an inch back' – unless the proposal for hiked fees was reversed. Aishe Ghosh, and her comrades in struggle, survived the brutal physical attacks by the

Hindutva mob; they stood tall. Her account in the book depicts the resilient struggles that Indian students are fighting in our time. She describes her personal journey to becoming an activist, and how this shaped her into a new individual with a sense of responsibility, empathy, conviction, and spirit to engage in a collective movement to defeat oppression and injustice.

This volume is enriched by the history and stories of the mass movements from two states, Kerala and Himachal Pradesh. While in Kerala, the progressive students' movement fought the pro-neoliberal INC governments, in Himachal Pradesh, the students' movement confronted both the INC and the BJP. In these states, the Left-led students provided an alternative, a different perspective, to create mass movements to counter the ruling class. While the students of these states walked turbulent paths, they successfully organized the students to build up a powerful resistance. Vikram Singh's critical piece offers an opportunity for the progressive and democratic students to reflect on the question whether there is a failure on the part of the progressive movements to galvanize the larger sections of the students into collective mass actions as the core issues of the students are being neglected, which, he argues, provides the impetus for an ideological battle. P.M. Ranjith highlights the impact of neoliberal policies on Kerala's higher education, and the resistance against these policies by the progressive students' movements since 1990. These allow us to think deeply about the nuances of organized students' movements and what such movements could offer to build a better future.

PART 4: INSPIRATION

We are honoured to have Radhika Vemula (mother of Rohith Vemula) and Fatima Nafees (mother of Najeeb Ahmed) speak to us for this book. Radhika Vemula lost her son to caste discrimination at UoH, and Fatima Nafees has been painfully waiting for her son – who disappeared from JNU under mysterious circumstances

– to return home. Their struggles began in seeking justice for their sons, but they became the inspiration for young men and women by setting examples of courage, compassion, solidarity, empathy, and leadership. We hope this book recounts the stories of the struggles that the brave students of India have fought and it provides a stimulus for students now and in the future to join the fight for a better society.

We hope that the stories of Indian students' movement(s) inspire our readers, and such stories are told and re-told. This book is our humble attempt to document the sacrifices made to make our educational institutions and society democratic in their genuine sense. It was both challenging and exciting to edit this volume as the authors and interviewees dealt with multiple issues while sharing their stories and reflections. This, amongst others, posed a great challenge for my co-editor Pindiga Ambedkar and me to thematically organize the book. However, we hope that, in some sense, we did justice to the essays and interviews by organizing them into five sections - separate yet integrated.

In the process of editing this volume, our ardent companion Deborah Veneziale (a communist internationalist living in Italy), who read the manuscript, meticulously penned her perspective as a mother:

> Our children are the future. Too often, our own dreams and aspirations are passed down to them. But regardless of the road they choose, we always love them and care for them. Thus, to watch in horror as their bodies are mutilated by those who are elected to protect them, and their minds are diseased by those who are supposed to teach them is worse than experiencing death itself. To send them off to fulfil their own dreams only to be told they have been murdered by the very institutions of learning that they aspired to be a part of is like twisting the knife into our hearts. To learn that your daughter has been assaulted by sexual predators and feels like a prisoner in her

hostel room, who calls out in the night shrieking in terror that they may return, whose physical damage may heal, but whose shining light is diminished forever – those things tear at the very being of any parent. It is impossible to recover from these events. The pain one experiences watching one's children suffer is unimaginable. To lose them to violence because they wanted a better life is inconceivable. The students' stories in this book represent a broad swath of young people in India, and their experiences meld together to create an image that mirrors the society in which they live. These students, who are the first generation to go to university and whose only desire is to go back home and help provide for the family who sacrificed so much so that they could attend; these students, who because of their caste, are intimidated, harassed, humiliated, and then ignored and left behind; these young women students, who because of their gender are treated like objects, abused, maimed, and left to be stigmatized the rest of their lives; and these students who believe that attending a university brings with it the responsibility to give back to society. These students, all of them, believe in the democratic ideal that education provides the promise for a new society based on equality and justice for everyone; these students tell the story of India's rich history of struggle for independence, democracy, and a new way of life that continues today. Reading these stories about Indian students' struggles against the depravities of neoliberalism whose communalism and anti-science and anti-reason ideologies attempt to cover up their economic devastation and political terror against India's peoples, is at once harrowing and uplifting. These struggles shine a light on the way forward for India and all her peoples.

Struggles for Equality

Justice for Rohith Vemula: Watershed Moment Within the Anti-Caste Students' Movement

Kuldeep Singh Nagi, Suddhabrata Deb Roy, Zuhail K.P.

Indian society is riddled with caste violence, initiated by historical forms of caste-based inequality and oppression. Though some may say that education rids individuals and society from such inhuman and historical forms of inequality and oppressive mentality, the reality is far from the truth that one constructs in their definitions of an educated society. The ethos of universities and educational institutions, supposedly pillars upon which a nation's conscience is premised, have repeatedly been undermined to satisfy the casteism that many Indians carry within themselves. University of Hyderabad (UoH) is no exception. Universities are not islands isolated from the broader society. They affect and get affected by what happens in society; caste-based discrimination and oppression is one such issue, among many others. UoH has seen many deaths by suicide over the past years, exhibiting both the subtle and blatant forms of structural violence that university spaces can inflict upon their students, especially those from marginalized backgrounds. Rohith Vemula, it must be remembered, was not the first student from a marginalized community to have died by suicide at UoH.

Senthil Kumar, a research scholar in the department of Physics, died by suicide in 2008 after swallowing a poisonous chemical. He took this drastic step when the department refused to allot him a new supervisor after the retirement of the original supervisor. Then in 2013, Pulyala Raju, a student from the Other Backward Classe (OBC) community studying MA Linguistics, died by suicide due to extreme academic pressure coupled with caste-based discrimination at UoH. Also, in 2013, Madari Venkatesh, a research scholar in the Advance Centre for Research in High Energy Materials (ACRHEM), died by suicide when he was denied the use of a lab and supervisors while his peers continued unfettered with their research.

Central Universities like UoH are uniquely placed in the country's educational fabric. With students and faculty coming in from different parts of the country, these institutions are the epitomes of the diversity that defines India. The student politics of UoH also reflects the diversity around them. Historically, it's been an institution that has always given a voice to students from marginalized communities, though not without conflict between the students and the administration. The left forces within the campus have time and again proved that with an adequate understanding of caste-based oppression, it is possible to forge a larger unity between the Left and the Ambedkarite forces premised upon a common agenda of universal social justice. Political students' organizations like Ambedkar Students' Association (ASA), Students' Federation of India (SFI), Dalit Students' Union (DSU), and others have been at the forefront of such struggles.

Time and again, these organizations have protested the entrenched structural inequality within the university system. For years, campus democracy, as a demand, has been a primary agenda within the students' movement. Democracy here is not used in the formal capitalist sense, but rather it is used as defined by Lenin – which speaks of democracy for all – especially for the marginalized communities who have, for centuries, been subdued by upper-caste and upper-class oppression. The administration, dominated mainly by right-wing people, has consistently opposed political and social movements of the students – individually or organizationally – aimed at ensuring campus democracy. Their excuses range from archaic heretical theories to legal issues which become mainstream under neoliberal capitalism. It is clear from the statements and activities of the administration that their support lies unconditionally towards maintaining an unequal and unjust societal-institutional framework.

Thus, Rohith Vemula's death by suicide in 2016 was not a sudden event. Instead, it was a culmination of the impacts of structural violence from forms of inequality, which run very deep within the system.

The events of January 2016 at the UoH are still fresh in the minds of those present on the campus during the incident, as well as those elsewhere who expressed solidarity with the students of the UoH. The nation's conscience shook when the news of the death of a promising young scholar, Rohith Vemula, was reported. Indian society, though permanently traumatized and characterized by caste atrocities, woke up to the fact that a university administration could so blatantly propagate structural violence, which could, in effect, lead a young Dalit scholar to end his own life in protest and desperation. Messages of solidarity began to flood in from all corners of India. Civil society groups from abroad and various left, progressive, and democratic groups from across the globe expressed their support for the movement led by the students of the UoH. The Joint Action Committee for Social Justice, formed to seek justice for Rohith Vemula, put up a unique, valiant, and united form of resistance. The movement, which germinated within the campus of the UoH, grew up to be a united national movement against caste oppression, bringing about a much sought-after unity of all anti-fascist, anti-caste, and anti-capitalist forces in the country.

The events of January 2016 at the UoH were largely influenced by the events of August 2015, when the Akhil Bharatiya Vidyarthi Parishad (ABVP), vandalized the screening of the film, *Muzaffarnagar Baaqi Hai* at Delhi University (DU). In protest against this act of vandalism in Delhi, the ASA at the UoH organized a protest screening of the same film in solidarity with the students at DU. The incident upset the ABVP-UoH unit so much that they even resorted to publicly shaming the members of the ASA who were associated with the event.

In a social media post, the then President of the UoH unit of ABVP, Mr Susheel Kumar, called ASA cadres 'goons.' Triggered mainly by the social media post, a confrontation took place between ASA and ABVP at the university. ASA asked Mr Kumar to delete his social media post and apologize to ASA for demeaning their organization and cadres.

According to the report filed by the security officer on campus, Kumar apologized to ASA and left the campus in a car. Ironically, without any pretence or pretext, Susheel Kumar got himself admitted to a hospital the next day and complained to the proctorial board that the ASA cadres had beat him. That proctorial board then was headed by Dr Alok Pandey, a strong supporter of the Rashtriya Swayamsevak Sangh (RSS). On 12 August 2015, the proctorial board submitted its first report to VC Prof. R.P. Sharma, stating that it found no evidence to prove that the complainant was beaten up. The report, however, also made atrocious remarks on the general state of student politics on the campus and suggested specific measures like banning organizations and restricting the mobility of these organizations. It called for the abolition of politics based on ideology and identities.

As per reports, Mr Susheel Kumar, with the help of a relative who was associated with the Bharatiya Janata Party (BJP), the political wing of the RSS, contacted Mr Bandaru Dattatreya, who was the Minister of State for Labour & Employment. Mr Dattatreya wrote a letter to the then MHRD Minister, Mrs Smriti Irani, on 17 August stating that the UoH's campus is a 'den' of casteist and anti-national politics. He urged the minister to take appropriate actions against the perpetrators.There are four letters from Mrs Smriti Irani to the university authorities asking for a strict probe into the affair.

Due to external pressure created on the proctorial board by the government, the report of the proctorial board's subsequent investigations, submitted to the VC on 31 August, stated that it had been convinced that Susheel Kumar was indeed beaten, abused, and was at risk on campus. While the first proctorial board decided to issue a 'strong warning' to the accused students, the second report's tone changed and recommended a complete suspension and social boycott of the accused research scholars, namely – Dontha Prashanth, Chakravarti Rohith Vemula, Pedapudi Vijay Kumar, Sheshaiah Chemudugunta, and Velpula Sunkanna for one semester. The report forbade these students to be seen in public spaces and even reside in university-managed accommodations.

The decision invoked strong resistance from the student organizations on the campus. It led to widespread struggles, which forced the then acting VC, R.P. Sharma and the most senior Professor on campus to revoke the suspension. He subsequently announced that a fresh enquiry would be made in the case. However, Appa Rao Podile, after becoming VC, violated that promise and decided to take action against the scholars. This move, by the administration, infuriated the already protesting students. In protest, the research scholars at the university decided to vacate their hostel rooms and stay in the *velivada* constructed at the North Campus Shopping Complex.[1] However, the university administration remained adamant and refused to meet with the students. The demands of the students' union and other progressive organizations on campus regarding the unconditional revocation of the suspension order fell on deaf ears. As a result, there was a further intensification of the struggle.

[1] *Velivada*: Telugu term for excommunicated people's ghetto.

THE FASCISTIC ONSLAUGHT ON CAMPUS DEMOCRACY

The Executive Council (EC) of the University had imposed a punishment with complete disregard for justice. The punishment of social boycott, which was meted out to these students, was not simply punishment, but rather it was a casteist mode of inflicting archaic forms of structural violence on students from marginalized communities. The continuous pains of persecution and subjugation, which the Dalit students face within universities, do not need an explicit mention. Over the years, our campuses have become, to a certain extent and due to continuous, radical, and militant student movements, spaces, which in a way, develop a feeling of community living and harmony among the students who come from various class, caste, and religious backgrounds. These spaces have been created through conflict with the system of bureaucratic avowal of caste-based systemic oppression within the universities. As one might emphasize, these spaces are heritages of radical student movements, which have been a thorn in the side of parties like the BJP and organizations that thrive on fascist ideologies like RSS's.

The current BJP government is on a rampage to destroy these spaces and convert them into hegemonic places suited to the needs of neoliberal capitalists and upper-caste Brahmanical people. The movement that followed the unfortunate institutional murder of Rohith Vemula put the caste question squarely at the forefront of the nation and media discussions, which had, in recent times, been pushed to the contours of academic debates. Rohith's death exposed the blatant lies and violence that the caste Hindu social order has normalized. Even though the students protested democratically, the movement and events occurring thereafter were taken as an excuse by the administration to introduce undemocratic and autocratic measures. The administration, led by Dr Appa Rao Podile, used the movement as an excuse to put in place policies that converted the cherished democratic space of the university into a mindless space. The norm became eradicating the free flow of ideas, the incitement of daily structural violence, and treating dissent like a crime.

The VC's lodge and the area surrounding it were previously accessible to students either for a stroll or for other democratic and public activities, and now it has been transformed into a military garrison with police check posts in front of the road leading to the lodge. Public events, along with academic lectures and discussions, in public spaces have been banned, and the administration has been implementing every possible move at its disposal to prohibit such events.

'Show cause' notices are served at will to organizers and participants alike. The gap between the administration and students has widened to the degree that the standard procedure of addressing students' grievances by the VC has been eliminated. Protests are now met with the Hyderabad police force escorting the VC from the campus without communicating with the students. This detachment between the VC and the students who do not subscribe to the dominant ideas in this casteist and classist social structure has been repeatedly promoted by the central and even the state government, which views the student movement as an obstacle in propagating their anti-people and anti-student policies.

THE UNITED RESISTANCE

The SFI and the ASA have played a pivotal role in the movement. Almost all the other organizations on the campus, except ABVP, have given continual support to the movement, including the DSU, the Tribal Students' Forum (TSF), the Bahujan Students' Front (BSF), the Telangana Vidyarthi Vedika (TVV), and the like. The students voluntarily boycotted classes. In response to the united movement of the student community, the administration cordoned off basic facilities like mess halls, and they threatened the students with a stoppage of electrical and water supplies throughout the campus. The then students' union, led by the SFI, virtually took over the university administration's roles. The students' union created community kitchens to maintain a steady food supply for the student body on campus. Along with that, the union ensured that other basic necessities, like electricity and water, were not disrupted at any cost through continuous communication with the administration.

During the movement, the administration harassed at least fifty students through various legal notices and means, which blatantly exposed the nexus between the administration and the undemocratic and bureaucratic BJP government in power. The Rao-Modi alliance left no stone unturned in unleashing an attack to defeat and crush the movement. The Left extended wholehearted and unshakeable support to the movement, both within and outside the campus. From organizing rallies in support of the movement to exposing the plight of the oppressed students in parliament, the left-wing parties of the country aligned wholeheartedly with the Ambedkarite forces and participated in the struggle both within the parliament and on the streets, battling the atrocious state machinery that the fascistic central government had let loose. After this watershed movement, the campus scenario has gone through some radically conservative and Brahmanical changes. Today the campus is witnessing a continuous curtailing of democratic and human rights as the administration hurls attack after attack to end student activism and dissent. Using tactics such as hikes in hostel fees and repeatedly increasing university tuition fees, the administration clearly wants to transform a free and open academic institution into a place reserved for the few. Under the current regime, whose character is fascistic and anti-intellectual at its very core, the very idea of a university is under attack. During their correspondence, Karl Marx and Friedrich Engels commented that student politics is the space where the battle of ideas occurs, which is the most critical characteristic of student politics. Whether illuminated by Bhagat Singh or Karl

Marx, student politics must revolve around one single point – the importance of ideas, debates, and dissenting views – everything to which the present government and appointed administrators of universities, from Jawaharlal Nehru University (JNU) to UoH, stand opposed.

THE DEMAND FOR AN INSTITUTIONAL MECHANISM TO END CASTE-BASED DISCRIMINATION

The Students' Union of UoH, in their statement from 2016 published in the *Economic and Political Weekly*, put forward the following demands as a framework for a broader struggle against deep-seated structural inequalities within Indian educational and institutional systems.

> To address caste-based and other forms of discrimination in higher educational institutions, the institutions must accept that discrimination on the basis of caste and other identities, in overt and covert ways, is a reality on our campuses. The Students' Union of UoH would like to suggest an institutional mechanism that shall ensure that these deep-seated social practices are addressed head-on.
>
> 1. We demand that each higher educational institution establish a 'Committee Against Prejudice and Discrimination' (CAPD). It must be in keeping with Article 15 and Article 21 of the Constitution of India, which together protect citizens from discrimination by the State or fellow citizens on the grounds of religion, race, caste, sex, or place of birth, and ensures the right to live with human dignity. The main focus of CAPD must be to look into complaints regarding acts of prejudice and/or discrimination against Scheduled Castes (SCs), Scheduled Tribes (STs), Other Backward Classes (OBCs), religious minorities, sexual minorities, women, transgender people,

racial, and ethnic minorities. CAPD must be structured along the lines of the Gender Sensitization Committee Against Sexual Harassment (GSCASH). CAPD must be widely representative (including women, OBCs, religious, sexual, racial, and ethnic minorities, etc.) while ensuring that at least half the committee comprises SC and ST members and is led by a person from SC/ST background. Student representatives must be part of the committee.

2. Immediately, higher educational institutions must collectively constitute a high-level committee to formulate rules for CAPD, and the committee must be given a clear vision and a deadline to submit its report.
3. A course should be introduced for all students in universities and colleges to increase their knowledge and understanding about the problem of caste, ethnicity, gender, and other issues. This course should be compulsory. Many countries such as the USA, Scotland, and England have introduced courses on 'civic-learning' or 'Citizenship Education' for students.
4. A module and administrative guidelines should be prepared to sensitize administrators and teachers at universities and colleges.
5. The current Remedial Coaching plans of UGC must be reformed, and funding increased to make them effective.
6. An Ombudsman must be appointed for each university for redressal of grievances by students as per the University Grants Commission (Grievance Redressal) Regulations, 2012.

The Thorat Committee was appointed to look into the deaths by suicide of Dalit students, and it successfully submitted its report, highlighting the forms of systemic and structural discrimination within educational institutions. Even at UoH, a committee was set up in 2014, which was supposed to look into discrimination based on caste. The recommendations of both, however, have largely fallen on deaf ears. The demand for the Rohith Act to combat discrimination in higher educational institutions, raised by the joint action committee for social justice, also met with a similar fate.

Rohith's death by suicide has exposed certain issues within the system that run deeper than what can be reformed merely through superficial measures but instead require a complete structural and ideological overhaul. The issues, which the tragedy has highlighted, are multifarious, ranging from using institutional murders as a political tool to altering the state of mental well-being among students of premier educational institutions. It is imperative to understand that Rohith was not an unaccomplished scholar; he was a highly influential and respected voice within the campus, both in terms of politics and academics. However, the causes that led to his death by suicide were extremely inhumane, and form a part of the larger structural and psychological paradigm within which Dalits in contemporary India continue to face oppression and exploitation at multiple levels and through multifarious methods.

'The University Mirrors Society's Caste System'

Pindiga Ambedkar

An interview with Dontha Prashanth[1]

The student movement at Univeristy of Hyderabad (UoH) is as vibrant and, in some cases, more prominent than at other universities in the country.[2] The students have waged battles against the administration on many occasions. This is because the students from marginalized backgrounds are vocal and assertive about their issues. But the watershed moment was the rustication of ten Dalit students who were protesting against the corruption in the university's hostel administration and the casteist posting of Dr K.Y. Ratnam to the sanitary warden from his earlier post of hostel warden in 2002. The students saw the move to change Dr Ratnam's position to that of a sanitation warden as an effort by the administration (Chief Warden's Office) to humiliate him; in the Indian caste society, this type of work is done by those lowest on the caste-hierarchy. The students presented their demands to the chief warden twice; however, their objections were brushed aside. So, the students protested, which resulted in a scuffle. The students were accused of violence and were debarred from the university for two years. All these students belonged to the Ambedkar

[1] Conducted on 27 November 2018 and updated in May 2022.
[2] UoH is popularly called Hyderabad Central University or HCU.

Students' Association (ASA).[3] Incidentally, the chief warden of the university at that time was Podile Appa Rao, who now happens to be UoH's VC.

Again in 2015, ASA was in the news when five PhD students (Dontha Prashanth, Rohith Vemula, Vijay Kumar, Sheshaiah Chemudugunta, and Velpula Sunkanna) were suspended by the university administration. This action was taken following a complaint filed by an Akhil Bharatiya Vidyarthi Parishad (ABVP) activist, Susheel Kumar, alleging that these students beat him up. However, the students refuted the allegations, and in the enquiry, the university's medical officer and the security officer stated that there had been no violence. Susheel Kumar had been operated on for appendicitis, which had nothing to do with any injuries. The real issue was that the ABVP had disrupted the screening of a documentary, *Muzaffarnagar Baaqi Hai*, organized by the Montage Film Society at Delhi University (DU); the ASA vehemently protested against this. In response to this protest, an ABVP activist accused the ASA leaders of being goons in a Facebook post.[4]

The administration was coerced by the local Bharatiya Janata Party (BJP) leader, Ramachandra Rao, who was also a member of the legislative council (MLC), after his meeting with the VC, in-charge, Prof. R.P. Sharma.[5] A committee was set up under the proctorship of Alok Pandey. After the enquiry found no evidence of violence, both the complainant and the ASA leaders were let off with a warning. Dissatisfied with the report, ABVP approached the central minister from Hyderabad, Bandaru Dattatreya, who wrote a letter to the Ministry of Human Resource Development (MHRD, now the Ministry of Education) seeking action against ASA. MHRD wrote letters to the university seeking action against the students.

[3] ASA was established in 1993.

[4] 'What Happened at Hyderabad Central University That Led to Rohith Vemula's Suicide?' *India Today*. 18 January 2016, https://www.indiatoday.in/fyi/story/what-happened-at-hyderbad-central-university-that-led-to-rohit-vemula-suicide-304365-2016-01-18.

[5] Ibid.

Later, a second report was submitted, which suspended the five ASA students, but it was revoked after the students protested. However, things spun out of control when Podile Appa Rao took charge of the university as VC. In December, when the university was on vacation, the five ASA students received the punishment that debarred them from their hostels, banned them from gathering in groups in common places, prevented them from even going to the administration office, and prohibited them from participating in the students' union elections for two years. They were allowed access only to the academic and library premises. ASA saw this as a clear diktat for the social boycott of the five Dalit students. So, the students erected a tent to make a *velivada* – a Dalit ghetto – similar to the Dalits' houses on the outskirts of the main village in India – in the common area of the university and began living there, out in the open, as a protest.[6] The social boycott of the students was condemned, and the students protest received broad support.

The students sustained the protest on and off for six months, beginning in August 2015, when the first proctorial committee was formed. From December onwards, the university was in a continuous protest mode. But the administration did not respond to their demands to revoke the social boycott and the suspension. Not able to bear this humiliation, one of the students, Rohith Vemula, penned his views in a letter and took his life in one of the hostel rooms. Seeing this institutional murder, the university and the country erupted into protests.

Unlike other central universities in India, this university has a dominant presence of marginalized students who represent a political force. ASA started as a pressure group to protect the students from the SC and ST backgrounds against harassment from the feudal forces on the campus. It was also established to help students get used to the university setting, as most are first-generation college attendees. ASA says that it introduces the writings and teachings of

[6] *Velivada* is a Telugu term for an excommunicated people's ghetto. It describes the Dalit ghetto outside of the main village area.

their role models – Babasaheb Dr B.R. Ambedkar, Mahatma Jotirao Phule, Savitribai, and other leaders – to ASA members so that they learn about their history and strengthen themselves to fight and survive at the university, which Prashanth says in the interview, 'is as feudal and discriminatory' as the outside world.

In this interview, Pindiga Ambedkar of the Tricontinental Research talks to Dontha Prashanth, the former President UoH Students' Union 2011-2012, and a senior activist of the ASA. Prashanth is a research scholar pursuing a PhD in economics and was one of the five students the university suspended under pressure from ABVP and BJP through MHRD.

When did you join the University of Hyderabad?

I joined the university in 2006 as an undergraduate student after graduating from Jawahar Navodaya Vidyalaya (JVV) in Rangareddy District.

How did you become an activist?

I learned about this university through a student, Vulli Dhanraj, who came to teach at our school. He was rusticated in 2002. He was one of the ten Dalit students rusticated from the university for protesting against the corruption that was going on in the hostels' administration department. The then chief warden is the same person, Podile Appa Rao, who had a role in the institutional murder of Rohith Vemula.[7]

After he was rusticated, Dhanraj joined our school as a guest history teacher. He was the one who asked the students to apply to the university. For the first time, the university was introducing an integrated program for class twelve pass-outs.

[7] ASA terms these deaths by suicide as institutional murders as the educational institutions are highly discriminatory towards the Scheduled Caste (SC), Scheduled Tribes (ST), and Other Backward Classes (OBC) students and create various roadblocks to pursue their education. With no grievance redressal mechanisms to address their problems, the students are forced to end their lives.

As we entered the university, the students from the marginalized sections had to grapple with the issue of the Reservation Policy in admissions. The peer circle from the privileged castes used to always question us, saying that we had taken away the opportunity of 'meritorious' students. Even I was, at one point, against reservations, thinking that they were terrible. Then, I used to take the side of my 'upper caste' friends, stating that reservations based on caste were wrong and reservations should be based on economic backwardness. I did not reveal my social identity in the initial phase of the university. In the beginning days, the students of the course divided themselves into groups. The ones who came from the urban areas belonged to one group. Those students who were from rural areas formed another group. Within this group, those from marginalized backgrounds formed a sub-group. This happened spontaneously due to pre-existing social conditions. I aspired to be part of the urban group initially. I used to imitate their patterns and their dressing style. It was material aspirations that lured me into this thinking.

However, through the ASA and their discussions, I started to understand how harmful these prejudices were. Yet, I did not identify with ASA immediately. Once you are associated with ASA, you are bracketed in the SC groups. ASA's orientation programs and thinkers like Katti Padmarao influenced me a lot.[8] From then on, I felt pride in being a Dalit, identifying with those struggles. We became accustomed to knowing our history and struggles. This was also the same time we were introduced to Dr B.R. Ambedkar. His quote, '[T]he backward classes have come to realize that, after all, education is the greatest material benefit for which they can fight. We may forgo material benefits; we may forgo material benefits of civilization; but we cannot forgo our right and opportunity to reap

[8] Katti Padmarao is an Ambedkarite and Telugu and Sanskrit scholar, He was one of the founders of the Dalit Mahasabha in the erstwhile Andhra Pradesh that was formed in response to the Karamchedu Massacre in 1985.

the benefits of the highest education to the fullest extent'.[9] These words created a spark inside me. I started reading him regularly and attended seminars and discussions initiated by ASA.

Before that, I was enticed by the material aspirations of the urban class. These values are picked-up by observing people. But after that, I started to take more interest in identifying with my social origins. Before joining the ASA, Dalit was a humiliating identity that I wanted to discard. But after that, I came to appreciate that the Dalit identity is the identity of struggle. I gained courage and started to speak more confidently in class and elsewhere. We were encouraged to speak and communicate openly. ASA promoted this culture among our students.

How did you take up active participation in students' politics?

This happened in phases. Senthil Kumar was institutionally murdered in the academic year 2007-08, and I saw how Senthil Kumar, a brilliant student, was forced to take his life. I also got the opportunity to watch documentaries like *Death of Merit* and *India Untouched*. These directly exposed me to the horrors of the caste system. After watching these documentaries, I realized that even though the students were fighting against the discrimination, these institutional murders were happening in the university. At one of the protests where the VC was present, Dhanraj, the senior leader of ASA, asked me to pose a question to the VC. This was my first public question and the beginning of my student activism. Later, during 2011-12, ASA had an alliance with the Students' Federation of India (SFI) for the students' union elections. Before that, due to the split in the progressive students' votes, ABVP was elected to the union in 2009-10. Until 2006, there was a University

[9] Dr Ambedkar speaking in the B.L.C. Debates, Vol. XXI, pp. 414-16, dated 5 October 1927. This speech was in support of the amendment to the Bombay University Bill moved by Mr Noor Mohmed to raise the number of nominated senators from 40 to 50. Reproduced in *Dr. Babasaheb Ambedkar: Writings and Speeches Vol. 2* 'The Bombay University Act Amendment Bill: 4' p. 62.

Discussion Forum, and all progressive organizations participated under that banner; only after 2007-08 did ASA start to participate in students' union elections independently.

ABVP had a core support group among the students, and it won successively in the union elections. Through these victories, they became highly arrogant, and they started beating up the students. Several student activists from SFI were beaten up. There was a major incident at H-hostel where some Masters of Computer Applications (MCA) students, particularly those who used to support the ABVP, had beaten up two Dalit students. Students were outraged after the incident, and as a counter to this assault and a form of resistance, the then ABVP president was roughed up. There was a series of protests. At that time, we realized there was a need for unity; a mutual understanding was reached between ASA and SFI. Two posts for SFI and four posts for ASA were agreed upon for the elections. In the first year, due to that united front, we (ASA) won the post of General Secretary and three other posts. The following year, we ran in the election for president, and I won the election as the President of the Students' Union, UoH. Being in the Union, it was easy for us to access the documents of the university regarding the intake of students, scholarships, reservations, and so on. We also saw the hypocrisy of some of the faculty members, who, while talking to students, said one thing but did just the opposite when submitting their views to the administration. We saw their betrayal when we were present at the Academic Council (AC) meetings.

Do you think electoral politics in the university spaces affect the marginalized students negatively, or is it a positive thing?

Electoral politics don't affect the marginalized sections as such. ASA has the position that electoral politics are the process of the movement, and you have to engage in electoral politics to be on the governing council here on campus. It is a form of struggle, and it is of the utmost importance because, at the end of the day, even if you are elected to the students' union, you'll have to struggle for the issues of the students with the administration and status-quoist.

ASA is not affiliated with or supported by any movement outside of the campus. Does the absence of outside support impact your struggles at the university adversely?

Our ultimate purpose is to protect the tiny space of education we have. If someone wants to choose politics as their ultimate cup of tea, they can certainly go and join a political party. To have an impact in eradicating discrimination, you have to be in the people's struggles and [with the people's] agenda. The objective of ASA is to protect the rights of marginalized students, in particular; that is the focus of ASA's activism.

Can you share some examples of how your representation in the students' union helped in the struggles?

The students' union was demanding that in addition to the interview process for the intake of PhD students, equal weightage should be given to Maulana Azad National Fellowship (MANF) candidates, similar to how the UGC-JRF functioned.[10] Recipients of the Rajiv Gandhi National Fellowship (RGNF) were also given the same weightage.[11] This demand, however, was undermined by the university faculty. The head of the Sociology Department, for example, appeared to be a somewhat progressive faculty member. He portrayed that kind of image, and some of his students were researching the question of Muslims and their socio-economic development. But, at the AC meeting, he opposed assigning a similar weightage to the MANF candidates. Taking their lead from him, other faculty also joined in and said that the exemption given

[10] This fellowship is given to religious minorities – Muslims, Christians, Sikhs, etc., to pursue their research in higher educational institutions.

[11] RGNF was introduced to help students from SC-ST backgrounds to avail themselves of fellowships so that they could pursue their research with little financial constraint. It was later extended to Persons with Disabilities (PWD) and OBC students as well.

to RGNF scholars should be withdrawn as well. So, nothing was resolved in the meeting.

Before the following AC meeting, we organized several protests and gave presentations to teachers seeking their support. Some teachers argued that RGNF was given to students without any merit criteria, even though their marks in attaining their Master's Degree were criteria for awarding the fellowship to the students. As part of mounting pressure on the administration, we met Asaduddin Owaisi, member of parliament, who was also member of the university court. He sought the university's response on the issue.

When the next AC meeting took place, students had gathered in large numbers outside the meeting's venue to express their support for the union's demands. The issues were resolved at the AC meeting. Both the RGNF and the MANF students who were awarded the fellowships were exempted from the entrance examination, like the University Grants Commission-Junior Research Fellowship (UGC-JRF) holders.

Around the same time, the administration proposed a fee hike of about 200 per cent. We fought and ensured that the fee hike was never implemented. But this also allowed us to study the arguments made by the administration that the UGC was reducing the funding, hence the need for the fee hike. We decided to do an investigation and found that the development grant, the maintenance grant, and the corpus fund could meet the university's expenses without putting the burden of increased fees on students.

In fact, the investigation helped me understand the importance of those grants and funds and their significance to the students. I remember that at about the same time, ASA had organized intense struggles on the campus around the BBL fellowships. By not sanctioning the full amount to cover or meet the mess expenses, the government clearly did not take into consideration the hardships of the social welfare scholarship holders.[12]

[12] The Post-Matric Scholarship that the state governments award the SC, ST, and OBC students (whose annual parental income is below two lakhs)

The lack of financial support for boarding and lodging became an excessive burden on the students, particularly those from marginalized communities. Given this context, the proposal was to either waive the payment of the mess bills or initiate a new scheme of scholarship, i.e., the BBL. This scholarship was instituted during the tenure of VC Seyed E. Hasnain (2006-11).

However, there was another issue; the social welfare department's rule stated that no student could have two scholarships simultaneously.[13] ASA immediately took the initiative both within and outside the university and met with the Department of Social Welfare officials. ASA pointed out a clause in the Department's manual which clearly stated that a student could accept boarding and lodging. Hence, the fellowship was named the Boarding and Lodging fellowship to ensure students receiving social welfare scholarships also received boarding and lodging. When I was the president of the students' union, there was an attempt to withdraw the BBL fellowship completely. We had to fight because we understood how this fellowship had come about. It was introduced due to the efforts of the marginalized communities. We fought back against its removal.

In 2012, the administration had still not implemented the reservation policy effectively in the students' admission process. There were lapses in the implementation of reservations. We also fought against this non-implementation of reservations in admissions. We organized two protests in front of the Scheduled Castes and Scheduled Tribes' standing committee of the university. There was no student representation on that university committee. Hence, we weren't able to access any of the official documents on the issue. So, that year we participated in two successive protests, and after the second protest, it was resolved that I would be invited

is funded by the Government of India and is only routed through state governments.

13 The Social Welfare Department was the State Government of Andhra Pradesh, which used to grant PMS to SC-ST students.

to the SC and ST Standing Committee as the president of the students' union. During my participation on that committee, I was exposed to the UGC guidelines on the reservation system and its implementation. If the seats were not filled, we could call for a special notification, alerting students that there was a backlog of seats for SC-ST candidates.

During my presidential tenure at the students' union, I represented the student body at a UGC committee chaired by Prof. Yogendra Yadav. It was a meeting to formulate guidelines on students' entitlements. Several students and organizations were members. We proposed certain things, which came out in a document called 'UGC guidelines on student entitlements. We submitted a collectively drafted letter to the committee, and some of our points were accepted.

This period also saw the death of two students, right?

In 2013-14, Madari Venkatesh and Pulleyala Raju were institutionally murdered. While I was the union president, the university tried to create a parallel body with the VC as the patron of that committee; we opposed it. They aimed to depoliticize the campus environment. After the institutional murders of Venkatesh and Raju, when committees were constituted for an enquiry, we ensured that there was adequate student representation so that the students' versions were also heard and documented. The resulting two reports stand out as clear testimony to the caste discrimination that occurred. In fact, after the Thorat Committee,[14] much of the disseminated information on caste discrimination was derived from reports written about UoH, Madari Venkatesh, Pulleyala Raju, and Senthil Kumar.

During the enquiry into the death of Madari Venkatesh, a protest took place; the committee found that on the question

[14] A committee was formed by the Government of India to look into the discrimination faced by the SC-ST students in the AIIMS, and measures to end the discriminatory practices were recommended.

of merit, he had achieved 100 percentile marks in his class 10th board exams. He had an excellent rank on the GATE, where only two students were admitted against the seven open seats. He was one of those two students, yet he was red-flagged and had to meet with the HoD to report his progress, while the other student was not obligated to do so.

Why was there a separate rule?

It is a sad and cruel story. He was forced to meet with the Department head because he was a Dalit. He was not allotted a PhD supervisor for two years. Even the students who were his junior were allocated, PhD supervisors. Despite that, he published his papers in reputed journals. His anxiety grew because his PhD was delayed due to the non-allotment of a research guide. Madari Venkatesh wanted to complete his PhD thesis and find a job. There was nothing at home to fall back on.

The anguish caused by not having an allotted supervisor was explained in the letter to the VC, and nothing happened. So, he took his life. We see it as an institutional murder. After Madari Venkatesh's death, we had several protests at the VC's office; we went to the department and collected several documents to prove how he was harassed at the institution and how he was selectively denied a supervisor.

How was Madari Venkatesh was pushed to the wall?

Despite his (Madari Venkatesh's) eligibility, the university's academic ordinances were not implemented. A Research Advisory Committee (RAC) was not constituted in his case. We exposed all these deliberate lapses and publicized the fact that we could also file a case of atrocity against the VC, as he was supposed to be the chairperson of the centre and the de facto chairperson of RAC. The VC failed his duties; he knew the pain from which Madari was suffering; he had read about it in the letter submitted to him by Madari.

This was not an isolated case; even after the institutional murder of Madari Venkatesh, two more students were found dead – one student from OBC and another Dalit student – both of whom were not allotted supervisors.

Even when supervisors were allotted, the students were harassed with 'non-satisfactory' reports. Whenever difficulties arose in the relationship between the students and their supervisors, the supervisor wrote 'not satisfactory' in the report, which spelt the end of the student's career. That's happening more regularly now.

How are they doing that? On what basis do they recommend such things? Do they not follow the rules? Do the research supervisors do that officially; can you cite some examples?

During the tenure of VC Podile Appa Rao, it happened much more.

The Doctoral Research Committee recommends that the student's acceptance for admission should be withdrawn, and the school board has the power to revoke the acceptance.

Unsatisfactory progress is cited as the reason for the withdrawal of the admissions acceptance. If a student is from a deprived community, having an SC/ST faculty on the RAC is mandatory. However, the policy is not followed.

In one example, a PhD student finished his four years of research, was always attentive to his research, informed his supervisor before leaving for the field, and attended his weekly progress seminars. In other words, his work was exemplary. The supervisor wanted the primary data from the student's research because it was related to folk studies and would provide substantial funding prospects. The student, however, had collected this data at his own expense; the data belonged to the student. He presented his research as a part of a study on Kalamkari (hand-painted art on fabric) design, which is now a significant trend. The student found that the Malas (the Mala caste is listed in the SC category) of

Andhra Pradesh were the original creators of the Kalamkari design and explored how a section of the Mala community's occupation was weaving. The student's guide disagreed and questioned him, 'How could Malas be weavers; they cannot be weavers!' The student, however, presented tangible evidence for his claim.

The guide is from a dominant caste group; he belongs to the Reddy caste. Entire folk culture studies were made possible due to folklore grants. Since the establishment of this department in 1990, not a single PhD scholar, let alone a Dalit, even a non-Dalit, submitted this type of research (till the time this interview was conducted). The guide obviously wanted to be the first; thus, his interest in taking the student's data.

The student waged a battle. I think that this case could become documented evidence if one were to study the discrimination and harassment that the student faced. After completing the requisite four years, the student wanted to finish his PhD. The student was not allowed to submit his PhD thesis, and he was asked to de-register from the PhD program despite having satisfactory work. The student was not allowed to enter the department; he was told, 'you are de-registered'. The supervisor refused to meet with the student to discuss his work. This was the same professor who supported VC Appa Rao during the Rohith Vemula movement. The student then filed a case in the anti-discrimination cell of the university. He also filed a complaint at the VC's office. None of these complaints received any response. He wrote two emails on the non-responsiveness of the people concerned.

After all that, a school-level grievance redressal committee was constituted. His only request was to change his PhD guide, as he faced discrimination. The supervisor had told the committee that 'the student did not know how to speak one word of English. He didn't know how to write in English, and his chapters must have been written by someone else'. The supervisor made all these false accusations.

Based on his satisfactory reports, the committee, to a certain extent, stated that the arguments of the supervisor were false. At the end of the day, the school board committee recommended that the student and the supervisor work towards the thesis's final submission. This was impossible. The board was again sending him back to the predator. The student was not okay with the recommendation and sought an appointment with the VC. The VC responded after receiving three letters from the student. The student was under the impression that the VC alone would be present at their physical meeting. When the student entered the VC's office, he saw the Controller of Examination, another faculty member, and the supervisor present in the meeting! They spoke in English, presuming the student did not understand them. He heard them say, 'We are all in this together. Let's see what they are willing to do'. The student again demanded that he wanted a new supervisor. From the beginning, his argument was clear: he wanted a different supervisor.

In the meeting, as the VC spoke to the student in English, the student comfortably responded in English, establishing that he was well-versed in the English language. He produced his grievance letters and a copy of his thesis. He showed them the doctoral committee reports, all of which were satisfactory. He also exposed how the guide was discriminating against him. In the meeting, the supervisor said that he would agree to supervise him provided the student gave him an apology letter. Even the VC strongly recommended that he offer an apology letter, but the student declined. Instead, he replied to the VC, 'As I have complained about his (supervisor) harassment and discrimination against me, what is the guarantee that my thesis will be accepted? The apology letter acknowledges wrong-doing on my part; my career would be ruined.'

The VC's office is acting as a cover for those who are harassing students. To all those who face caste discrimination, the VC mediates against and suppresses those complaining against casteist actions.

UoH is a politically vibrant campus where the voices of the marginalized are mainstream. So why do you think that students still suffer in silence? The students here are very vocal and are struggling against the administration's discrimination; how is it that the faculty continues to get away with this discrimination, which forces the students to take their own lives? What prevents student organizations from knowing what's happening at the school level or how it happens?

If we look at the institutional murders that have repeatedly happened on campuses, particularly at UoH, Rohith Vemula's institutional murder must be viewed from a different perspective than the institutional murders of Madari Venkatesh, Senthil Kumar, Bal Raju, and others.

In Senthil's case, his fellowship was stopped. He was the first Dalit student from his entire community in Tamil Nadu to study for a PhD. When his PhD admission was about to be withdrawn because he could not pass one of the coursework examinations, Senthil's hopes were shattered. For Dalits, who have no land back home, higher education is the only vehicle with which to attain their emancipation and employment. For Dalits, entering the university is their ticket to a better life. But when one enters the university space and is confronted with constant discrimination and harassment, the student's situation becomes untenable, and their dreams are completely destroyed. There are different forms of struggle that one could take up; but when one feels that their options to fight discrimination and injustice have been exhausted, institutional murder is the only alternative.

The Madari agitation did force the administration to make changes. Certain changes were made, but those changes were not permanent because the majority of people in the administration are people with Brahmanical interests who do not want change and will not change. In fact, after these institutional murders, at a meeting of the university faculty, a casteist professor stated, 'What is the point in talking about all this; one who has merit will survive, and those who do not, will lose the competitive race'.

Do you think that due to the lack of faculty from SC and ST backgrounds in the departments, students are not able to fight the casteist faculties?

Yes, but even if there were faculty from SC and ST categories, the majority of the faculty is from the dominant social groups (non-SC-STs). The DRC is composed of professors and department chairperson, all of whom are non-SC-ST members. How many professors do we have that can question the VC, the Academic Council, and the Executive Council? The university is a microcosm of the social domination in the villages; the university mirrors society's caste system. The dominant castes have come to urban spaces, and their *agraharas* are no longer in the forests.[15] Now they exercise their control in the universities and the institutions. The situation has become even more difficult for us [marginalized communities]. Even in our case, if you look at the committee, the chief proctor, Alok Pandey, is part of a right-wing organization. The first report completely acquitted us, but without any evidence, the second report suspended us.[16] We had to fight to remove the suspension order.

The campus was at a boiling point with the death of Rohith Vemula; VC Appa Rao went into hiding. When things returned to normal, he came back to the post of VC, on the instructions of MHRD and local BJP-ABVP leaders. After the VC came back, he would have meetings with his supporters, but these meetings were quickly uncovered by the students. They protested at the venue,

[15] *Agraharas* were the income producing land-grants of the twice-born castes (brahmins) of southern India that were exclusively theirs and lower castes were not allowed to pass through those streets. They were most often close to the forests and the Brahmin teacher would offer his teachings there.

[16] 'What Happened at Hyderabad Central University That Led to Rohith Vemula's Suicide?' *India Today*, 18 January 2016, https://www.indiatoday.in/fyi/story/what-happened-at-hyderbad-central-university-that-led-to-rohit-vemula-suicide-304365-2016-01-18.

and the administration used the police force to quell them. The VC could take these actions because he had the power to do so.

Similarly, in the other case we discussed, it was really difficult for a student to fight back against a supervisor for six months. Yet, his thesis wasn't submitted. There are a few who are able to fight, but many who undergo discrimination and harassment cannot.

In many universities in India, student organizations like ASA can fight the Brahmanical forces at the student level, but when it comes to the administrative level, there is a power imbalance. If the teachers from SC-ST-OBC backgrounds are vocal against discrimination, do you think it might make a difference?

Initially, ASA also represented the voice of the teachers, because there were hardly any teachers from these social backgrounds due to the non-implementation of reservations. ASA fought at the university level to implement the reservation system at the faculty level. The few teachers that were there from our communities supported us. Their numbers were small, and yet they organized and fought against the administration. The Senthil-Balraj agitation was a combined protest by the SC-ST Teachers' Forum and ASA. Even in our case, the SC-ST Teachers' Forum was with us; they also had written a letter to the VC.

If teachers from marginalised sections are members of the administration's committees, can it be assumed that they can prevent discrimination against students?

Yes, I will give you an example. Professors Laxminarayana and Deepa Srinivas were present at the first proctorial committee. The registrar had sent them a letter stating that they were co-opted members, and hence, they had no voting rights. They attended the meeting, and the first report was reasonable. At the second meeting, there was no representation from the SC-ST faculty, and it was only Alok Pandey and two others who decided the case and suspended us. They decided to boycott us socially, and it came from the Executive Council, which had no representation from SC-ST faculty.

You are a senior student of the university, have you observed any change in the politics of the campus and the student movement?

Particularly after BJP came to power at the centre in the year 2014, we saw changes immediately. With the appointment of Podile Appa Rao as the VC, the administration went after the students' demonstrations. Before VC Rao's appointment, open discussions were held with administration officials, and public hearings were possible. After he was appointed VC, the faculty was informed that he did not encourage accepting memorandums from students or having open conversations with students on issues. He also said he would not encourage one-on-one discussions or protests. This was the attitude with which he began his job. At that time, we were in the Students' Union and the United Democratic Front was elected.

During 2005-2006, ABVP on campus was waiting for an opportunity to create havoc within the student movement; they had invited their leaders to the university. In the process, they defaced the portraits of Dr Ambedkar by hiding his portraits with their flags. ASA resisted them. ABVP was waiting for a chance to hit back, and with the BJP in power at the centre, this time, it was easy for them to come after us.

Appa Rao was appointed VC as a result of his network among the top leadership of the BJP. As soon as he assumed power, having prepared everything in advance based on the two letters that the MHRD sent, he constituted a sub-committee of the Executive Council, keeping us all in the dark, and they passed the orders to punish us. We received the orders that our hostel rooms were being blocked and that we were to be socially boycotted on campus. A seven-month struggle ensued, beginning in August 2015 and ending in January 2016. During this phase, when the suspension was revoked, we were victorious, but then the administration attacked us. The student community was well aware of the facts of what exactly had happened in the incident. Five of us, the active members of the organization, were punished. In this context, Rohith wrote his letter on 18 December 2015 and other letters later on.[17] Despite the commitment and dedication to the struggle for university education, there is hardly any room to manoeuvre when the entire regime is operating against you. Rohith's death was an institutional murder. What Rohith wrote in his last letter was evidence of this.[18] After Rohit's death, the campus erupted in anger. Students from across the country were protesting against the injustice meted out to the five students of ASA.

Because of the students' demonstrations, VC Appa Rao, in one of his interviews, said that he would resign if the government asked him to. But the ruling BJP wanted him to continue. If he had resigned, the government would have been on the backfoot. He continued as VC; this fortified all the casteist forces. He did everything he could to damage the institution, to damage the student community, especially the marginalised sections, and yet, he was able to continue because of the support from the BJP. For the student community and ASA, fighting against a powerful regime was difficult when the whole State machinery was behind the VC. The students, however, will not be deterred. The struggle against the casteist forces at the university and across the country will continue.

[17] In this letter to the VC, Rohith had asked the university to allot poison and a rope to every Dalit student at the time of admission to end their lives, as the administration does not support marginalized students when they are humiliated. See: Teesta Setalvad, 'Rohith's Death: We Are All To Blame'. *Sabrangindia*, https://sabrangindia.in/article/rohith-death-we-are-all-blame.

[18] The Wire Staff, 'My Birth Is My Fatal Accident: Rohith Vemula's Searing Letter Is An Indictment Of Social Prejudices', *The Wire*, 17 January 2019, https://thewire.in/caste/rohith-vemula-letter-a-powerful-indictment-of-social-prejudices.

What are your views about the differences among the student organizations?

There are differences between student organizations on an ideological basis. However, there are issues around which we would unite and fight back together against the anti-student policies.

Dialogue, Dissent, Struggles: Chronicles from the Indian Institute of Science

Subhankar Chakraborty

One evening in early February 2015, after the sun had set in Bangalore, there was a rather unusual sight on the quaint campus of the Indian Institute of Science (IISc). The roads inside IISc, refurbished only recently, displayed an obviously new, thin coat of tar. The natural brick colour of the walls around the arterial roads shone more brightly, and the mundane dividers glistened in black, white, and yellow. Then, much like the overnight paint and tar coats, police rushed onto the campus, security tightened, and drones flew over.

Prime Minister Narendra Modi, buoyant from his 2014 election victory, visited the campus with an entourage of ministers. Understandably, visits by heads of state, ministers, Nobel laureates, and international dignitaries and envoys are not uncommon at IISc, but this paraphernalia was a spectacle.

A few hundred meters away from the Prime Minister's programme venue, a group of students and post-doctoral researchers gathered in protest 'against the lack of scientific temper reflected in recurrent comments made by the Prime Minister and the representatives of his government. There were also active voices against the saffronization of the curriculum, which would hinder the scientific thought process for generations to come', the press release read. Greeting the Prime Minister with a protest on a campus where organized students' movement is absent is an uncommon sight.

Barely three months before this protest, Modi had publicly presented *Karna* of the literary epic *Mahabharat* and the Hindu God *Ganesha* – a deity with an elephant's head on a human body – as evidence of ancient India's advances in genetic sciences and plastic surgery, respectively! This wasn't the first time, nor would it be the last time that Modi, his cabinet, and party colleagues publicly pronounced obscurantist views.[1]

With Rashtriya Swayamsevak Sangh (RSS), the fountainhead of its political arm, Bharatiya Janata Party (BJP), ascending to power, the legacies of a forceful endorsement of obscurantism began haunting scientists and academics.

In the previous BJP-rule (1999-2004), Atal Vihari Vajpayee as Prime Minister and Murli Manohar Joshi as the Minister of Human Resource Development (HRD), the agenda of pseudoscience got a push by its insertion into the formal curricula of the universities. Astrology was introduced by the University Grants Commission (UGC) under Ministry of Human Resource Development (MHRD), making scientists like Pushpa Bhargava and others approach the High Courts and the Supreme Court. Several prominent scientists from IISc, like researchers and scientists from many other notable scientific research centres, were vociferous in their criticism of inserting 'Vedic astrology', 'Vedic mathematics', and 'Vastu' as part of university courses.

Early in his tenure, assured of BJP's strength inside parliament, Modi picked up from where Vajpayee-Murli Manohar Joshi had left off by injecting the instruction of irrationality and obscurantism in the universities.

1 Sanjay Kumar, 'In India, Hindu Pride Boosts Pseudoscience,' *Science*, 363, no. 6428, (2019): 679-80. https://doi.org/10.1126/science.363.6428.679.

Although the assault on reason and scientific temper is not very uncommon in public discourse in India, it attains a significance when executives and elected officials turn to the spokespersons of the occult. After every preposterous proposition put forth by these reactionary forces, public protests erupted, demonstrating that students and teachers play an important role, not only in articulating argumentative public debate based on reason but also in their refusal to accept these as the new normal. This defiance was reflected in the protest that Narendra Modi faced.

As scientific temper is central to the vocation of the sciences and education, one would imagine that the rightful space to engage in public debate, raise the alarm, and protest when there is an assault on reason would be the universities and research institutions. However, this is not solely vocational; a critical public engagement on scientific temper is as historical, political, and social as it is scientific.

> The applications of science are inevitable and unavoidable ... But something more than its application is necessary. It is the scientific approach, the adventurous yet critical temper of science, the search for truth and new knowledge, the refusal to accept anything without testing and trial, the capacity to change previous conclusions in the face of new evidence, the reliance on observed fact and not preconceived theory ... Too many scientists today, who swear by science, forget all about it outside their particular spheres. The scientific approach and temper are or should be, a way of life, a process of thinking, a method of acting and associating with our fellow men ... It is the temper of a free man. We live in the scientific age, so we are told, but there is little evidence of this temper in the people anywhere or even in their leaders.[2]

[2] Jawaharlal Nehru, writing in 1944, articulated his thoughts on scientific temper while incarcerated in Ahmadnagar Fort Prison. Subsequently published as *The Discovery of India*, Calcutta: The Signet Press (1946).

REASON UNREASON: STUDENTS' STRUGGLES AGAINST OBSCURANTISM

Remaining in the dark closets of one's vocation or perhaps only engaging in vicarious events of a scientific nature allows one to distance oneself from social and political engagement and continue to work in the sciences.

One could argue that working scientists have played a rather ancillary role in people's engagement with scientific temper, both historically and in contemporary times.

To illustrate this, readers may find this narrative interesting. At the end of 2012, two years before the protest against the new Prime Minister, in an increasingly polarized environment, *Concern,* a broad-based Left students' group in IISc, which was formed in the mid-90s and existed on campus for more than two decades, organized a screening of Anand Patwardhan's celebrated documentary *Ram Ke Naam*.

Ram Ke Naam (1992) – a masterpiece of documentary filmmaking – stands as very important material and a visual narrative of the Babri Masjid demolition, the widespread riots, and the events surrounding it. The film captured the faces of bigotry, the language of hate, the helplessness of fear, and the visceral scale of the destitution that the organized communal riots had on the Muslim community in India. The film exposed how the demolition resulted from and had a significant impact on the profound political polarizations within Indian society and how those effects shaped the history of India in the coming decades. This film remained authentic documentation of the assertion and ascendancy of the Hindutva-communal forces in Indian polity.

For these reasons, the film, even though widely watched, discussed, taught in several universities and courses across disciplines, remains a flashpoint for attacks on students who organize screenings, teachers who teach about its significance, and people who gather to watch by the groups and individuals who align themselves with the ideology of RSS. Very few legally cleared films in world cinema can perhaps match the persistence of the acerbic attacks it receives, where each screening is a potential threat, a struggle, and thereby a counter assertion, even nearly three decades after its first screening!

Therefore, it is understandable that the students of a left group like *Concern* would find this impactful and necessary to screen, and engage with the country's contemporary history.

Contrary to the culture of IISc, where organized disruptions are rare, a motley group of students and researchers aligned with Hindutva politics put their efforts into disrupting the screening. The organizers thwarted the attempt. The vehemence of this Hindutva-aligned group to establish that the documentary peddled lies to malign the prominent leaders of the BJP like Atal Vihari Vajpayee, Lal Krishna Advani, Murli Joshi, Kalyan Singh et al., the RSS, and the Vishva Hindu Parishad (VHP), even though their public rallies, addresses, and meetings spoke for themselves in the film, exposed the real purpose of this disruption.[3] It was a – 'how dare you' – that relied on force rather than reason! One agitating researcher, who identified himself as a PhD student, kept shouting that there was archaeological evidence, dating 9.5 lakh years ago, of the presence of *Ram* in Ayodhya, implying that the demand – *mandir wahin banayenge* (the temple will be built there) – a slogan that communicated the political demand and ensuing terror succinctly, was indeed evidence-based!

Now, one can easily brush this aside as a ridiculous one-off statement had we not witnessed that courtrooms after courtrooms, public figures, cultural icons, and so on have succumbed to these myths.

3 Ravishankar, Ra. responds to Aishhwariya Subramanian, 'Sparks Fly at IISc over Anand Patwardhan Documentary on Babri Masjid Razing,' kractivist.org, 15 December 2012, https://www.kractivist.org/sparks-fly-at-iisc-over-anand-patwardhandocumentary-on-babri-masjid-razing/.https://www.kractivist.org/sparks-fly-at-iisc-over-anand-patwardhan-documentary-on-babri-masjid-razing/.

Much like the social and political contexts laid the groundwork for education, it is no different in the sciences. Thus, one can practice science and technology without being analytical about one's surroundings.

At the same time, we have also witnessed the growing disquiet among researchers and scientists in the past few years. As obscurantism assumed assertion in the polity, the rationalists were murdered, attacked, and threatened regularly; myths were peddled from the podiums of science congresses; more students and scientists rallied in public protests. Even under tremendous intimidation, this is continuing.

The students' protests or agitations are not unusual in these 'premier science institutions', at least in that they range from the issues emanating from and related to the specific institutional concerns to national political questions. They are, however, often irregular in the absence of an organized students' struggle. Thus, it may be prudent to explore the nature of political spaces in these institutions.

WHOSE STRUGGLE IS IT ANYWAY?

The political spaces within the campuses at the research institutions are important to understand for the students' engagement with democratic processes. At the same time, equally meaningful is recognizing the ideological axis (or lack thereof) along which students engage within their institutions and with the society at large. This article will attempt to explore this, drawing from the narratives of protests.

In the structure of the institution, the students' council – a democratically elected body – represents the students of IISc. The students' council is supposed to take up issues concerning the students with the administration. In reality, however, students' council often functioned as a mouthpiece of the administration; it disseminated the administration's decisions among the students.

The activities of students' council were largely limited to organizing various cultural events and voluntary donation events like blood drives, clothes donations, notebook donations for nearby schools, once-a-year/abandoned bicycle clearance drives, and a few seminars/events on 'career opportunities' or 'counselling'. Though an elected body, often the posts were not contested, and the individual student who would file nominations for the posts of Chairman, General Secretary, Academic Secretary, Women's Secretary, Hostel and Amenities Secretary; and more recently Undergraduate Secretary would get elected uncontested. In most instances, students' council would function as a club with an institute appointed faculty advisory committee to guide students' council members. Thus, students' council would often fail to take a position on the students' interests where it is contradictory to that of the administration. On numerous occasions, the individual students or a group of students reacted to the pertinent issues and took them up with the administration, while students' council remained a bystander. There were instances when students' council joined the students' agitation reluctantly at later stages.

In 2013, for instance, the administration moved to withdraw subsidies, thus, privatizing the students' mess. This aligned with the MHRD directives under the then second United Progressive Alliance (UPA-II) government led by Dr Manmohan Singh. The UPA-II was pushing aggressively for privatization of higher education since it came to power in 2009. The students at IISc, apprehensive of hikes in mess fees, began an agitation. Even before that, the efforts to privatize the services had begun. A couple of years before this, around 2011-2012, the institute slowly started deregularizing the mess workers, with privatizing the mess and outsourcing the workforce. A section of students protested at that time too, when one of the C-mess workers was served a deregularization notice. The students' council kept its distance. It was the directives of the MHRD that the institutes were implementing. In the mould of neoliberal austerity of cost-cutting, the UPA-II government was laying off workers, privatizing utilities and services, outsourcing, and contractualizing, which furthered the commercialization of campuses and brought uncertainties to workers' livelihoods and students' services. Studies have shown that it is not only inefficient to privatize these services, but it also does not reduce costs. The workers in the mess, sanitation, security, construction, and other services are, in turn, left at the mercy of the contractors, where institutes no longer take any accountability for the working people who serve these institutions. The experience and work of the workers' forum *Hamara Manch,* at the Indian Institute of Technology Kanpur (IIT-K) reflect the pitfalls and grave injustice of privatization of campuses. Since their inception, newer institutes like Indian Institutes of Science Education and Research (IISER) have been created with privatized workforces in the services and utility area. However, the work of *Hamara Manch* (at IIT-K) and the struggles elsewhere also provide a spasmodic yet significant and burgeoning narrative of sections of students' and scientists' support towards concerns of workers on their campuses. The support often stems from and becomes publicly visible when there are immediate and correlated effects for the students like withdrawing subsidies and privatizing the mess services, thus contributing to the increase in mess fees and/or when there are tragedies involving human lives, like accidents or the death of workers. For instance, on 30 June 2019, the newly constructed iron gate of IISc's main entrance came crashing down on the on-duty security guards, killing Gautam Biswal, a migrant worker from Odisha and severely injuring two other guards. The administration showed no urgency and went behind the procedural curtain. But the students pulled down the veil, demanding immediate suspension of the contractor and manufacturer. They demanded setting up a committee with student representatives so that the institute could look into its engagement with contractors and how it was addressing the labour issues. A large number of students joined this agitation in support of the workers. They stormed the director's office and intensified the struggle for transparency in the investigation, which extracted promises from the administration at the end of three days.[4]

In 2012-2013, there were several smaller and larger students' protests at IISc on mess subsidy withdrawal and its privatization impact. Several emails (the author was part of several email conversations) by the students involved in those protests and newspaper reports of the period establish that the administration had to withdraw or silently shelve several orders in the face of these protests and demonstrations. A large section of students was able to identify the central government's role in these privatization moves. In contrast, a smaller section was able to understand that the neoliberal policy trajectory withdraws subsidies, increases mess charges, contractualizes workers, and hikes tuition/admission fees, and were all beads in the same garland.

In the 2013-2014 Students Council elections, which happened before the large agitation against the mess subsidy removal notification in early 2014, a group of students contested who had progressive agendas. Annuradha Rakesh, a graduate student from Management Studies, and Femi Olu, a Nigerian graduate student from Materials Engineering, led the campaign contesting for Chairperson and General Secretary, respectively. They put together a panel with a specific agenda. This election was interesting in several ways. This election was held with a backdrop of protests against the mess privatization efforts. During the course of the campaign, the contest was divided between certain progressive agendas on one side and a *status quoist* formation on the other side. Equally important was that, for the first time in IISc history, a woman student and an international student were contesting for chairperson and general secretary, respectively,

[4] Ralph Arakal Alex, 'IISc Bengaluru Students' Protest Enters Third Day Over Security Guard's Death,' *The Indian Express*, 04 July 2019, https://indianexpress.com/article/cities/bangalore/iisc-bengaluru-students-protest-on-safetyconcerns-in-campus-5813556/./

representing an alliance of candidates. Their agenda reflected clearly that 'the administration cannot compel students to support mess privatization without due democratic consent'; they would not meekly communicate the administration's decisions to the students, nor would they play a role in placating students' voices. Both of them lost the election to the *status-quoist* alliance, but they were able to generate important democratic discussions around the narrow window of a campus election.

The 2014 spring semester, despite a meek SC, witnessed a spirited students' agitation on campus. With the administration adamant in withdrawing the mess-subsidy, the students from different messes and their mess committee members came forward and took up the issue. For a campus known for its indolent students' agitation, it took the administration by surprise when around 800 students marched to the main administrative building. They refused to negotiate with the registrar; with their slogans echoing amongst the high ceilings, they made the director listen to their grievances and apprehensions and sought the mess-subsidy withdrawal order removed. For the moment, the administration blinked.

This agitation exposed the students' council yet again. Students were charged up about this issue, and they could observe SC's reluctance to raise issues that sharply concerned the students. The 2014 students' council elections were around the corner. The candidates in the 2014 election emerged from this agitation. Kallol Roy, a graduate student in Physics, and Anindita Brahma, a graduate student from the Ecological Sciences, led an alliance of candidates contesting for the Chairperson and General Secretary, respectively. Both were visible during the agitation, and, more importantly, so were all members of the alliance. Thus, when they campaigned among the students, they were identified as those who had questioned the administration, in contrast to the other section, who were closer and more aligned to the outgoing students' council members and lackeys for the administration.

The progressive alliance formed the students' council with a 4-1 majority and probably elected the first woman General Secretary in the history of IISc's students' council. This is significant for two reasons. First, the agenda was dominated by the recent experience of the agitation, and the candidates emerged from this agitation. In other words, candidates who won were motivated by the dialogues during the agitation. They were keen that students' council must unflinchingly represent students' issues and not be a consenting body. Second, IISc, like most other science and technology research institutions in India, is gendered with a heavy male bias. Though the tendency is comparatively subdued among students compared to faculties, women have rarely contested in posts other than for Women's Secretary, let alone assumed office, with the significant exception of Annuradha Rakesh as the Chairperson candidate the previous year. The campaign turned polarised in the run-up to the election, targeting the progressive alliance as a left-wing panel in a largely politically apathetic campus. Whereas the alliance of candidates shared common views of raising pro-student concerns and progressive values, it was not an organized left alliance. The progressive alliance won with two female candidates – Women's Secretary and the General Secretary – and two male candidates, Chairperson and Hostel Secretary – for these central panel posts.

The 2014 students' council became proactive in taking up students' issues with the administration. In its tenure, three major initiatives of students' council, concerning students' welfare and responsible activism, warrant highlighting. The new students' council took on the mess subsidy issue, which had carried them into office, with the administration and further pushed them to shelve the move. They took up a fellowship discrimination issue set in motion by MHRD's whimsical diktats and were part of the country-wide agitation. And, they confronted head-on The Art of Living Foundation, a business enterprise operating at IISc, generating money using the IISc infrastructures.

SOME GET MORE, SOME GET LESS: INDIA'S UNDERPAID SCHOLARS

In February 2015, a protest was brewing across the country. Research scholars called for a protest action opposing differential disbursal of stipends to students supported by different funding agencies.

India pays its research scholars very poorly. Particularly, the students pursuing their PhDs at Indian universities live on a meagre stipend, often irregular and supported mainly by the universities or department grants. The students in centrally funded research institutions such as IISc, Indian Institutes of Technology (IITs), National Institutes of Technology (NITs), and IISERs, the Council for Scientific and Industrial Research (CSIR) institutions, the Department of Atomic Energy (DAE) institutions, and the Department of Science and Technology (DST) institutions receive more regular and comparatively higher stipends as compared to the researchers at Indian universities. However, these stipends too were not revised regularly. Their demand for a hike in the stipend was long overdue.

The MHRD and then Minister, Ms Smriti Irani, was sitting on MHRD's promises. Different funding agencies came up with varying implementation dates for the stipend hikes! This meant that students in the same institutions and even in the same lab would get different pay based on which funding agency supported them. Researchers called for a demonstration in front of the MHRD building in Delhi. They were arrested.[5]

While one could observe that these protests by the students of India's *elite* scientific research institutions overlooked the more significant crisis of struggling researchers at Indian universities, it was also the time when discrimination was institutionally accentuated, further based on who was funded by which

[5] Priyanka Pulla, 'Indian Grad Students Take to Streets over Miserable Pay,' *Science* 23 February 2015, https://doi.org/10.1126/science.aaa7894.

scholarship. In practical terms, it meant that peers working in the same lab or the same department would get different stipend remunerations!

The carrots of certain fellowships, soaked in meritocracy, are left to rot on these campuses. At the same time, in consecutive budgets and actual funds disbursals, the scholarships for the Scheduled Castes and Scheduled Tribes (SC/ST) students are squeezed. Discrimination is institutionalized within institutes and departments, and such scholarship cuts jeopardize social justice objectives in Indian higher education.

However, these protests emerged as immediate responses to the MHRD's missives; protests around regular and reasonable stipends continued to erupt across campuses. IISc's students' council extended its total support for the agitation, mobilized students, went for mess campaigns, and even some members of the extended students' council joined the hunger strike. The students' council called for General Body Meetings (GBM) and drew up the campus-specific agitation programme for this nationwide protest. As the campaign intensified, the students were mounting pressure on MHRD and were vocally opposing the Modi government's anti-student stance. However, there were students with links to the Akhil Bharatiya Vidyarthi Parishad (ABVP), an RSS affiliate organization, trying to limit this agitation to the departmental notifications of the MHRD and not a protest against the policies of the Modi government. In contrast to the previous year, IISc's student council protested with the students. The protest venue in front of the main administrative building garnered wide attention. Also, since the protest engaged in a sit-in and relay mode for over a fortnight, along with a hunger strike, slogans, posters, songs, performances, and street theatre, it created an atmosphere of dissent and democracy where many students participated. The students forced the administration to visit the protest venue and communicate students' grievances to MHRD. The protest finally made MHRD relent by withdrawing the circulars they issued earlier of increasing the fellowship for a certain section of students and not addressing the long pending demand of fellowship hikes for all categories of students.

India's research scholars are still severely underpaid. And, the inequality in fellowships between universities and research institutions (and across disciplines), analogous to the increasing income inequality in the country, continues to exist. This students' agitation did not address those concerns, nor did it try to bridge the widening gap between the peers of universities and institutions in terms of stipends. This agitation had limited influence and outcome. However, at IISc, it created an avenue to reignite the spirit of the 2014 agitation and to continue to draw more students into policy directives or issues that affected them.

THE CLOAKS OF THE QUACKS AND HOW THE ART OF LIVING FOUNDATION OPERATES

The vocation of sciences does not implicitly ensure engagement in scientific temper and rationality. The common cultural practices of most laboratories often do not encourage students to engage intellectually with scientific temper beyond the narrow regimes of objectivity set as gold standards for experimentations and research designs for the problems that the laboratories/groups are working on. Thus, when The Art of Living Foundation (AOL), a large business enterprise of a Hindu Godman (guru) 'Sri Sri' Ravi Shankar, who touts himself as a humanitarian and spiritual leader, enters the institutes like IISc and 'takes classes' on yoga and meditation, one can understand why engaging in scientific temper must be necessary for scientific institutions.

The AOL and other such enterprises entered IISc and similar institutes through their network of followers on campus. After an informal session, they would start advertising, often with posters or broadcast emails (that the followers would share), on how their meditation methods helped reduce stress and why they were scientific (one needs to sell this point, after all, in a science institution). The advertisements generously highlighted all the institutions, such as IITs, some foreign universities, or some private software companies, where they claimed to have conducted sessions similar to IISc, thus claiming fame while validating their activities by peppering the ads with the name of the institutions. Elsewhere, in a similar business ploy, they would use IISc to secure credibility.

Of course, there is no free lunch. AOL charges students for the meditation/yoga/stress-buster courses. Using the institute's facilities, they conduct their sessions, create a cult following, and generate revenues for the organization.

When the new students' council assumed office in 2014, they acted on some of the students' complaints. The Students' Council objected to the operations of AOL within IISc. They queried why AOL was charging students, and students' council questioned their permission and impunity of operations using the institute's facilities. The students were apprehensive about the Hindu religious views the group espoused with its dubious claims of 'scientific method' of practice in a secular higher education institution. The students' council brought these apprehensions and the students' objections to an external private body using institute facilities for monetary gain to the administration. The students' council steering committee passed a resolution in its meeting not to endorse the functioning of AOL within the campus.

Based on the complaints and Students' Council's apprehensions, the administration banned AOL from using IISc facilities for monetary gain.

This attracted the wrath of some of AOL followers, which included a few students and had the tacit support of a few faculty members. These AOL followers gheraoed the General Secretary, Anindita Brahma, in front of the students' council office and demanded that students' council withdraw its decision of not endorsing the AOL on campus. The General Secretary and students' council (barring one ABVP member) stood their ground. Around the same time, the General Secretary thwarted a similar attempt, this time directly by the RSS, to misuse an institute hall for a political brainwashing session under the guise of cultural celebration. Along with a few alert students, she flagged this to the administration and made them step in, preventing a closed-door, openly hate-filled religious session. Some of the most prominent supporters of AOL were common participants in the RSS's failed meeting.

It showed that in the face of festering religiosity and organized obscurantist practices on campus, a responsible representative students' body along with alert and rational students together could thwart such an agenda and bring institutional accountability to the limelight. Thus, after four years of banning AOL at IISc, in 2019, when 'Sri Sri' Ravi Shankar was invited on campus by a handful of influential members of the faculty, including a serving deputy director of IISc, more than 700 students, researchers, and alumni wrote to the director asking IISc to dissociate from the event.[6] Under pressure and criticism, the IISc administration had to distance itself from the event. Even though the deputy director and a few faculty members behaved as 'devotees to a Godman', the intense criticism rekindled the steadfast position the 2014 students' council took in ousting AOL officially from the campus.

The snub that AOL and RSS received at the hands of IISc students in 2014-2015 made them contest the 2015-2016 students' council election as an organized force. Informally among the students, they became the AOL panel. This tremendously polarized the election, much more than any other students' council elections held in the last decade. Amiya Banerjee, a graduate student from Nanoscience and Wasimakram Binnal, a graduate student from Management Studies, led a progressive alliance as the Chairperson

[6] The Wire Staff, 'IISc Students Protest Sri Sri Talk on Campus for 'Unscientific' Views,' *The Wire*, 11 October 2019, https://thewire.in/education/iiscstudents-protest-sri-sri-talk-on-campus-for-unscientific-views.

and General Secretary candidates, respectively. The campaign was heightened with issues on scientific temper, whether religious organizations should find space on an educational campus, and on parity in fellowships and so on. The campaign in this election extended beyond the messes and hostels, reaching out to students in the labs. The progressive candidates defeated the entire AOL panel with a thumping 5-0 majority in the central posts.

Though the 2015 election brought the much-needed debate on what a scientific institution should be and was contested on students' issues beyond their immediate and narrow demands, the intense engagement was for a shorter period. In the absence of an organized students' movement, the democratic discourse often takes a backseat except during a period of reaction or when the issues affect students more intimately. One can observe this phenomenon by noticing how oblivious a large section of students at IISc remain to the Students' Council's elections and activities in general or when observing a pattern of voting along regional linguistics lines during the elections.

I had heard this on numerous occasions when several working scientists boasted how institutes like the IISc, IITs, institutes set up under the DST, Department of Biotechnology, CSIR, DAE and, more recently, the IISERs 'don't have students' politics'. They often were scornful toward the universities, a handful of which had vibrant students' movements still aspiring to shape the agenda of education, questioning policies, and not readily succumbing to the asymmetry of power in academia.

THE SPECTRE OF A UNIVERSITY IN A SCIENCE INSTITUTION

There are often distinctions made between universities and research institutions. It rests mainly on the quality of research output as a standalone index, conveniently creating social capital for merit. It overlooks education's (and universities/institutions) rather crucial social function in teaching, learning, and training students from the vast, diverse sections of society.

I found this rather interesting when I came across consternation expressed by senior professors and people higher up in the academic hierarchy. I will pick an inane one. IISc does not have a humanities or social sciences department. For a long time, powerful sections in decision making resisted these fields. One anxiety that withstood the test of time was that if humanities or social sciences were introduced, it would become like any other university. A few in positions of power agonized that 'IISc would become a JNU'! This *spectre* of universities is real, and the exceptional view of these institutes runs deep, even though significant sections of the faculties remained alumni of public universities – in India or from abroad!

It is also interesting for another reason. P. Balaram, a former director of IISc and who was instrumental in setting up the IISc Archive, in a talk organized by the Archive at the National Centre for Biological Sciences, elucidated the formative years of IISc. With a keenness to document an institutional history, which is largely absent among the educational administrators and establishment scientists in India, Professor Balaram and his colleagues could locate several of the earlier documents in setting up the IISc. These are critical in understanding not only the institutional history but also, possibly, of higher education in colonial India at a phase when the national freedom struggle was aspiring and preparing itself for post-colonial institution building. The draft plan conceptualized IISc as a university, with not only humanities and social sciences as integral parts but also medical sciences, a vocation amputated largely from the university education in India and left to lurch in its professional ambit. In 1898, Burjorji J. Padshah, a key architect in the establishment of the Indian Institute of Science, working with Jamsetji Tata, drafted a proposal that conceptualized the institute with three departments:[7]

[7] P. Balaram, 2018. NCBS Archives Public Lecture Series: The Conception and Birth of IISc. https://www.youtube.com/watch?v=horcEiRiHh0.

1) Scientific and Technical department, with sub-departments in Physics with Mathematical Physics and Electrical Engineering, in Chemistry segregated into Advanced Inorganic Chemistry, Organic Chemistry, Analytical Chemistry, and Agricultural Chemistry,
2) in Medicine with sub-departments of Bacteriology, Hygiene and Physiology, and Pathological Chemistry, and
3) in Philosophy and Education with sub-departments in Methodology of Education, Ethics and Psychology, Indian History and Archaeology, Statistics and Economics, and Comparative Philology.

Thus, this contemporary perception and vision regarding scientific research institutions stand in contrast with the historical project of institution building.

There are certain parallels with the technical institutions that one can observe within Indian scientific establishments. The N.R. Sarkar Committee was set up in 1945 to review the state of technical education in India. In the 1948 interim report, the committee astutely noted 'the narrowness common among students in technical education'. As the Harvard anthropologist Ajantha Subramanian in her book *The Caste of Merit: Engineering Education in India* noted in drawing the history of establishing the IITs, the committee envisaged new institutions to 'integrate mathematics, science, and humanities with the specialized professional subjects'.[8] Half a century ago, both the N.R. Sarkar Committee and Burjorji Padshah identified the Massachusetts Institute of Technology or John Hopkins University as 'the exemplar model' with a mix of applied and theoretical, humanities, and social sciences.[9] However,

[8] Ajantha Subramanian, *The Caste of Merit: Engineering Education in India* (Massachusetts: Harvard University Press, 2019), p. 67.

[9] Kim P. Sebaly, 'Tata Steel and Higher Technical Education in India: The Padshah Plan, 1916–21,' *History of Education* 17, no. 4 (1988): pp. 309-20, https://www.tandfonline.com/doi/abs/10.1080/0046760880170405.

Subramanian highlighted the debate that was a precursor to the formation of the IITs and raised the apprehensions that 'the existing institutions are likely to stagnate and decay while the newer institutions will work in an atmosphere of isolation'.[10] Scientists like Nazir Ahmed and Meghnad Saha argued for '*a closer alignment between scientific and technological research and education and the existing network of national universities*'. Still, as Subramanian observed, the apprehensions 'on the potential for institutional isolation, limited impact, and undemocratic limits to access went largely unheeded'.[11]

Though these are not the concerns or issues to which the students' movements are paying attention, they reflect the spaces in the academies where they are operational. Creating a public understanding of higher education that rests and nurtures a monolithic notion of merit devoid of democratic involvement has helped operationalize these concerns. Since their inception, a large number of the scientific establishments of research institutions have remained isolated from society without a vibrant democratic engagement both within and outside.

GUARDING THE TRENCHES OF THE IDEA OF A UNIVERSITY

While working at IISc, one can acquire a desolate engagement with democracy. But the bulwark of institutions protected by order of merit could not suppress the students who challenged the order and marched against the regimes. In 2016, when Rohith Vemula succumbed to an institutional witch-hunt and humiliations at the UoH; and when the bots reached a university gate baying for the blood of the students and thumping to shut down Jawaharlal Nehru University (JNU), its students arrested, assaulted in public court, and the Modi-government unleashed the full might of the State where ministers became indistinguishable from trolls,

[10] Ajantha Subramanian, *The Caste of Merit*, pp. 66-71.

[11] Ibid., p. 74.

the spring of solidarity wasn't far away at IISc. The idea of a university was under unprecedented assault. And students at IISc, like the students on campuses across the country, were counting themselves in the resistance.

In the immediate aftermath of the institutional murder of Rohith Vemula, the students at IISc joined forces at a demonstration in Bangalore's Town Hall, where a large number of students gathered from across the research institutions, colleges, and universities in Bangalore. *Concern* organized a condolence meeting on campus, which was attended by students and scientists.

When the campuses were churning with demands of justice for Rohith Vemula, articulating a sharp narrative of struggles for social justice, JNU came under an unprecedented combined attack from the State and RSS. The Bangalore town hall swelled with students from IISc, the National Institute of Advanced Studies, the Jawaharlal Nehru Centre for Advanced Scientific Research, the Raman Research Institute, the National Centre for Biological Sciences, the Indian Statistical Institute, the National Law School of Indian University, the Bangalore University, the Azim Premji University, the Institute for Social and Economic Change and from across many other colleges. Close to 400 prominent scientists-researchers wrote a letter to JNU's VC expressing 'deep disappointment with your actions in the events leading up to the arrest and detention of several students', calling on him to protect the students and the university.[12] Many students and scientists of IISc signed the petition, and many students joined the protest demonstrations in the streets. The media widely covered the town hall gathering of researchers and scientists. With escalating attacks on JNU students and teachers in Delhi and the attack on the Jawaharlal Nehru University Students' Union (JNUSU) President

[12] Jacob Koshy, 'Scientists, Academics Protest JNU Student Leader's Arrest,' *The Hindu*, 18 February 2016, https://www.thehindu.com/news/national/Scientists-academics-protest-JNU-student-leader%E2%80%99s-arrest/article14084639.ece.

in the court, students at IISc, led by the group *Concern,* initiated a petition on the campus addressing the President of India. Students were collecting signatures in front of the messes when they came under attack from right-wing students on campus. Infuriated by the media reports of the large turnout at the town hall protest earlier and seeing the posters calling to – *Repeal Sedition Law, Stand with JNU, Free the Students* – a group of RSS-ABVP supporters pounced on the students. They tore up the signature sheets, physically abused and threatened students, provoked the organizers, and branded them as 'anti-nationals'. This physical altercation was rather unprecedented at IISc. With the ongoing state-supported violence at universities becoming a public spectacle, police entering campuses at the slightest provocations, and violent mobs shaking campus gates, the situation alarmed the students and scientists at IISc. Understanding the intent of this attack and the provocations, the students of *Concern* displayed the utmost maturity and restraint. They immediately approached students, scientists, and the administration, asserting their right to peaceful demonstration and the signature campaign. While the administration was mulling over permission and procedural issues, several members of the IISc faculty came out in strong support of the students. They could no longer ignore the vicious campaign by RSS against the universities, knowing that if left unchallenged, IISc could become a target of mobs, trolls, and hate politics.

A group of faculty rushed to the director and strongly backed the signature campaign as a democratic exercise on campus. A senior mathematician of international repute argued against permissions and procedural quagmire; he asked, '... could students henceforth need permission from the director or deans for every petition they float?'. The administration capitulated. *Concern* went on with the signature campaign. It became evident to the students and scientists that in a polarized country ruled by the politics of hatred, no campuses were immune or protected.

In the subsequent years, the universities across the country came under uglier, more desperate attacks, as if it was raining assaults. Throughout 2019, IISc students regularly responded to these attacks. When police lathi-charged students on the streets of Delhi for protesting against fee hikes at JNU and other universities, the IISc march called for putting an end to commercialization; when the BJP MP Babul Supriyo led a frontal attack on the students and teachers of Jadavpur University (JU), IISc rallied in solidarity with Jadavpur. Within months, mobs attacked Jamia Millia Islamia (JMI) and Aligarh Muslim University (AMU). Students at IISc staged a sit-in demonstration near the J.N. Tata statue. If the attacks made it clear, on the one hand, that no campuses are immune to the organized politics of hate, on the other hand, *students established that no campus would shy away from standing in solidarity.*

FATALITIES OF MERITOCRACY

For society to accept the triumph of capital, many myths must be spun to disguise the exploitation and injustice. What the landed gentry, the kings, and nobility exploited with their accumulation and inheritance of the power of wealth, and by using existing – and creating new – social divisions for centuries to maintain that power, under capitalism, it all sharpened.

While capitalism rests upon creating and enforcing inequality, the people are fighting for the dignity of labour and life, equal opportunities in education and healthcare, and other social and political rights. People of colour asserted these demands through relentless struggles worldwide, fighting sharply in Europe and North America. The movements seeking gender equality, caste equality, and the recognition of and restoration for indigenous people are asserting their demands for justice, asking *why are there so few of us in the universities and so many of us in the sweatshops.*

Universities are not shielded from these social and political contexts. The myth of merit offers a powerful trope that negates history, ignores multiple and critical pedagogic practices, and spins injustice, yet it triumphs, becoming reasonably socially acceptable through valorizing a few individuals alone. Generations have been lost to this fallacy, while the myths of merit continue to flourish. In the science vocations of higher education, this is nakedly visible. Merit construes a conduit to obfuscate this.

Investigating the racial disparity in income, covering almost the entire population of the United States from 1989 to 2015, a group of social scientists and demographic researchers discovered that 'the black Americans and American Indians have much lower rates of upward mobility and higher rates of downward mobility than whites, leading to persistent disparities across generations'.[13] The social disparity is a decent predictor of who becomes an innovator or a scientist and who grinds away in sweatshops. One would think that this is obvious. However, these studies use population-level (census scale) empirical evidence combining inter-generational income estimates, census data, taxation, and employment data to establish how equal opportunity remains elusive to the millions of marginal people and their families. This affects not only their livelihoods in their lifetime but also deeply impacts their children and grandchildren and so on.

There are broad similarities or patterns of subjugation and extermination. This design is not limited to North America or erstwhile colonial nations.[14] In India, we see an abysmally low representation of Dalit and Adivasi students in higher education in sciences, engineering, and medicine, even after almost three decades of the post-Mandal framework of reservations.[15]

[13] Raj Chetty, et al., 'Race and Economic Opportunity in the United States: An Intergenerational Perspective,' *The Quarterly Journal of Economics* 135, no. 2 (2020): pp. 711–83, https://doi.org/10.1093/qje/qjz042.

[14] Anand Teltumbde, *The Persistence of Caste: The Khairlanji Murders and India's Hidden Apartheid*, (New Delhi: Navayana, 2011).

[15] Priyanka Pandey and Sandeep Pandey, 'Survey at an IIT Campus Shows How Caste Affects Students' Perceptions,' *Economic and Political Weekly*, 53, No. 9, (2018), https://www.epw.in/engage/article/Survey-at-an-IIT-Campus-ShowsHow-Caste-Affects-Students-Perceptions. Also see S.

Not only is there disproportionately lower representation, but Dalit and Adivasi experiences within the scientific research and higher education institutions remain growing testimony of institutionalized discrimination and neglect.[16] The students from socially marginalized sections who enter institutions like IIT, IISc, IISER, or Tata Institute of Fundamental Research (TIFR) find themselves out of place, which presupposes a hostile culture of merit. These hostilities are often subtle, tacit, but on many occasions – public.[17] When you do well (in class, on an assignment, or working through a problem), 'you are brilliant (for your background)', 'you are different', 'oh, you're good in math, chemistry, biology', 'didn't expect you to do this'. These are the compliments in disbelief or surprise shrouded in caste and social prejudice. These are somewhat subtler. Often someone who does not have a nuanced understanding of how caste prejudices and discriminations are accentuated might miss them. But for Dalit, Adivasi, or other marginal caste students, these are forms of psycho-social trauma within the framework of the institutions. If you don't do well in a class or a course or solve a problem, you run the danger of validating caste notions!

Do Dalit and Adivasi researchers escape social stigma in scientific establishments? No. The stigma haunts them in

Rukmini, 'India's Unequal University System,' *Mint*, 9 September 2019, https://www.livemint.com/news/india/still-too-few-dalits-in-indian-colleges-1568013598781.html.

16 Satish Deshpande and Usha Zacharias, eds. *Beyond Inclusion: The Practice of Equal Access in Indian Higher Education*, (New Delhi: Routledge, 2013) Sukhadeo Thorat and S. Madheswaran, 'Graded Caste Inequality and Poverty: Evidence on Role of Economic Discrimination,' *Journal of Social Inclusion Studies*, 4, no.1, (2018): pp. 3–29, https://doi.org/10.1177/2394481118775873.

17 S. Srinivasa Rao, 'Structural Exclusion in Everyday Institutional Life: Labelling of Stigmatized Groups in an IIT,' in *Sociology of Education in India: Changing Contours and Emerging Concerns*, ed. Geetha B. Nambissan and Srinivasa Rao (Oxford University Press: 2012), pp. 199–223. https://academic.oup.com/book/4186/chapter-abstract/145995578?redirectedFrom=fulltext. Ajantha Subramanian, *The Caste of Merit*.

classrooms, laboratories, and private spaces – hostel rooms, public spaces of the mess, dining areas, and playgrounds. The sociologist of education from JNU, S. Srinivas Rao, drawing from his ethnographic research at IIT-M, shows how the institutions become festering grounds of social stigma for Dalits and Adivasis.[18] The narratives bear testimonies to how Dalit and Adivasi students and even faculty have to carry these stigmas like the proverbial cross. This affront to the students' and faculty's dignity and equity forces them to withdraw socially, taking shelter in a much smaller homogeneous group. Institutions turn into trauma centres, and individuals struggle and graduate with bruised self-esteem and dignity. These sociological perspectives are essential because they do not treat the scientific establishments in isolation, as chambers of merit, where grades or academic outputs are the sole measures of an individual. Instead, these perspectives allow us to situate importance to the narratives, often ignored as individual 'problems', and draw evidence from it to link with the social inequality and caste hatred prevalent in society and reflected in the institutions. Most importantly, the narratives of these traumas, their documentation, the tireless struggles that students' organizations and individuals take up against this inequality, the infinitesimally incremental advances, the more overwhelming heartbreaks – all are constitutive of the demands for democratic and inclusive systemic reforms.

In addition to fighting the odds of social stigma, the economic hardships Dalit and Adivasi students face are palpable. Though this reality befalls a much larger section of the students coming from economically weaker sections across castes, the intergenerational mobility of Dalits and Adivasis remained stagnant for decades and, in recent years, even regressed. After coming to power in 2014, the Narendra Modi-led BJP government purged the

[18] S. Srinivasa Rao, 'Structural Exclusion in Everyday Institutional Life: Labelling of Stigmatized Groups in an IIT,' in Nambissan and Rao (eds.), *Sociology of Education in India*, pp.199–223.

Planning Commission. Since then, the designated allocations in the financial sub-plans for SC and ST students were systematically eroded, with efforts to relegate them form an integral part of financial planning to certain programmatic disbursements. By doing so, the State was able to abdicate its responsibility and negate the necessary, proportionate population-based allocations to mere token and whimsical disbursements. Already, these are reflected in a reduction in budgetary allocations and subsequent expenditures. The fellowships are in decline, and the support that allows Dalit and Adivasi students to continue education is nearly non-existent.

Access to higher education is one of the significant avenues for economic opportunities and intergenerational mobility. Similar to what was discussed earlier about racial segregation and economic opportunities in the USA, in India, much of the inequality between the SCs, STs, and OBCs with that of the upper castes in terms of land holdings or enterprise ownership (i.e., stable and sustainable economic opportunities) reflect the perpetuation of inequality.[19] Though the empirical data is not on the scale of the studies examined in the USA, several of the surveys of the National Sample Survey Organization (NSSO), whether they reflect household consumption, household expenditure, access to assets or assets ownership, provide a picture of the depth of this inhumane inequality.[20] Thus, it is not surprising when studies conclude'[that] the inequality in per capita consumption expenditure is due to inequality in asset ownership (agricultural land and enterprise) and higher education'.[21]

In a scientific establishment like IISc, we often hear voices against reservations. 'Reservation should not be based on caste' or 'Reservation should be for the economically poor', and other such

[19] Sukhadeo Thorat and S. Madheswaran, 'Graded Caste Inequality and Poverty,' pp. 3-29.

[20] Raj Chetty, et al., 'Race and Economic Opportunity in the United States,' pp. 711-83.

[21] Sukhadeo Thorat and S. Madheswaran, 'Graded Caste Inequality and Poverty,' pp. 3-29.

assorted illiterate social justice views spew forth on campus, both from students and faculty members. The caste blindness in peer groups has a debilitating effect on students from the marginalized sections. Thus, when a group of students formed the Babasaheb Ambedkar Study Circle (BASC) at IISc in 2018, it was precisely to bring conversations on caste and the project of social justice to the forefront. Such efforts had earlier amalgamated in the formation of Ambedkar Periyar Study Circle (APSC) at IIT-M, and Ambedkar Periyar Phule Study Circle (APPSC) at IIT-Bombay and, more recently, at IIT-Gandhinagar. The experience of Dalits and Adivasis on these campuses and their flagrant absence in scientific establishments even after three decades of a reservation system precipitated in shaping these anti-caste students' groups.

SUITABLE CANDIDATES NOT FOUND, AND THE MISSING SCHOLARS

It is evident that the glaring absence of Dalits and Adivasis has not bothered India's scientific establishments; neither has the absence of women. Institutions and academies remained non-committal to any structural changes toward addressing social marginalization across various axes.

In *Dispersed Radiance: Caste, Gender, and Modern Science in India*, the scientist-turned-science historian Abha Sur of the Massachusetts Institute of Technology unpacked the gender and caste hegemony in the first half of the last century.[22] Sur elucidated the work of scientists, particularly that of two influential scientific thinkers, Meghnad Saha and C.V. Raman, within the social and political context of the times. Raman, in particular, discouraged women students from joining IISc; he enforced strict sex segregation in his lab and had only three women research students

[22] Abha Sur, *Dispersed Radiance: Caste, Gender, and Modern Science in India* (New Delhi: Navayana, 2011).

in his whole academic life.[23] In Sur's reconstruction of a critical history of Raman's women research students, Lalitha Doraiswamy (*nee* Chandrashekhar), Sunanda Bai, and Anna Mani, none of them received the recognition that they deserved as scientists. After finishing her work with Raman, Lalitha married the scientist Subhrahmanyan Chandrashekhar and did not pursue scientific research professionally. Both Sunanda Bai and Anna Mani worked for substantial years with Raman; none received a doctorate. Sunanda Bai died by suicide, and Raman never supervised a woman student again. Anna Mani went on to work extensively on meteorological instrumentation and weather, and retired as the Deputy Director-General of the Indian Meteorological Department.

These examples are not the idiosyncrasies of the individuals. *Connect*, a magazine of the publication cell of IISc, covered the institute's outlook on gender through a series of articles and interviews.[24] Writing the cover article, Deepika S. drew attention to the historical context of allocating resources for women students, their narratives, and the recruitment of women faculties at various levels chronologically.

> On the day IISc first opened its doors to students, as the Institute's Annual Report for 1911 tells us, one hostel block was ready for occupation. What the Annual Report doesn't mention, however, is that the 'students' hostel' was only meant for men. In 1909, plans had been made for staff quarters, two blocks of student quarters, quarters for 'servants, sweepers and maistries', and even quarters for police. But it would take around three more decades for a women's hostel to feature in the Institute's plans.[25]

[23] Ibid.

[24] S. Deepika, 'Women and the Institute' *Connect*, 5, no. 2, (June 2018): pp. 2-3.

[25] Ibid.

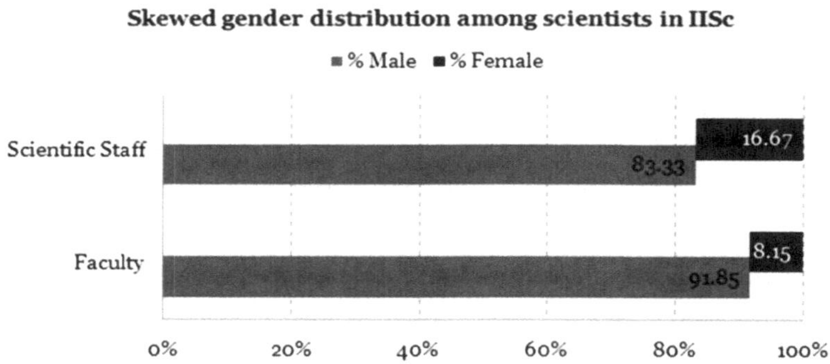

Figure 1: Gender distribution among the faculty and scientific staff members at IISc reflects a flagrant skew typical in scientific establishments in India. (The data is based on the serving faculty and staff as of 1 July 2021)

If women did not feature in an institutional plan for the sciences in India in the first half of the twentieth century, it was by design that they were excluded. If women do not represent the proportion of the population in Indian science and research institutions today in the twenty-first century, that design will continue and adhere. In both instances, meritocracy continued to overlook and supersede the project of equal opportunity.

The past four decades of faculty recruitment at IISc reveals this reactionary occluded view on gender and caste. Out of the 466 serving members of the faculty, there are only a handful of women scientists, 38 serving at IISc as of 1 July 2021 (Figure 1) – a mere 8 per cent. There are only two OBC and Dalit women and no Adivasi women on the faculty at IISc. Of the sixty-six serving officers across departments, eleven are women scientists, around 17 per cent among the scientific staff. There are only three Dalit women who are scientific officers, while none are from OBC and Adivasi social backgrounds.

The scientific establishments and academics, particularly in North America and Western Europe, are unable to ignore the near-total dominance of men. While #WomenInSTEM is becoming a contemporary rallying point, institutions are justifiably questioned

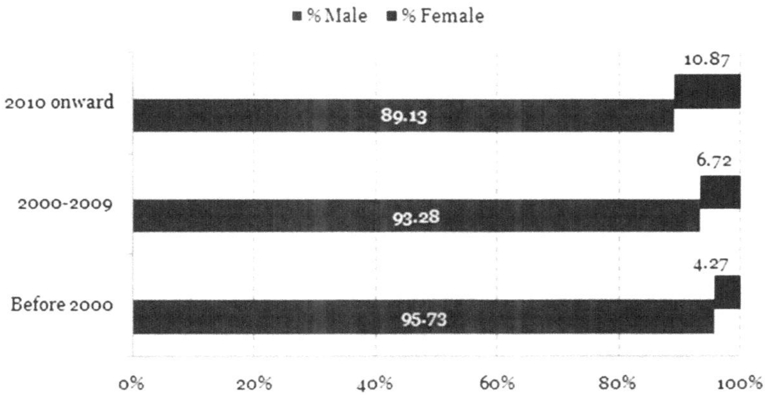

Figure 2: Gender distribution in faculty recruitment over four decades in IISc. (The data captures members of the faculty recruited over four decades who are serving as of 1 July 2021)

for their commitment to the call for *diversity*. And, when diversity is the call, along with gender justice, strong voices challenge white domination. In India's scientific establishments, gender equality has been a point of discussion, particularly in the last half of this decade. Looking at the timeline of recruitments at IISc, the previous decade witnessed incremental progress, even though nearly 90 per cent of the recruits were men (Figure 2).

However, Dalit-Lives-Matter or Adivasi-Lives-Matter hasn't emerged as a force knocking at the doors of the academies. IISc is representative of India's scientific establishment's failure and total non-commitment to the social justice project. More than 94 per cent of the faculty are from upper castes, of which upper-caste men alone consist of around 87 per cent. Of the 466 serving faculty members, 12 and 13 are from OBC and Dalit social backgrounds, respectively (Figure 3). Only two Adivasi scientists are serving at IISc. It was fourteen years ago when an Adivasi was last recruited, and the previous recruitment was twenty years ago, almost a generation!

Among the non-teaching posts of scientific officers, almost 55 per cent are from upper castes, while Dalits and Adivasis comprise

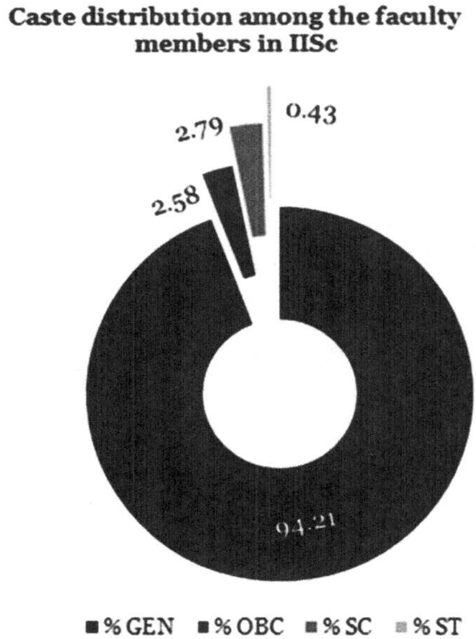

Figure 3 (above): Caste distribution of members of the IISc faculty reflect near homogeneity and domination of upper castes. (The data is based on the serving faculty members as of 1 July 2021.)

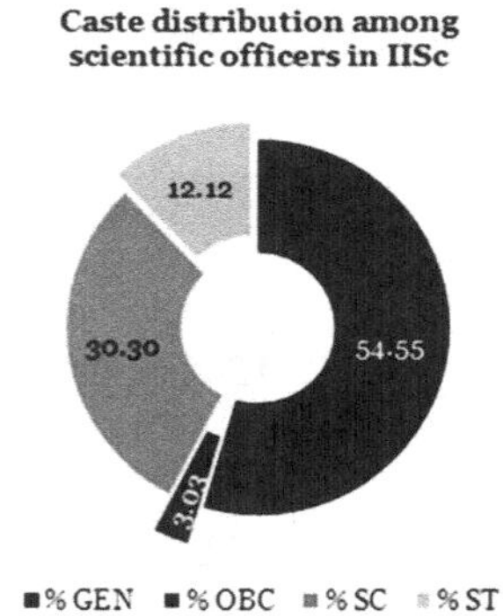

Figure 4 (above): Caste distribution of scientific staff at IISc. These non-teaching posts comprise less than 15 per cent of the serving members of the faculty and are far and few between. (The data is based on the serving staff as of 1 July 2021.)

30.30 per cent and 12.12 per cent, respectively, among the serving sixty-six scientists (Figure 4). The scientific officer posts are far and few between, and a department typically has only one or two such positions. Though there is a significantly higher representation of Dalits and Adivasis than the proportion among faculty members, scientific officers are not in positions of authority in departmental decision making, as those committees are primarily drawn from faculty members.

The history of faculty recruitment at IISc establishes the ongoing hegemony of upper castes in India's scientific establishments, and there is no epiphany in sight. The decadal breakup (Figure 5) also shows the lack of institutional mechanisms to address this discrimination. Of the recruited faculty before 2000, who are currently serving, more than 98 per cent were drawn from the

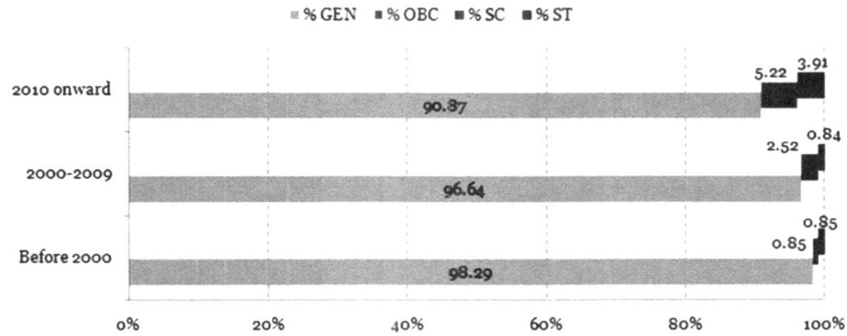

Figure 5: Caste distribution in faculty recruitment over four decades in IISc. (The data captures members of the faculty recruited over four decades who are serving as of 1 July 2021)

upper caste (Figure 5). To add insult to injury, of this 98 per cent, only five women scientists were recruited, and after adding all reservation categories together, there was only one Dalit member recruited as faculty in the entire decade of the 1990s. Things didn't improve. In the first decade of 2000, only four faculty were recruited across all reservation categories, three Dalit and one Adivasi faculty out of 119 recruitments in ten years. No faculty were recruited from an OBC background in the 1990s and 2000s. Between 2010 and July 2021, out of 230 recruitments, 12 OBC and 9 Dalit faculties were recruited, corresponding to 5.2 per cent and 3.9 per cent, respectively, of the total recruitment of the period (Figure 5). No Adivasi faculty were recruited during this period. Thus, there continues to be the absence of an inclusive policy, and, therefore, all the talk on the institutional policy of diversity and occasional showcasing of individuals or running hashtags remains pretentious.

IISc is not an aberration. A decade of recruitment data from the oldest IIT, IIT-Kharagpur, substantiates this systemic exclusion (Figure 6). On 6 November 2019, the registrar of IIT-Kharagpur responded to a request from an Under Secretary of the Ministry of HRD, detailing the caste categories of a decade of faculty recruitment from June 2008 to October 2019. No Adivasis

Systemic bias in faculty recruitment in IIT

IIT Kharagpur faculty recruitment data for the period June 2008 - October 2019

Total GEN OBC SC ST

	Total	GEN	OBC	SC	ST
2008	8	8	0	0	0
2009	23	23	0	0	0
2010	20	18	2	0	0
2011	9	9	0	0	0
2012	10	10	0	0	0
2013	47	45	2	0	0
2014	25	24	1	0	0
2015	31	28	3	0	0
2016	41	37	4	0	0
2017	29	29	0	0	0
2018	80	77	1	2	0
2019	59	50	8	1	0
Total	382	358	21	3	0
% of recruitment		93.72	5.5	0.79	0

Source: Council of Indian Institute of Technology • Created with Datawrapper

Figure 6: Caste distribution in faculty recruitment over a decade in IIT-Kharagpur with a yearly breakup.

were recruited into IIT-Kharagpur out of the total of 382 teachers who were recruited in this period; only three Dalits were recruited (<1 per cent). During this same period, if IIT-Kharagpur followed the mandated reservation of 27 per cent for OBC candidates, 15 per cent for SC candidates, and 7.5 per cent for ST candidates, it would have had a maximum of 103 teachers from backward castes, 57 teachers from Dalit communities and 29 teachers from the Adivasis. However, this is a crude estimate and might not reflect the roster-system that the IITs are supposed to follow.[26] For instance, it was not clear immediately how many of those recruitments were advertised and under which category those vacancies were, or what was the backlog of vacancies across all categories during this period and did the institution take any measure to address the

26 Reservation roster is an application to determine the reservation of posts in a cadre for different categories with reference to the applicable percentage of reservation.

backlog of vacancies in the categories of SC, ST, and OBC.

'Suitable candidate not found' is the customary response from India's scientific establishments when confronted with the obscene bias against the socially and historically marginalized. For years, this, too, remained the standard response for not recruiting enough women in STEM. It becomes an important question, therefore, how have the institutions evaded India's laws on reservations? Are they not following the roster system of recruitment? And, if not, how are they circumventing this? These are some of the questions the Left and anti-caste movement organizations assertively pose.

EMBRACING AMBEDKAR-PHULE

In debunking the prejudice in *science* that was ever so eager to explore the biological basis of intellectual superiority and, therefore, of merit, and less so in comprehending the palpable and evident correlates of social inequality in opportunities, what the Harvard evolutionary biologist and palaeontologist Stephen Gould wrote remains an important pointer even in contemporary India.

'I am, somehow, less interested in the weight and convolutions of Einstein's brain than in the near certainty that people of equal talent have lived and died in cotton fields and sweatshops.'[27]

Gould's words are proverbial; caste hegemony makes up the largest proportion of the Indian population outcast in science, whether in recruitment or training. That it gets ignored by institutions for decades speaks to the nature of India's scientific establishments. In February 2021, in the upper house of parliament, the CPI(M)'s MP, Elamaram Kareem, sought answers in a series of questions on the current status of reservations in Indian scientific establishments. The Minister's response reflected how top-tier institutions like IISc are falling short of implementing affirmative

[27] Stephen Jay Gould, *The Panda's Thumb: More Reflections in Natural History* (New York: W.W. Norton, 1980, 1992).

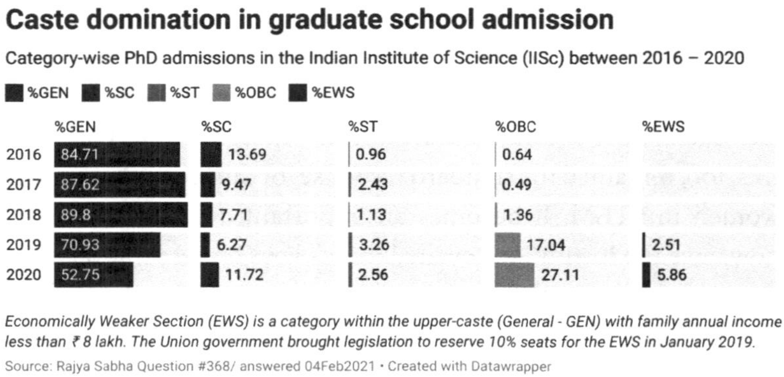

Figure 7: Caste distribution in PhD programme admission in IISc for 2016-2020.

action measures. During the five years between 2016 and 2020, the Dalits, particularly Adivasi students, were underrepresented in selecting PhD candidates, and there existed a systemic upper-caste bias (Figure 7).[28]

If the missing scholars from the margins are a concern, the institute is non-attendant to the dialogue on caste. How would an institute meaningfully commit to diversity if it stays away from the concerns of the marginalized? In one of the initial reading sessions of BASC in 2018, a key organizer succinctly expressed the group's purpose as he envisioned it: 'Dalits have been reading Ambedkar for decades now. But, has the upper-caste engaged with Ambedkar? Would it be possible for Dalits and backward caste people to annihilate caste? Is it not all the more important for people from upper castes to understand sociology, history, and the narratives of caste oppression? Ambedkar said *educate*. Should upper castes not educate (themselves on caste)?'[29]

The BASC is a small group of student-researchers. They

[28] The analysis is based on a question posed by the MP Elamaram Kareem in Rajya Sabha and answered by the Minister of Education on 4 February 2021. See: Question 368 of Elamaram Kareem at https://rajyasabha.nic.in/Questions/MemberWiseSearch#.

[29] This is part of a conversation from a weekly meeting of BASC at IISc in 2018 where the author was present.

engaged in a serious reading on caste. It is important to observe the emergence of similar groups in a few of the other campuses across India. Such groups often provide and subsequently create a space for dialogue on caste. Other than studying caste, BASC engaged in organizing students and mobilizing opinions on issues related to the campus and beyond.

In contrast to organized students' movements, these groups are nascent and largely depend on a few students to organize activities to engage others. Further, on a campus where Dalits and Adivasis are stigmatized, unless the organization emerges as a force to be reckoned with, it does not always exude confidence among Dalit and Adivasi students to publicly rally behind. Among the sections of the already stigmatized Dalit and Adivasi students who found the group to be an ally, there was still apprehension in publicly showing their association, fretting about their peers' or supervisor's reaction. More profound sociological observations and studies are necessary to understand the stigmatized marginalized section's nature of engagement with democratic and progressive spaces at IISc.

HUM DEKHENGE – WE SHALL SEE

Organized students' movements are largely absent in the scientific establishments in India. So is a collective organized effort to initiate dialogues discussions on contemporary and historical questions concerning science, technology, national and international developments. Organized movements on campuses played this historical role, connecting the campuses with the larger society and engaging in democratic processes. The significance of a broad-based students', researchers', and scientists' organizations lies here.

These dialogues were integrally present within several of these scientific institutions during the anti-colonial struggle and post-independence. The World Federation of Scientific Workers, originally a trade union of scientists, technicians, and researchers, later, when transformed and founded in July 1946, brought scientists across different nations and colonies together in associations with internationalist ideals. Internationalism is integral to science in its worldview and praxis. This view was organized and created collaborations, mature debates, and platforms to share ideas in the anti-colonial and anti-war struggles in 1940, both in the colonial nations and in the colonies waging an anti-imperialist liberation struggle. The Association of Scientific Workers of India (ASWI) emerged in India on the heels of independence with Jawaharlal Nehru as its founder president, which included the active participation of leading scientists of the time. Scientists like Meghnad Saha actively campaigned for the ASWI through his writings in *Science and Culture*, and ASWI could galvanize the imaginations of the younger scientists and scholars who would go on to lead India's scientific establishments like Satish Dhawan and Pushpa Bhargava, among others.[30] Not limited to the leading scientists, ASWI emerged to capture the broader base of scientific workers in India in the 1950s and 1960s. As ASWI units were established in colleges and universities across the country, science teachers, scientists, students, and young researchers joined. J.D. Bernal, J.B.S. Haldane, and Joseph Needham actively collaborated with ASWI.

Thus, there were vibrant dialogues within scientific establishments on scientific temper, democracy, institutional planning (which led to the expansion of scientific institutions and infrastructures), against wars, and in strong solidarity for peaceful coexistence. These also laid the foundations for the people's

[30] In October 1946 issue of *Science and Culture* (Vol. XII, No. 4) Saha called attention to the scientists and educators the necessity of unionizing with an editorial titled 'A plea for an Association of Scientific Workers'. In the same volume, J.D. Bernal explained further the objectives of ASWI with an article, titled 'Organizations of scientific workers' delving on the praxis. See: Meghnad Saha, 'A Plea for an Association of Scientific Workers,' *Science and Culture*, XII, No. 4, (Oct 1946): 157. J. D. Bernal, 'Organizations of Scientific Workers,' *Science and Culture*, XII, No. 4, (Oct 1946): pp. 158-160.

science movement in India. Since the 1980s, and particularly with the formal embracing of the neoliberal trajectory in the 1990s, India's scientific establishment witnessed a distancing from the legacies of the anti-colonial struggles and of planning for national self-reliance. While embracing neoliberalism, the top scientific agencies in India imported a managerial framework in science with a thoughtless imitation of the American scientific establishments. The designation of *principal investigator* adorned scientists in every institute in India. This is not a semantic issue. There is a systematic push for scientists to consider themselves managers, managing their own research groups and projects. Thus, what started as a prerogative of accountability in research projects for funding agencies, turned out to be a career profile for a scientist. It is, therefore, a long way from scientists or scholars considering themselves as scientific workers or thinkers to get sized into the boxes of principal investigators!

Are scientists citizens of a democracy? Once, perhaps, unimaginable, this is now a bona fide question. As the vocation of sciences in general and institutes in particular turn increasingly regimented, the project of building democratic citizens recedes within the campus boundaries. This has a far-reaching tragic consequence. Inquiry and critical thinking are foundational to science. If the motivation for public engagement limits its bounds to the customary acknowledgement of public funding, scientists continue to be co-opted as a messianic apparatus of the State rather than qualifying for their social role as critical thinkers.

At the same time, some of the most placid campuses feel the ripples, if not outright waves, when students resist. When students organize, they push back. They created space where scientists could incubate themselves in the democratic citizenry rather than staying apathetic, isolated, or oblivious. The range of protests over the last decade at IISc is a testimony to students' engagements with the democratic process, their reflections and responses to injustice, and their embrace of progressive ideas even in the absence of organized movements. These narratives from IISc would presumably stay in the margins of the vibrant democratic student movement in the country, as many campuses and stubborn student organizations faced the wrath of a Hindutva neoliberal state and violent fundamentalist mobs but stood unvanquished. Nonetheless, these are the narratives of promise and hope.[31]

[31] I thank the following for their inputs in shaping this article: Anindita Brahma read a section of the draft, and her comments were invaluable. Discussions with Alakta Das helped me verify a period in the timeline of events at IISc. The section of the data covering the status of reservation in IISc – capturing the gender and caste composition – is part of a more extensive (yet to be published) study on scientific establishments in India, and I immensely thank the many sources who shared their observations, data and insights, and who wished to remain anonymous.

'Only When a Daughter is Safe, She'll be Able to Study': The Struggle for a Safe Campus at Banaras Hindu University

Satarupa Chakraborty

An Interview with Mineshi Mishra[1]

The Banaras Hindu University (BHU), or the Kashi Hindu Vishwavidyalaya, is one of the oldest universities in India, located in the 'holy' city of Varanasi (it is also known by the names of Banaras and Kashi) in Uttar Pradesh. The university was established in 1916 by Pandit Madan Mohan Malviya, who was a part of the Hindu Mahasabha. With the independence movement as the background, this university soon became an important centre of learning. Along with contributions in various fields of knowledge building, '[it] has produced many great freedom fighters of modern India.'[2]

In contrast to the history of this university, in subsequent years and most recently, the university authorities, like most other authorities in institutions of higher learning across India,

1 Conducted on 24 January 2019 and updated in May 2022.

2 'About BHU,' Banaras Hindu University, https://bhu.ac.in/index.php.

are unwelcoming or scornful when their students participate in politics on campus.

In 2017, when the country was witnessing protests by the students, a disturbing incident of sexual harassment took place at BHU. While these incidents were rampant, the women students suffered in silence. However, due to years of accumulated anger over the regular occurrence of molestation and stalking, the students collectively revolted against such crimes. The university women provided leadership to the protest that soon drew enormous support from the larger community of students. Their placards highlighted the slogan '*Bachegi Beti, Tabhi Padhegi Beti*' (Only when a daughter is safe, she'll be able to study), and it struck a chord with the larger society.[3]

Instead of standing with the students who were protesting against gender violence, the university administration played a disgraceful role in downplaying the incident. The VC of the University, Girish Chandra Tripathi, in fact, stated, 'This was not a case of molestation; this was a simple case of eve-teasing'.[4] He believed that the protesting students were deliberately staging the protest a day before the Prime Minister's visit to the city. There was an attempt to turn attention away from the actual cause of the protest instead of addressing the students' demands. The administration labelled the students as 'leftists' simply because they demanded a transparent inquiry into the incident and sought measures to end such harassment on the campus.

In order to understand the protest, we spoke to a student who was part of the movement. This interview attempts to record

3 Supriya Nidhi, ' 'Bachegi beti, tabhi padhegi beti': BHU students up in arms against varsity administration,' *National Herald*, 24 September 2017, https://www.nationalheraldindia.com/national/bachegi-beti-tabhi-padhegi-beti-bhu-students-up-in-arms-against-varsity-administration.

4 Alok Pandey, "Simple Eve Teasing': Varanasi University (BHU) Vice Chancellor Questions Protests,' NDTV, 26 September 2017, https://www.ndtv.com/india-news/just-eve-teasing-varanasi-university-bhu-vice-chancellor-girish-chandra-tripathi-plays-down-protests-1755086.

the historic protest at BHU in 2017 – the changes this students' resistance brought to the campus and the nature of assaults the students had to confront. It also documents the journey of Mineshi Mishra, who, after joining BHU in 2015, became an activist.

In 2017, the BHU students started an agitation after an incident of sexual harassment reportedly took place on 21 September 2017. Could you elaborate on the incident? How often do such incidents take place on campus?

A female student at BHU was returning to her hostel in the evening around 7:30 pm. When she was about halfway from hostel, near Bharat Kala Bhavan (the university's museum), a group of men drove up on their motorbikes and surrounded her. The men on the motorbikes molested her – they groped her. She fell to the ground. This incident took place much before the usual hostel closing time. Such incidents are very frequent at BHU. I, too, witnessed such incidents before 2017.

On the evening of 21 September, our proctor was present near the spot where the incident occurred, but he did nothing; he was a mute spectator. The administration has never made any attempt to investigate incidents of sexual harassment or violence. As a result, these incidents have become a regular phenomenon and are considered 'normal' on the campus.

Can you reflect more on the complicit role of the BHU administration on such issues and the nature of the BHU administration that you have experienced?

The BHU administration chose to remain silent whenever a case of sexual harassment occurred. This attitude encouraged men with a sense of entitlement to do whatever they wanted. While the university proctor is appointed to intervene in such matters, they have chosen not to perform their duties. Conversely, they often interfere in activities that their responsibilities do not entail. For example, they are often seen controlling and redirecting the routes of the rickshaw pullers and auto drivers, whereas there are designated personnel to perform these tasks. If the administrative officers find a couple (a man and a woman) wandering around, or simply a man and a woman hanging out together as classmates, they immediately start harassing them – threatening them with reprisals. It has, in fact, become a practice that they (the administrative officials) would physically remove these couples and take them to the proctor's office. They would make the students write an apology letter with a declaration that the behaviour would not be repeated. Sometimes, the administration even calls the students' parents to harass them further. So, the administration is always keen on moral policing and harassment of the students, but they have no interest in stopping incidents of sexual harassment even when they witness them directly.

On the evening of 21 September, our proctor decided not to involve himself in the incident as those men were not easy to deal with. Directly following the incident, the woman went to the proctor's office and reported everything. Instead of supporting the student, the proctor accused her of instigating the incident. He said that she was at fault for having gone out in the evening instead of being in the hostel, and this incident would not have happened if she had been in the hostel.

Women's hostels, in most universities, have specific rules. Are there such rules at BHU women's hostels as well? What is your opinion about such rules in women's hostels?

Yes, specific rules applied to women's hostels. Those rules, in my opinion, are very regressive. For instance, BHU has a curfew for the women students that requires all women to return to their hostels at a specific time. My hostel had an 8:00 pm closing time. Other hostels, including the one I am staying in now, close at 10:00 pm. The women's hostel at the medical college used to be open 24/7. The Indian Institutes of Technology (IIT) women's hostel closes at 10:00 pm. There is no consistency. Such rules are not there for the men's hostels, and no one cares if the men are in their hostels after 10:00 pm. Whereas, for us, the rules exist and must be strictly adhered to.

Additionally, there are also rules regarding how a woman should be dressed. Wearing shorts is not allowed even within the common areas inside the hostels. Varanasi gets hot during the summer. Initially, four of us used to share a room with a single fan, which was not sufficient. For practical reasons, we needed to wear short and loose-fitting clothes. But more importantly, why should a warden or an administrator decide what clothes I should wear? Women students were harassed and threatened. The administration told women hostelers (indiscriminately), 'What kind of woman do you want to portray yourself as? If you go out dressed like this, men will molest you'. So, in essence, they were saying that a woman student is responsible for anything terrible that happens to her.

While I was residing at the hostel, the warden seized my phone on two instances and did not return it for five days. It demonstrates their mentality. They assume that if a student is talking on the phone after 10:30 pm, she must be in a romantic relationship, which is not allowed under their 'norms'.

I think that such rules need a radical change, as these rules often lead to moral policing of women rather than addressing the real problems. These rules were not part of the hostel's manual, but they were prescribed, unwritten rules which everyone had to follow without question. We were verbally informed about the 'rules' during the admissions process – the 'what we can and can't do rules', and the wardens followed them strictly. If anyone did not follow these unwritten rules, the woman student would be ridiculed in front of everybody in ways that no one would dare to break the rule again. Therefore, those hostel rules often lead to harassment and moral policing of the women students. I think that these rules must change. In a university, a man and a woman should have equal rights, and rules should be formulated based on this principle. I want that equal right.

Does BHU have elected students' representatives or a union?

There is no students' union at BHU. Some organizations such as the Akhil Bharatiya Vidyarthi Parishad (ABVP), the National Students' Union of India (NSUI) and Samajwadi Chhatra Sabha (student members of the Samajwadi Party) are present there. But there is no elected union.[5]

Does the absence of a students' union make it difficult for students to have a democratic space within the university?

It has affected us substantially. For instance, when we want a space on campus to organize meetings or cultural programs, we are denied the space. Yet people from political parties (often members of the BJP) have come to BHU several times, made speeches in the lecture halls, and the VC attended those events. So, when it comes to inviting a Bharatiya Janata Party (BJP) person to the university, the VC opens up the campus space; but we have no space when it comes to representing our voice. Anybody who differs from the BJP's political viewpoint is not provided space. If we hold events, we are told that we are politicizing the campus, which is against the rules.

Is there a complaints' committee or gender sensitization cell on the campus? Is there any record of complaints of sexual harassment?

As far as I know, there is no record to be found. There is no committee such as a Gender Sensitization Committee against Sexual Harassment (GSCASH). There is no record of how often

[5] Elections for a students' union were banned indefinitely by the BHU VC Y.C. Simhadri, on 20 February 1997, following large scale violence during an election rally, which led to the death of a student at the university.

incidents of sexual harassment take place. Due to the fear of victim shaming, many women often choose not to file a complaint. When filed, complaints are often dismissed, and the administration tries to 'settle' cases rather than investigate them.

The cases, therefore, are not registered. That is why I strongly feel that there is an imminent need for GSCASH. Students should have an institutional body where everyone can put their confidence and trust. Most of the incidents are not reported because women feel that the administration is not trustworthy. Due to this, they had no faith that justice would prevail. So, women either choose to deal with the situation themselves, or they do nothing at all and suffer in silence.

There is an internal complaints committee at the university, which exists only on paper. There are neither meetings nor gender sensitization classes held. Practically, this committee does not address complaints. It just exists on paper, and university students have little or no knowledge of it.

Massive resistance from the students followed this incident of sexual harassment. We saw in the media that women were leading the protest. Can you explain how the protest began? What were the initial demands to the administration?

Immediately after the incident, the victim returned to her hostel and shared her horrifying experience with her friends. They complained to the warden. The warden, however, dismissed them and the incident. Clearly, he was attempting to cover up the harassment incident.

In response to the cover-up by the administration, hostel students staged a protest on the evening of the incident. The next day they decided to move their demonstration to the BHU main gate and requested others to join them. Women students joined in huge numbers. I was an undergraduate student at that time. I went to the protest site in the afternoon along with my friends. The protestors were discussing the need to file a complaint with the police. Also, the students demanded that the VC address the issues of sexual harassment on campus and the need for strict action by the administration – as such incidents were common and needed to stop.

Every woman could relate to the incident. The common question was: 'Why are these incidents so frequent on the campus? Why are the proctors not doing anything about these attacks against women, even though a significant amount of the university's budget is slated for the gender fund?' The demonstrators demanded that the VC explain what steps were being taken to investigate incidents of sexual harassment, and what steps he took specifically regarding the latest incident? Students demanded that the VC put an end to the harassment culture and the assurance that no more incidents would occur in the future.

How did you get involved in the protest and become a key voice? Can you share some experiences?

When I went to the protest, I realized that although the central demand was focused on the incident of sexual harassment and the need to end it, many other issues were being raised as well. For instance, if a media channel would ask a student at the protest to speak about the demands, the student would also talk about ending the curfews at the hostel; others would raise the point that the VC should meet with the protestors and address the issue. But a clear charter of demands was yet to be formulated. At that moment, it became clear that a complete list of demands was necessary. I volunteered to prepare such a list of demands. So, by the first night of the protest, we had our list of demands printed in a pamphlet. The pamphlet was circulated to all the students present at the protest. We also requested for their support and asked for their inputs to modify the demand charter if necessary. The students agreed with almost all the demands; we had a starting point to build a consensus for shaping the protest.

Was there any central slogan to articulate all the demands of the students? Could you elaborate on the charter of demands?

The demands were formulated at the protest; they came from the students who had faced harassment either physically or morally. So, our slogan was focused on '*Swatantra, samta, suraksha, siksha, avam shanti*' (freedom, equality, security, education, and peace). The key demand was to ensure legal action against the culprits of sexual harassment and the irresponsible proctors of the university. In order to attain gender sensitization on campus and to check sexual harassment, we demanded a functional GSCASH. We highlighted the curfew and demanded the revocation of the rule to access the university facilities just as the men did. In addition to these demands, we included the proposed installation of more lights, increased security, and the establishment of helpline numbers, managed by women on campus. These were some of the central demands.

Your charter of demands proposed the idea of instituting the GSCASH. You, too, mentioned the need for having a GSCASH. How did you find out about the GSCASH, as it is institutionalized at only a few universities, such as Jawaharlal Nehru University (JNU) or the University of Hyderabad (UoH)?

Initially, I did not know about GSCASH. So, in the charter of demands, I first proposed that a body, as per the UGC recommendation, be established at the university. During the protest, I discussed with a senior who first introduced me to GSCASH. I read the rules of GSCASH at JNU and UoH and found them very useful for dealing with many of the problems that existed at BHU. I was not the only one; most students in the protest were not unaware of GSCASH. During the protest, we got an opportunity also to educate ourselves.

The women led the protest. Did it bring any change in claiming the physical space by women on the campus? Can you share your experience?

The curfew was enforced during the protest, but remarkably, the women students stayed there at the protest even beyond the curfew (8:00 pm). The hostel gates remained open; the women students would return for dinner and then go back to the protest. Seeing women students roaming around the campus, even after 8:00 pm, was an unprecedented occurrence to witness at that time. There was such a fierceness among the women. The best thing the protest did was to create a space for women on campus, which liberated the women from their fear. Until our protest began, the campus was a regular site of harassment. But things changed once women started participating in the protest in large numbers. Those who might have been involved in harassing women were now afraid of doing so. The women were not afraid to take a step forward or speak up against any incident of harassment should someone be so inclined. We generated this strength from the protest. There was a strong feeling of unity.

What were the challenges the students faced amid the protest? How did the students react to those?

Challenges existed, of course. From the beginning of our protest, the administration tried to cover up the incident of sexual harassment. They also tried breaking up our protest following the 'divide and rule' policy. For instance, professors were sent to BHU's Triveni hostel, where they attempted to separate other protestors from the Triveni hostel residents by calling the protest solely a hostel issue. The hostel wardens were asked to advise the women students not to participate in the protest. They tried to divide our solidarity – to break the bond between the women in the protest. Then the administration tried to isolate the women protestors from the men protestors, describing the issues as women's issues only and questioning why men would protest on their behalf. The administration directed professors to restrict students from leaving their classes to protest. They also locked the doors of the washrooms to discourage women from staying at the protest site for long durations. The administration adopted such petty tactics in their attempts to stop the protests.

But we responded to all those tactics by continuing a unified protest. We said that anybody who supported the protest could participate. It didn't matter if the person was a woman, a man, or a transgender person. However, there were efforts to incite violence in the middle of the protest. Provocateurs were sent in to start a fight amongst the protestors, citing the so-called violence; the police were called in to respond with a lathi charge. The administration tried to project our protest as violent, and they justified their actions by saying there were disturbances at the protest. We, however, resisted such attempts by intervening so that our protest remained peaceful. Therefore, despite all their attempts, our protest continued. We were able to communicate with our people and maintain our unity.

The Akhil Bharatiya Vidyarthi Parishad (ABVP) has a significant number of members in BHU. What was their role as a students' organization during the agitation?

Initially, they were part of the protest. But once the administration's intervention started, their support also dwindled. ABVP enjoys certain benefits on campus from the administration. When the administration admonished them for their participation, they simply pulled back. In fact, they tried their best to stop the protest at that point. But the protest had already escalated, so they could not stop it – their attempts failed.

In recent times, we witnessed that whenever a movement escalated, the administration of various universities, and the ruling party, targeted the movement by circulating negative propaganda. You, too, hinted at this earlier. Could you elaborate a bit more?

When their 'divide and rule' policy, and their violence and provocations failed, they adopted the policy of negative propaganda as their tool to sabotage the protest. We were branded as 'leftists' and as 'opportunists' because we 'chose' to protest during the prime minister's visit to Varanasi. They accused us of ruining the university's image and condemned us as puppets of outsiders and leftists at JNU, who they said were controlling the protest. However, even this narrative failed. The protesting students could relate to the issues involved. That's why this propaganda against the protest had little impact.

The media was focused on BHU at that time. One day, suddenly, the statue of Dr Radhakrishnan at the BHU gate was found defaced. Immediately, the administration blamed the protesters and continued their drivel about how the protestors wanted to destroy the image of BHU. The funniest part is that the statue is so high that one needs to climb a ladder to reach it. Later, an investigation was undertaken, and it was found that their allegation of our involvement in the defacement was false.

How were the decisions taken during the protest, and how were the strategies formulated?

After the protest began, we formed a Joint Action Committee (JAC) with more than a dozen members. JAC did not start the protest. It was an organic protest that developed through the spontaneous participation of students. But later, after JAC was formed, it played a pivotal role in shaping the entire protest. JAC is not a political organization. JAC is a group of progressive students. Students of all political organizations were part of JAC. Those who were not affiliated with any political organizations, such as me, were also a part of JAC.

For any movement, an organizing committee or a leadership group is essential. Otherwise, the protest could not have been sustained, given the administration's crackdown attempts. For instance, when the administration tried to spread false propaganda, the JAC promptly clarified in response. It provided the necessary leadership to shape the protest, which was essential. Activities such as putting up posters, initiating creative campaigns, and laying down a charter of demands, were taken up by JAC. The committee comprised both men and women, although except for Shivangi Chaubey and me, the majority of JAC's members were men. However, the decision was taken that the women would lead the protest. It was the women who were standing at the forefront. JAC shaped the protest and protected it from outside forces.

You have talked about the campaigns and circulation of movement materials. What types of channels did you use to popularize the campaigns?

BHU Buzz played an essential role at that time.[6] It is a platform on social media that was started two or three years ago. It delivers news on BHU. As many students are Facebook users, this platform was helpful to our protest. It served as a means to inform the students about the events. BHU Buzz has a good reach. So, we had a platform to communicate with a large number of students and the general public to clarify the false propaganda against the protest. In fact, some students sent the videos of violence by those who wanted to destroy our protest, and the videos of the lathi charge by the police to the BHU Buzz platform to publish. Using our page, we issued appeals to the protesting students to not be provoked by those who came to incite violence as the administration would take steps against our peaceful protest. We were sure that our voice would reach a large number of students, and we were correct. Also, the videos, which BHU Buzz published, reached news portals and media channels. So, it turned out to be an effective medium of information and communication.

[6] BHU Buzz is a Facebook page and describes itself as 'a social media platform for students of BHU to interact with each other through blogs, videos & other mediums'. It also provides regular updates about events, seminars, and other happenings at BHU. For more: https://www.facebook.com/BhuBuzz

Sustaining a protest for long sometimes tires out the protestors, especially when the attacks are vicious. How did the students maintain the protest amid the administration's crackdown and other challenges?

We, the protesting students, were branded as being 'anti-student'. They alleged that we were protesting for publicity and were the representatives of leftist ideas. The administration said that we were there to ruin BHU. It was not easy for us, as one had to attend to many things to keep the protest successful. For instance, we had to ensure continuous discussion with everyone participating in the protest. Since this protest was not led by a single leadership group or a political organization, every decision had to be made via constant discussion until there was a consensus. Then, we had to coordinate with the media and ensure that false propaganda never went unchallenged. All of this was quite tiring and time-consuming. We did not have any leadership experience before the struggle; we were just a group of people with a certain energy level, which helped keep the protests going. It was undoubtedly difficult. But ensuring a democratic process helps keep a protest alive. We were few but consistent and faithful. We felt tired many times. But it was worth our effort.

Was there any victimization of the protestors after the protest? Did you get targeted due to your participation in the protest?

Yes, there was the victimization of the students. They have targeted a few in particular.

When the protest began at its initial stage, I did not want my identity as a JAC member to be disclosed out of fear of repercussions. However, after about six months, I had to attend a TV interview as a JAC member. Immediately afterwards, I started facing a lot of harassment and victimization on campus. The fear of being victimized and falsely targeted had already dissipated by then. I was ridiculed in my class by my professor. I was ridiculed in my hostel with allegations that I wanted to be on TV, that I wanted publicity, and that I was ruining BHU's image. I was verbally abused in my practical (laboratory) paper, and my project file was not accepted. I went through all this. I knew that they couldn't do anything more than that.

After a year of protest, Zee News came to the campus and interviewed some professors. The chief proctor was appointed after the protests began, and she made a very shameful statement – saying the protest was staged, and we were given pizza and pepsi to sit in the protest. Even though she was on leave during the protest, she claimed to have seen trucks full of pizzas coming onto campus, and the students were taking them. Students were furious after the statement came out in the media. So, they protested outside her office; those students faced complaints. A committee was set up to investigate them, and the committee was highly biased, as she was in charge. She lodged a First Information Report (FIR) against the students, with the charge of an 'attempt to murder'. Those students were innocent, but eight of the protesting students were barred from the university.

How long did the protest continue? How did it end?

The protest continued for about four days. After the police lathi charge, the BHU administration announced class adjournment sine die, and the women students were asked to move out. We were asked to vacate the hostels. It was the period around the Durga Puja festival vacation, and the students had already submitted their leave applications to the hostels. But after the lathi charge, leaving the hostels was made compulsory; those about to leave in two days were asked to move out immediately. When we were immediately asked to leave, some of us went to Delhi. My friends from JAC and I went to Janatar Mantar in Delhi and held a protest there.

The lathi charge led to a class adjournment sine die in the university. How do you view this?

A lot of students were injured in the lathi charge. The lathi-charge was done to prepare the ground for the class adjournment sine die. However, the lathi charge further energized the students. The anger of the students after the lathi charge made all of us more determined to stand up for our demands.

Was there anything concretely achieved after the protest?

We achieved a substantial amount, but it was not necessarily concrete. At a university where there were seldom protests on such a scale, having led this was a big thing. For the first time, the issue of gender inequality within the university came to the forefront. Moral policing reduced substantially. After the protest, the housekeepers could not continue their disrespectful talk to the women as they feared our protest.

If you want to see some sort of changes in your university, what would be those changes?

At our university, harassment has been a chronic problem. So, we demanded the installation of CCTV cameras on campus. They've been installed, but they are of no use because those cameras were installed in front of the hostel gates. It was done to keep an eye on the movement and activities of the women students! Therefore, the installation of cameras became an instrument to practice moral policing. They were not installed to keep us safe. We wanted the cameras installed in places where the incidents of molestation and harassment were rampant. We wanted them to catch the perpetrators effectively. Things have been done but unjustly.

Even though you were not associated with any political organization, the issue for which you fought was political. How do you view yourself politically now as compared to before the movement?

I think I see myself as having grown up. When people ask me about my politics, they have a preconceived notion. I have become politicized in people's minds. I have become a leftist for some people because I am definitely not a rightist. And because I am not a rightist, I am leftist. That is the lens through which most people view me. However, I see myself as being pro-Constitution and pro-people. The protest politicized me in different ways. I have been introduced to a diverse range of people with varied ideas. For example, JAC had a lot of students from different political backgrounds. I have been exposed to these ideas through the students I met.

As I told you, in the initial days of the movement, even ABVP members were supportive of us, although they disassociated themselves from us later. I believe that people, in general, are not bad. Most people are good people, and they can set out to do good things. Ideologies create differences. An ideology can have certain good things and certain flaws. I think sticking to one is not the right thing to do. I prefer not to be associated with any one ideology. My identity as a free person, not part of any political party, helped me immensely in the entire process. If my identity had been attached to a political party, it would have been way easier and manageable for the administration to paint me with that brush. Since I was not from any political party, I could connect with everybody, with students in general, and with people from different political parties. Saying that I am not political is not accurate. I am political. While I am not part of a political party, I have a strict set of ideas and principles. But I think that one has to be political. JAC itself, in that case, is political. If it were not political, it could not have built that wall of resistance. One has to be political to be in a movement.

As a youth in India, do you wish to see a change in the universities and the institutes? And if so, what would you like these changes to be?

I think every protest lays a path for the next one. The issue of curfews was raised during the 24/7 library movement. The students demanded that, along with the library, the gates of women's hostels should remain open 24/7. But this was not achieved by the students then. It came through a process, a movement, and it happened now. GSCASH should be set up in every university, including BHU. We know, however, that it will take time to set them up. This goal cannot be achieved instantly. The students must continue to protest and raise the demand for a GSCASH if it is to be established. But I think that needs to be done.

Also, I would like all youth to be political. That is very important. When a student is asked not to be political, that student is being deceived. Those who ask students not to be political are being political. By asking students not to be political, it becomes easier for the administration and the status quoists to never address the rights of the students. When we joined BHU, we were asked to sign an affidavit; our parents were also asked to sign. We had to declare that we would not take part in any protest against the administration. If we did participate, the administration had a right to take action against us by removing us from the hostels. So, they make up such rules for their benefit. The students and youth must, therefore, be political.

A Fight for Gender Justice: Paving the Path for Progressive Politics at Pondicherry University

Jishnu E.N.

> We had seen boys making vulgar comments at girls on the streets; we could not imagine that we would experience the same, followed by rape threats inside our university, known to be a prestigious central university in India. That pains and harms our self-esteem even if no one else has heard them abusing us.
>
> Kavya M.

Pondicherry University (PU) – a Central University established by an Act of Parliament in 1985, located on the Chennai-Puducherry East Coast Road – is the most prestigious central university, after UoH, in southern India.[1] The university has ninety-five affiliated colleges, making it one of the largest affiliated institutions of higher learning in southern India. As per the latest annual report of 2017-18, the university has 6,353 students enrolled in various postgraduate and research programs.[2]

[1] Pondicherry was renamed to Puducherry in 2006.

[2] Thirty Second Annual Report (2017-18), Pondicherry University. http://www.pondiuni.edu.in/sites/default/files/Annual%20Report%20English-12112019.pdf

Students from all across India come to pursue higher education at PU, and most of them love the campus. However, certain problems have persisted at the university which are discomforting for the students.

The university has a history of rowdy elements disturbing the campus atmosphere. They are backed by local party units of the bourgeoise political parties, active in Puducherry's politics. Within the university, the instances of promoting the culture of hooliganism are witnessed time and again. It is commonly believed that many of the Department of Physical Education students have been used by local parties and even by the university's administration to maintain a culture of terror. For instance, in 2014, a student questioned food quality and inadequate hostel facilities. He was later threatened and attacked physically inside his hostel room. This attack was organized to silence any critical voice.

Until 2015, the local assailants would bring liquor onto the campus to drink. This made the campus unsafe, particularly for the women students. The security staff was inadequate and incapable of dealing with these outsiders and often clueless about what action they should take when any untoward incident happened.

In an instance during 2016-17, a group of students was abducted from the campus by another group of students, and they were taken into the forest area within the university. They were tied up to a tree and were beaten until morning. The victims were even threatened with death and having their bodies thrown into the sea. The perpetrators were emboldened as they had support from some local goons.

There were several cases of molestation that went unreported. The students refrained from reporting these disturbing events as they feared retaliation from the abusers. The incidents of sexual abuse became regular occurrences on campus; both people from within and outside the campus were responsible for the growth of this horrific culture. To add insult to injury, even the police, rather than register complaints, if and when someone did file a complaint, tried to 'settle' the issues without holding the abusers accountable. In fact, they threatened those who tried to help the victims. Instead of addressing the real problems, the university's administration installed a gate to separate the boys' and the girls' hostels. The Students' Federation of India (SFI) organized a protest against it during 2013-14. The protest was mainly organized to keep the gate open 24 hours a day, while the administration closed the gates at 9:00 pm. The SFI named it the 'gender gate', which soon became a popular term within the university.

Amid the prevailing violence on campus, there have been protests by the progressive section of the students. But the struggle for gender justice in 2013, led by two students, Kavya and Vidya, changed the environment on the campus altogether. This significant struggle continues to inspire the students at PU even today as it has not only challenged the prevailing culture of violence at the university, but contributed to raising students' consciousness on the question of gender.

THE STRUGGLE LED BY KAVYA AND VIDYA

Kavya M. and Vidya T. Appukkuttan were admitted to the university in 2013 for postgraduate studies. Hailing from the rural areas of Kerala, like many of their friends, it was the first time they had left home and their native state to pursue higher education.

On 21 September 2013, they were walking towards their hostel mess around 8:00 pm. Two male students made snide comments about them while passing by on their bikes. Kavya and Vidya were quick to react, asking the men what their problem was. In response, the male students uttered some abusive words to Kavya and Vidya. Kavya recalled the incident and stated, 'When we told them that this was not the way they should talk, one of the guys threatened to rape us. He said that sometime during the two years of our course at the university, he would assault us physically at any cost. He also used some vulgar gestures towards us.'

As first-year students on campus, they were naturally frightened and initially decided not to file a complaint. The two perpetrators belonged to the Department of Physical Education, known for its notorious record of abusing and beating up students. They were powerful. They were part of a vast nexus with the support of the university administration, local politicians, and goons. They were capable of doing anything they wanted.

Kavya recalled, 'The day after the incident, the same person who threatened us, came and told us that if we filed a complaint, he would assault us sexually. And later, I found out from Monu (another friend who was with us on the day of the incident) that Jithu (one of the abusers) warned him that if Vidya and I went ahead with the complaint, he (Jithu) would stigmatize our image as "the girls who were sexually assaulted by Jithu" on campus.'

Notwithstanding the chilling effect of the threat, these two women filed a complaint against the perpetrators. Kavya and Vidya did not know then that it was just the beginning of a long battle. The SFI stood firmly with them, although the organization's unit was still in its formative stage on the PU campus. The then SFI office bearers were beaten black and blue in their hostels. The attacks continued until 2017.

Initially, the university did not take these physical assaults seriously. Thus, they continued. The SFI began protests, which led to a large demonstration against the *Goonda Raj* (rule by the Goons). Around 600 students participated in the protest. It forced the administration to start the enquiry process. However, they were lackadaisical in their approach. The physical attacks on the students and the neglect from the university administration left the students with no other options but to go to the police. As the protests grew bigger, the media too began to cover the struggle.

THE ROLE OF THE ADMINISTRATION AND THE STUDENTS' RESISTANCE

Prof. Chandra Krishnamurthy was the VC of the university when the incidents of harassment and threat took place. However, she was not on campus; the students demanded that the VC act against these attacks once she returned. They expected that justice would prevail, that she would act and stand by Kavya and Vidya, if not as the VC, at least as a woman. However, to their shock and dismay, Prof. Krishnamurthy abused Kavya and Vidya at their first meeting when she called them to discuss the incident. Instead of standing by them and taking action against the culprits, the VC criticized the complainants. Prof Krishnamurthy did not ask them anything about the abuse they faced on campus. However, she blamed them for the university's 'bad reputation' created by the news media.

Due to the pressure from the protesting students, the university was forced to constitute an Enquiry Committee to look into the matter. But shockingly, the Enquiry Committee was constituted under the university's Anti-Ragging Committee. This was done because the administration was trying to establish that it was not a case of sexual harassment.

The entire enquiry process added to the harassment of Kavya and Vidya. Kavya describes her experience:

> The committee questioned us for hours. They spend the entire time of the enquiry to try and establish the abusers' version of the incident instead of paying attention to our complaints. They asked me repeatedly if I abused Sreejith's [one of the abusers] mother. They spoke on behalf of Sreejith and came up with a bizarre defense that Sreejith was reacting to my actions against his mother. I was shocked. The day we were harassed was my first encounter with him [Sreejith]. When

> I asked them why would I do that, they had no answer. Why would I abuse his mother? In the final meeting of the Enquiry Committee, I had to scream at them and left the room in tears. This sham of an enquiry was double harassment for us.

Vidya also had a similar experience with regard to the enquiry. She shared her account: 'The first question they asked me was if we belonged to SFI. Their intention was not to investigate the matter, but to try and establish that the complaint was an attempt by SFI to gain ground on campus.'

This narrative was spread to influence a section of students so that the complainants were discouraged and defamed. It is because of such an attitude by the administration that there have been multiple incidents of sexual abuse on campus, yet women do not feel confident to file complaints. In the name of interrogation, the complainants are further harassed after they file complaints.

As Kavya and Vidya stood up against the abusers strongly, they had to face attacks from all sides. After the harassment received from the administration, a student from the perpetrator's gang filed a counter-accusation that Kavya made casteist remarks against him using his caste (Dalit) identity. He was a Dalit. After the so-called enquiry, the registrar issued a show-cause notice on 25 October 2013 to eleven students – the majority of them were SFI members. The notice accused the students of engaging in a 'group clash and hurling abusive and derogatory words against each other'. It added that these students had been found 'to be instigating the students to join the respective factions and creating a tense situation on the university's campus'. The order also alleged that the students had not sought redress within the university's internal mechanisms, instead, they sought redress from outside agencies. According to the order, this act was an attempt to 'denigrate the university's reputation'. We have already seen what the 'redress mechanisms' of the university did to the complainants.

The students had no intention of subjecting themselves to the harassment of the university administration.

Eight were suspended on 1 November 2013, including Kavya, Vidya, and Sreejith. Except for Sreejith, all others were SFI activists who stood with the women students to fight the assault. Three others were warned, one of whom included a friend of Sreejith.

Soon after this unjust enquiry, SFI decided to start a hunger strike. SFI also organized a protest march to the Ministry of Human Resource Development (MHRD) in the national capital and submitted its demands to the MHRD. The striking students received massive support from across the country.

THE HISTORIC LEGAL BATTLE

The historic legal battle began in parallel with the ten-day-long strike. Initially, the Puducherry High Court and the Madras High Court single bench ruled in favour of the university. A judge once told Kavya and Vidya to submit a letter of apology to the university and seek the revocation of their suspension at the mercy of the administration. The only impression that one could have been left with from the courtroom was how deeply rooted patriarchy was in Indian society. The judge was not worried about delivering justice to these two students or their well-being and safety, instead, he was worried that they would not get good marriage proposals if they had gone ahead with the court case on sexual harassment. The university's story, presented in court, was that Kavya had a relationship with one of her abusers, and it had turned violent, resulting in the clash between different groups of students.

Vidya and Kavya began the hunger strike. Kavya continued the strike for three days, while Vidya continued it for seven days. The strike began as the university issued the suspension order. The fight was also directed against all the malicious campaigns that the people in power ran. Nothing could stop the movement. Although

PU was not a campus where students had earlier witnessed such actions, it gathered support from the students. To a great extent, the movement became a reference point, which broke the fear among the students.

The Division Bench of the Madras High Court set aside the orders of the university, as did the Single Bench on 4 December 2014.[3] Justice V. Ramasubramanian, in the historic judgment against the Pondicherry University on *M. Kavya vs Chairman, University Grant Commission (UGC)* case, stated, 'The [Enquiry] Committee [of Pondicherry University] stressed the stereotyping effects and the woman's right to a fair and just trial and indicated that the judiciary must take caution not to create inflexible standards of what women or girls should be or what they should have done when confronted with a situation. Eventually, the committee held that the complainant had suffered re-victimization through stereotypes and gender-based myths. I think the case at hand is also one of re-victimization or secondary victimization by the institution in which the petitioners happen to be students.'

The court pronounced, 'The handling of their [Kavya's and Vidya's] complaints by the university has made the remedy worse than the disease and added insult to injury.' Appreciating both the women students, the court also stated, '... [that] the petitioners alone stood their ground and refused to tender an unconditional apology as per the order of the appellate authority, namely the VC, goes to show their courage of conviction and a refusal to compromise at the cost of honour'. It further added, 'the petitioners have overcome the normal tendency and temptation of lesser mortals, especially girl students whose whole career as well as life may be at stake, to surrender to the power of authority. This could not have been possible unless they had felt genuinely offended. Therefore, the ordering of a proper enquiry alone and that too after setting at naught all the humiliation to which the

[3] *M. Kavya vs The Chairman*, UGC, 4 December 2014. See: Indian Kanoon, https://indiankanoon.org/doc/143339158/.

petitioners have been subjected will restore the confidence of the girl students on the campus that there is gender justice. Otherwise, the morale of the other girl students would go down, and this will prove to be a retrograde step for gender equality'.

The Division Bench also asked the university to pay 25,000 Rupees to each as compensation for the injustice toward Kavya and Vidya and ensure that they complete their courses on time. The verdict was reserved on 17 November 2013, and it was only pronounced on 4 December 2014. By then, Kavya and Vidya had lost a semester. The court asked the university to hold special classes for them. As Vidya could not go home during the suspension days, she had to stay at the hostel, where she faced abuse from the security staff. She was forced to move out of the hostel at midnight one evening. The court asked the university not to deny the women access to any facilities to which they were entitled, such as hostel accommodations, participation in seminars, workshops, sports activities, etc. Along with scrapping all disciplinary actions against both the students, the court also said that the university must amend its rules and ordinances, including the definition of sexual harassment of one student by another, and protect the victims and ensure they face no further victimization. The protest concluded after Kavya and Vidya secured the victory through the legal battle.

THE FIGHT FOR GENDER JUSTICE STRENGTHENED THE FIGHT FOR DEMOCRATIC RIGHTS AT PU

PU did not conduct students' union elections until 2012. A massive fee hike, of around 200 per cent in some courses, was implemented between 2007 and 2013 during the tenure of the highly renowned VC Prof. J.A.K. Tareen. He is credited, and rightly so, for the university's development in terms of new courses and infrastructure. During his tenure, he recruited a large number of permanent faculty, which included a significant number of women professors. However, he, too, was an autocrat. He opposed student representation through elections. During his time, the students organized a massive protest against the poor quality of food and lack of other facilities in the hostels. It even evoked the support of the day scholars, and the protest escalated to the scale that the university was shut down for a day. SFI was the major force behind this protest. SFI slowly began to show its presence on campus by late 2011. Initially, it was challenging. SFI slowly began organizing protest rallies and posters on campus despite the opposition and harassment from the university security staff and administration. The first aim of the SFI-PU unit was to convince the administration to hold students' union elections. After numerous applications were filed under the Right to Information (RTI) Act 2005 and several sessions of discussion thereafter, Prof. Tareen agreed to hold elections in October 2012.

After Prof. Tareen's term ended, Prof. Chandra Krishnamurthy became the VC at PU. During her tenure, a section of the teaching faculty wanted to oust her as they had lost their voice and representation in the administration. At the end of 2014, they held a rally against the VC in which they used their students to show strength. When they sought the help of SFI, the organization decided to extend its support and found common ground in the fight against the VC.

The anti-Chandra Krishnamurthy protest widely acknowledged the Kavya-Vidya movement. Among the significant demands of the protest were: a progressive sexual harassment prevention committee, sensitization among students about the importance of reporting sexual abuse, and guaranteeing the safety of students, especially women students on campus.

The university's protest movement started gaining momentum after the struggle by Kavya and Vidya. The students held massive protests post-2015, with thousands of students participating in the protests. As a result of the pressure, the university withdrew the appeal against the Madras Division Bench in 2016 and accepted the verdict.

The university witnessed various protests for gender justice after that historic movement. The students waged protests against moral policing by the security staff and biased hostel rules, especially for the women's hostels, which led to mass gatherings and protests on the university's campus. Progressive politics gained ground within the campus, which led to the historic victory of progressive students in the union election during 2015-16. To establish campus democracy, SFI, along with the newly formed Ambedkar Students' Association (ASA), decided to eliminate the anti-student faction and with the help of progressive students, SFI-ASA registered the victory and representation in the union.

In February 2016, hundreds of women students gathered outside one of the hostels after an outsider molested a resident in front of her hostel. The SFI-led council swiftly intervened and led the students to the main gate, demanding justice. Students joined the midnight march by defying the unjust hostel curfew. Due to the pressure from the students, the then in-charge VC, Dr B. Anisa Khan, was compelled to come to the protest venue to meet the students at midnight. The student demonstrators were not activists. But they had the consciousness to fight against the injustice. Though the students' council was leading this struggle, the students gathered in front of the hostel independently. The Kavya-Vidya movement has played a significant role in educating the students' community to realize their rights and fight for them with determination. It also helped the elected council channel the students' anger along the right path and reach its logical conclusion. The movement for gender justice, led by Kavya and Vidya, and with the support of SFI, strengthened the student struggles within the campus. It was followed by many protests, which ensured that the security for students' safety was strengthened. This was the long-standing demand of the students, and it was achieved.

As a result of the Kavya-Vidya movement, the student community realized the need for reconstituting the Sexual Harassment Prevention Committee (SHPC) at the university. It was not functional when Kavya and Vidya faced the abuse. The SFI-led council put forth a significant demand to reconstitute SHPC. The students' council also demanded representation through a separate election of the students on SHPC. PU students are yet to achieve this demand, although the struggle continues.

The brave movement for gender justice helped formulate the students' charter of demands, including the need for more representation in the other governing bodies of the university, which the students' council took up later. Democratic election to these posts and power to the elected representatives is a must to ensure the proper functioning of such committees.

From the absence of student politics on campus to the presence of more than half a dozen students' organizations, PU has successfully created a political atmosphere on campus. Although the students' organizations are still 'banned' on campus, political discussions are now part of the university culture. In the recent past, the students of PU extended solidarity to many national movements, including Justice For Rohith Vemula, Hok Kolorob, Occupy UGC, and so on. SFI played a vital role in the major shift in campus culture. From starting an organization, holding protests, campaigning, using flags inside the campus, meeting the demands of the student's community, or its intervention in the first council to try and formalize several things – the organization guided the movements. Thanks to these brave women, Kavya and Vidya, for leading the historic fight that changed, for the better, so much at the university.

Kavya says, 'I have learned from the movement that no protest is easy. If we have to demand our rights, there is no shortcut. We dealt with multi-faceted pressures, and we were able to overcome them as we knew we were right. And we got support from the student community. That sense of justice and support is the key. As we believe – *The people united shall always be victorious.*'

Breaking Silence: Shubh Laxmi's Struggle in Assam

Sangita Das

Assam, one of the seven sister states of Northeast India, is often cut off from the news headlines of the national news channels and papers. Therefore, discussions of the state's vital issues have remained primarily absent from the national debate. Even within the state, there has been a lack of sensibility on the part of media and the political leadership to address critical issues and attempt to bring them to public discourse.

The question of gender relations or crimes concerning violence against women is one such issue that has been systematically excluded from public discourse. As a result, these crimes have not only increased in the state, but this forced public silence has created something more concerning: the perpetrators of these crimes have been left unchecked, and women have been conditioned to think that they are the wrong-doers as opposed to being wronged.

The problem, therefore, is exacerbated. We see complacency in addressing the issue of sexual harassment on the one hand and an overwhelming lack of understanding about what constitutes sexual harassment, often not understood even by the women, on the other hand. Based on our experiences, we find that this ignorance persists even among the educated section of the population, which creates fertile ground for these attacks to increase and normalizes the occurrences of sexual harassment within the state.

The latest data published by the National Crime Records Bureau (NCRB) 2021, is revealing. For four years in a row since 2017, Assam recorded the highest number of crimes against women. To hoodwink the people of the growing crimes against women being discussed in Assam, the Bharatiya Janata Party (BJP) made tall claims, crediting the party to have undertaken the sensitization campaign to such a height that women are now coming up to register the cases, and hence, the state records the highest crime rates against women. However, we should be aware that BJP is a party which operates on the principles of the Manusmriti ('Code of conduct' of Hindus provided by Manu), and has dark records of its leaders publicly making sexist and misogynistic remarks, and rallying for the rape accused. The BJP's claims that the increase in crimes is a result of sensitization is nothing but total hogwash.

The state's political leadership clearly failed to initiate measures to end crime against women. Even earlier, during the Indian National Congress (INC)-led government's tenure, a spike in crime against women in Assam was recorded, one of the worst records after Delhi, according to a 2016 report.[1] Comparing this record with the recent figures, we find that the criminal cases against women further increased from '126.8 in 2016 to 143.3 in 2017, to further 166 in 2018 and 177 in 2020 – the highest numbers recorded in India, higher than the Indian average of 56.5'.[2] Although the government is out and out publicizing its 'sensitization' drives, it's unwilling to provide a secure place for women in the state.

[1] India News, 'Nearly 41% women face sexual harassment at workplace in Assam, says study,' *Hindustan Times*, 4 June 2019, https://www.hindustantimes.com/india-news/nearly-41-women-facesexual-harassment-at-workplace-in-assam-says-study/story-r1fytxZj9wphzinbFhrSJN.html.

[2] Mythreyee Ramesh, 'Why Assam Recorded Highest Crime Rate Against Women For 4th Consecutive Year,' *The Quint*, 18 September 2021, https://www.thequint.com/neon/gender/assam-highest-crime-against-women-ncrb.

An incident in September 2021 left us shocked and anguished when a young woman candidate was humiliated and harassed in the examination centre in Assam's Tezpur for the dress she wore. The girl who had travelled nearly 70 kilometres to reach the examination centre from her home in Biswanath Chariali to write her entrance exam for the Assam Agricultural University (AAU) Jorhat was asked by the invigilator to leave the hall.[3] When the candidate argued that no dress code was mentioned in the admit card, the invigilator told her that short dresses were not allowed inside the examination centre premises. From the examination centre, she was accused of lacking common sense. She was humiliated to the extent even by the controller of examination that she could not appear for the examination unless she wrapped a curtain around her leg. Later, when her father complained citing that incident as a case of mental harassment, this issue created a lot of debate and people expressed their concerns on social media. However, everyone who stood by them, were trolled on social media; sexist and vulgar comments were made. I too was subjected to such a notorious attack after I expressed my views condemning the harassment and humiliation of the young woman candidate. When I went to file a complaint to the cyber-cell in the only woman police station in Guwahati, I faced harassment from the police. I was asked to provide the location and other specific details of the persons who abused me on social media, whereas it was the duty of the police to investigate the matter with the links and proofs I attached with my complaint letter. This incident not only shows the level of sensitisation in the state where people in position, such as, the controller of examination lack basic understanding of dignity, choice, and rights; but it also is indicative of the role of the police who are supposed to provide security to the victims of crimes.

[3] Tora Agarwala, 'Assam: 19-year-old in shorts made to take exam wrapped in curtain,' *The Indian Express*, 17 September 2021, https://indianexpress.com/article/north-east-india/assam/assam-19-year-old-in-shorts-made-to-take-exam-wrapped-in-curtain-7513464/.

Guwahati, the state's capital has become one of the most unsafe cities with rising number of crimes against women. One can imagine the scale in which crime is growing in other parts of the state. Yet, in fact, a minimum, i.e., to activate a toll-free number for women to seek instant help is not put in place. Years of horrifying cases indicate more towards the need of sincere measures to be instituted rather than rhetorical speeches and claims.

Lately though, some public discussions on gender have taken place in Assam. Protests organised by women groups saw large scale participation of the girls and women. Why do we see this change? Is it because, suddenly, the sensitisation in the state reached its peak as the ruling BJP's ministers and leaders would blatantly claim? Or is it because of a certain objective reality within the state that the women are pushed to raise their voices against crime against them?

It is important to reflect on the nature and the instances of crime in the state in order to understand that if anyone is serious in addressing the problem of crime against women, it would need consistent and sincere efforts at multiple levels.

SOME CASES OF SEXUAL HARASSMENT IN ASSAM – WHAT DO THEY REFLECT?

One example is the molestation case in 2012 in Guwahati. There was a huge public outcry after a seventeen-year-old girl was 'stripped' and 'molested' outside a bar by a group of more than a dozen men in one of the wealthier neighbourhoods of Guwahati.[4] This incident should not be seen as an isolated incident. For instance, in November 2020, a report surfaced where a young woman registered an First Information Report (FIR) against her

[4] IANS, 'Outraged India demands action against monsters who molested 17-year-old girl in Guwahati, activists publicly shame suspects by putting up hoardings in the city,' *India Today*, 13 July 2012, https://www.indiatoday.in/india/northeast/story/guwahati-molestation-case-activists-put-up-hoardings-of-suspects-109301-2012-07-13.

father, the principal of a college in Guwahati. The accused was arrested by order of the Chief Judicial Magistrate Court on charges of sexual harassment of his daughter. It was shocking to hear of a father turning out to be an alleged predator, repeatedly exploiting his daughter from 2004 to 2011.[5] Additionally, the young woman's mother (who held the position of deputy secretary of the higher education department) had also been physically harassing her and mentally torturing her. Such cases may be viewed as extreme examples of the scale of violence against women, but these incidents result from a certain mindset and system that considers a woman as an object. Therefore, women are more likely to be harassed – at home, on the streets, on public transport or in workplaces – rural or urban – by the 'educated' or the 'uneducated'. These cases reflect the negligence on society's part as a collective to rise against crimes against women and involve itself in the process of gender sensitization, standing against the patriarchy rooted in our society.

Even people who grew up with a good understanding of gender could not speak about the molestation they faced at a tender age; a hesitation in raising one's voice in opposition to these crimes against women automatically developed. Without the strength and support to publicly denounce these crimes, women began to feel 'impure'. Society, including one's peer group, made women feel even more vulnerable, and this vulnerability, on account of their gender, is experienced by women throughout India. Within this environment, gender sensitization is essential. In Assam, an agitation in 2017 taught us the importance of gender sensitization, and that agitation, with the slogan – Stand with Shubh Laxmi – helped generate a wave of interest in advancing the idea and work on gender sensitization.

[5] Sentinel Digital Desk, 'Girl's FIR lands father in jail on the charge of sexual harassment,' *The Sentinel*, 8 December 2020, https://www.sentinelassam.com/guwahati-city/girls-fir-lands-father-in-jail-on-the-charge-of-sexual-harassment-515138.

SHUBH LAXMI'S STRUGGLE

Shubh Laxmi was an activist of the SFI. At about 21 years old, she was molested on the streets four times. On 8 February 2017, Shubh Laxmi posted on Facebook about these experiences. The post went viral on social media, and it led people to raise questions about the security of girls and women in the state. On her Facebook wall, she wrote:

> They come under the cover of darkness, their faces hidden behind their masks. They come on bikes at reckless speed. I try to move to the side of the road, but they follow me. They fondle my breasts and drive away. I freeze and stand very still, thinking what just happened. It feels like the sting of a caterpillar. I return to my room. They come under the cover of darkness, their faces hidden behind their masks. I try to move to the side of the road, but they follow me. This time I wear my bag in front instead of on my back. They come closer to me and press my butt. I again freeze and stand very still, thinking what just happened. It pricks like a thorn. This time I don't wait for the darkness. I return without completing my work. I am back by 4:00 pm. I say to myself, 'someone please save me' They have come today also. Someone speaks in my ear, '… will … you' … 'Will … you till … widens'. Today I try to rip them off me. But in seconds, they disappear. I puked today.
>
> My room is on DC [Devicharan Baruah] Road, Jorhat. I walk down this road. I am sexually and mentally harassed to such an extent that I feel like locking myself in the room. I am always in an anxious state. Until now, this type of violent harassment has happened to me at least four times. Not only me, but most of the girls who walk down this road are also harassed. No girl comes alone after 6 pm on this road. I know I can do nothing by posting this on Facebook. But despite what happens today, I feel very insecure. I am terribly angry, but I

am also terrified. I fear, will they tear me apart someday??
(Original post in Assamese)

The fourth incident she faced took place on 7 February 2017 in Jorhat. A group of young men would roam around near the girls' hostels or near paying guest accommodations in Jorhat and other towns in Assam. They would know the whereabouts of the girls and women; they would know their arrival times at their hostels.

Like in Jorhat, these incidents happened in other parts of Assam. There are regular incidents of molestation on the streets throughout Assam. Due to the unsafe streets, especially at dusk, girls and young women choose to return to their hostels or rooms in the daytime.

It is important to highlight in this context that a report of the Assam State Commission for Women (ASCW) in 2014 raised concerns regarding the safety of girls and women on the streets. The commission, therefore, demanded more street lights across the state as a measure to ensure their safety. ASCW recommended this after, 'a study revealed that 51 per cent of crimes in Guwahati take place due to ill-lit streets'.[6] The recommendation, however, still lies dormant; it has never been implemented.

In Jorhat, after the Shubh Laxmi incident, the entry time of girls and women into their hostels was advanced. Even the girls staying in their own homes preferred to confine themselves or were forced to confine themselves at home after a certain time. This 'caging' or imprisonment of women, out of fear that someone would harm them, cannot be seen as a solution to the problems. Rather, the question needs to be raised as to why girls and women are forced to confine themselves to their houses or hostels after a certain hour in the evening.

[6] Pranjal Baruah, 'Streetlights necessary for women's safety: ASCW,' *The Times of India*, 23 July 2014, https://timesofindia.indiatimes.com/city/guwahati/streetlights-necessary-for-womens-safety-ascw/articleshow/38907383.cms.

PROTESTS AND SOLIDARITY

After the Facebook posting, however, there was a spontaneous protest on 8 February 2017 in Jorhat and students from every college participated. Following that, protests spread throughout Assam. By 10 February, there were protests all over the state by students from various colleges and students' organizations. Shubh Laxmi's courageous act created a spark and put the question of gender sensitization front and centre. Her Facebook post about the harassment had been shared by over 3,500 people.[7] SFI in the Jorhat district organized protest rallies demanding street lights in every nook and corner, proper patrolling, and the establishment of a Gender Sensitization Committee against Sexual Harassment (GSCASH) on every campus. The students' union of Jagannath Barooah College and students from different colleges in Jorhat spontaneously participated in the rally. Media also gave wide coverage to the issue. The outrage on social media was also immediate. There was a Twitter storm with the hashtag #VoiceofShubhLaxmi.

The first woman Superintendent of Police (Jorhat), Sanjukta Parashar, through a public post on social media on 14 February 2017, extended unconditional solidarity with Shubh Laxmi. She wrote,

> She has expressed herself quite clearly, the pain and the anguish of being sexually assaulted, the trauma of feeling lonely, and the frustration at the inability to get help. Her words are a cry for justice, a cry for putting an end to such heinous acts by men. It becomes very easy for a woman to blame herself as the society tries to instill such thoughts in us as children.

[7] Ratnadip Choudhury, 'Groped By Bikers, Shrugged Off By Minister, She Fought Back On Facebook,' NDTV, 18 February 2017, https://www.ndtv.com/india-news/groped-by-bikers-shrugged-off-by-minister-she-fought-back-on-facebook-1660744.

> We won't be parked cars; we, as capable and competent women, will go to schools and colleges, to markets and to our jobs. We are not to blame; our clothes are not at fault; we won't apologize for being women.
>
> I am appalled that such an act took place. I am proud that she had the courage to speak up against this atrocity. I am confident that Assam police will be able to find the offenders, prosecute them, and bring them to justice.
>
> I am with Shubh Laskhmi.

A leading news channel in Assam, *DY365*, even aired a day-long programme, on Valentine's Day, titled 'Support Shubh Laxmi' asking people to support her. There were spontaneous 'people's meetings' in different places where feminists and other intellectuals from various fields participated. The pressure was so great that Assam's Director General of Police, Mr Mukesh Sahay, announced that a *suo motu* (on its own motion) FIR was registered with regard to the assaults on Shubh Laxmi.[8]

Programmes were organized on college campuses and in the streets. The core issue of these discussions was mainly centred around the harassment of women and the lack of gender sensitization. These programmes were organized by SFI with the help of other students, intellectuals, and many in civil society under a common slogan of 'We support Shubh Laxmi, Unite Against Sexual Harassment'. The students rallied around this slogan in their colleges. Students initiated signature campaigns, open field discussions even outside the campuses, and the submission of protest letters to the authorities.

The often neglected Assam found their issues being written and talked about in national newspapers and on TV and radio

[8] 'Jorhat Girl Recounts Abuse in Viral FB Post, BJP Min Blames Her,' *The Quint*, 15 February 2017, https://www.thequint.com/voices/women/jorhat-girl-subhalakshmi-in-assam-recounts-molestation-in-viral-facebook-post-bjp-minister-blames-her.

channels. The questions of gender, the security of women, and the rise of crime against women were the focus. Civil society played an important role during the agitation. The demand to set up GSCASH on the campuses was recognized by the student community, and after the agitation, especially in the colleges of Jorhat, complaints committees were also formed.

Due to the protests in support of Shubh Laxmi, a message was publicly broadcast on the necessity of reporting cases of molestation and sexual harassment. The hesitation and fear that a girl or woman has or the humiliation she faces during any harassment, could be overcome, due, in large part, to Shubh Laxmi's courageous public post. The impact of such a brave act was immediately felt when we witnessed the huge participation of girls and women, regardless of age – from 10 to 80 years old – in the public meetings.

This scale of spontaneous participation of girls and women protesting against sexual harassment had been missing in Assam for a long time. Shubh Laxmi's public exposure of this crime was the catalyst for a movement.

They came out into the streets not only to protest, but to speak openly against the patriarchal feudal society. Though the committees are not functional on many campuses, at least students are now aware of GSCASH, and the agitations forced the Assam Education Department to alert all the college administrations regarding the formation of GSCASH. The 'Stand with Shubhlaxmi' agitation was a milestone in creating gender sensitization across Assam, but the technical aspect of committee formation is still a challenge on many Assam campuses.

THE RESPONSE OF THE RULING PARTY

While the whole of Assam was rallying in support of Shubh Laxmi, instead of tackling the issues of the rampant eve-teasing and molestation occurring in the state, the ruling party, through its cadre, started a counter-campaign on social media.

Questions like, 'Why didn't she go to the police station first?'; 'What was the necessity of posting on Facebook?' and 'After such a degree of harassment, can a person write such a beautiful post on Facebook, I feel it's all made up?' spammed over social media. These posts were obviously intended to solicit comments from people of the Sangh Parivar (an umbrella of Hindu nationalist organizations) who still believed in the Manusmriti. To defeat these Sanghis, regardless of political affiliations (except the BJP), people from all democratic and liberal organizations started countering the Sanghi propaganda. This was a critical stage of the agitation.

Assam's Legislative Assembly was in session on 13 February 2017. A lawmaker echoed the demand for justice for 'Shubh Laxmi' in the assembly, and the question of women's security was also raised. Women members such as Pramila Rani Brahma, and an ally of the ruling government, supported Shubh Laxmi's fight and said that measures had to be taken to ensure the safety of women. A Member of the Legislative Assembly (MLA) admitted that she, herself, had been a victim of such harassment. But a reactionary comment from the then Parliamentary Affairs Minister, Chandra Mohan Patowary, a member of the ruling party, led to an outburst of public sentiment. He stated 'She [Shubh Laxmi] is a member of SFI. Everybody knows that. She has [made a mistake] by posting her experience on the social networking site. She should have gone to the police first.'[9]

Due to a number of factors, it is very difficult for women to deal with the fear and trauma of being sexually harassed. First, there is the trauma of the actual sexual harassment. Second, the outlook of patriarchal society tends to make the women (who are the victims or survivors) the culprits. Third, there is a feeling of impunity that is nurtured within society and favours the perpetrators; and finally, the sense of shame that a survivor is made to feel. All these

[9] Abdul Gani, 'Assam Minister's Sexist Jumla Draws Flak,' TheCitizen.in, 15 February 2017, https://www.thecitizen.in/index.php/en/NewsDetail/index/3/9952/Assam-Ministers-Sexist-Jumla-Draws-Flak?infinitescroll=1

and more make it very difficult for a woman to speak up.

For instance, a student from Dibrugarh University was reportedly sexually harassed repeatedly from October 2016 onward, two months after she joined the university to pursue her master's course. As she reported, 'He used to call me several times during the day, at odd hours, saying that he would give me good marks and I would be able to complete my MPhil and PhD from the university if I spent time with him at his cabin. This continued for nearly three weeks.'[10]

There were allegations of inappropriate physical contact by the professor, which, after a point, became unbearable for the student. The student filed a case against the professor on 15 November 2016 with the university's registrar. But, as soon as the enquiry began, the professor took voluntary retirement.

To everyone's shock, he was then appointed as the VC of the newly formed Majuli Cultural University by the former Chief Minister of Assam, Mr Sarbananda Sanowal of the ruling BJP.

While her complaint was registered, she got repeated calls from other professors who were supporting the accused and urged her to withdraw the complaint. Even though an FIR was registered, there was no action taken against him. Instead, he was rewarded with a promotion to lead a university as VC.

The role of the BJP, therefore, on questions concerning gender justice is known to a wide section of the population. When a woman challenges patriarchy, misogyny, and sexual assaults, the foundation of those who believe in Manusmriti is shaken.

BREAKING THE SILENCE – A REMARKABLE STEP FORWARD

Shubh Laxmi was no longer an individual; she had become the

[10] India News, 'Sexual harassment charge returns to haunt VC of Assam's Cultural University,' *Hindustan Times*, 8 June 2019, https://www.hindustantimes.com/india-news/sexual-harassment-charge-returns-to-haunt-vc-of-assam-s-cultural-university/story-feqa2PfDKDvOu7u1Drvu3N.html. 1

symbol of the resistance against crimes perpetrated on women. The 'Stand with Shubh Laxmi' agitation inspired many girls and women across the state. Young women began to come forward to register complaints against these crimes, something very rarely heard of before. After the Shubh Laxmi posting, another molestation occurred in Jorhat. In another example of how Shubh Laxmi's brave act inspired others, the young girl gave her deposition at the Police Station about the molestation she faced on the road. Once a complaint is registered, local media usually reports on it. When these types of experiences are made public, girls and women are traumatized a second time, because Indian society tends to judge a girl or a woman and assassinate her character rather than hold the perpetrator and the regressive ideas and practice of the society responsible.

Society still believes that it's a matter of shame to publicly announce that we have been harassed, sexually as well as mentally. Girls are asked by their parents to stay silent, out of fear that their family's dignity and respect will be impacted adversely. In schools, biology teachers skip the section on the human reproductive process. Only 'fertilization' is mentioned in the textbooks because it's embarrassing to discuss 'sex' in public. These are examples of how deep patriarchal values are embedded in our society's thinking. Only a rupture or confrontation with these above values can happen when they are in direct conflict with the values of the newer generation that has been exposed to the modern values of equality, dignity, and self-respect. The need to confront and speak out about these indignities in public is an outcome of the changing values. The agitation 'Stand with Shubh Laxmi' was able to bring people from different arenas under one umbrella; still, sadly, it seemed that many people just felt pity for her. The 'Stand with Shubh Laxmi' movement, however, created a spark in Assam to speak out against sexual harassment.

The fight for gender sensitization became even stronger. With the continued movement and pressure by SFI, the Directorate of

Higher Education was forced to issue notices to every college in Assam to form cells that would deal with the question of gender and sexual harassment.

There are committees in the colleges, but they are either not functional or don't work effectively. The importance of gender sensitization was realized both at the institutional and organizational levels. The students have become very aware of the harassment that takes place in educational institutions by some faculty; they understand the need to report this harassment to the authorities, and they realize they must form committees against sexual harassment and bring about continuous gender sensitization. As a result of the movement, in Jorhat, on almost every dark street corner where students move about, the street lights were installed; it was a step forward for the people of Assam to become aware of the crimes against women.

The battle of gender sensitization has a long way to go, but through movements, such as Stand with Shubh Laxmi, a ray of hope spreads. It must touch every level of society and must be organized in such a way that the diverse, unheard voices of India are heard. The fight is not against a particular gender; it is against the patriarchal and feudal system, and thus, sensitization is a process that must be internalized by all people regardless of gender.

Struggles Against Authoritarianism

Memories from the Hok Kolorob Movement at Jadavpur University

Gitosri Sarkar

Jadavpur University (JU) has always been appreciated and admired by a range of people and the media. The opinions and views expressed by the students and teaching faculty at the university have always gained space in public debate due to the strength of their arguments. This space, however, shrunk in recent years. The media, an essential tool in forming public opinions and narratives, has been running a vilification campaign against the university. The corporate media has begun to show the university's cherished students' movement in a negative light to champion the ruling class opinion. Thus, movements have become synonymous with 'disturbance' in their propaganda. These attempts gained considerable traction within a section of people who have always viewed the students' involvement in politics as objectionable.

The students know that these attempts need to be countered. They raised questions: why are movements/protests/resistances targeted as 'disturbances'? Whose interests are being served when students are being called 'anti-nationals'? Why is curbing dissent so fundamental for certain political formations? The answers to these questions are found in our history; the ruling class is never comfortable with the questions or resistance that challenge their ideology and anti-student actions. To understand the reasons for these attacks on JU, it is worth briefly revisiting its history. We take pride in our history; our pledge is to continue the struggles.

JU draws its legacy from the struggle against imperialism and the Indian Freedom Movement. In 1906, the National Council of Education (NCE) was set up as part of the Swadeshi movement to challenge the hegemony of British colonialism and promote science and technology.[1] The NCE established the Bengal National College and Bengal Technical Institute as per the mandate. These two institutions were merged, and, in 1955, JU was born. It was formally established as JU a few years after Indian independence.

An institution that is forged in the fire of the anti-colonial struggle and is never afraid to rebel against the draconian behaviour of the rulers can never be permanently put down and suppressed. We learned these lessons from our history. The seeds of struggle for autonomy and freedom of expression that were sown many years ago are manifested in JU's present-day students' movements. JU students have always had to pay the price for the courage to ask questions and take a righteous stand. With the Indian National Congress (INC)'s rule in West Bengal, the attacks against JU continued. In fact, the period of the INC's rule under the Chief Minister, Siddhartha Shankar Ray, can be characterized as a regime of 'semi-fascist terror'. In response to this authoritarian rule by the INC's, in the 1977 state assembly elections, the people of West Bengal gave an astounding mandate to the Left Front, rejecting the INC. JU students continued their struggles even during the Left Front government.

In the early 2000s, the students agitated against a proposed fee hike by the administration. The students thoroughly debated the issue, and it was never resolved. Finally, a phased fee hike was introduced. However, the students' struggle ensured that

[1] The Swadeshi movement originated from the anti-partition movement in Bengal (1903-1908). During the movement, a 'Boycott resolution' was adopted on 7 August 1905, calling for boycotting Manchester cloth and Liverpool salt. See: Bipan Chandra et al., *India's Struggle for Independence* 1857 – 1947, (New Delhi: Penguin Books: 1989), pp. 124-127.

students from the economically and socially backward sections were exempted from paying the hiked fee. This agitation happened when the Left was in power in the state. During the time of the Left Front government, there was no attempt by the government to scuttle or tamper with campus democracy or campus autonomy. In fact, not only Students' Federation of India (SFI), which was close to the ruling Communist Party of India (Marxist) (CPI(M)), but all other student organizations functioned at full strength; these student organizations were represented in the departments of the Faculty Council of Science, and Engineering and Technology for several years. In 2011, the All India Trinamool Congress (TMC) government came to power; in contrast to the Left Front government, they unleashed continuous onslaughts on the democratic rights of the students. With the post-2011 change in government, the TMC captured the leadership of all educational institutions.[2] These attacks intensified. Later, when the Bharatiya Janata Party (BJP)-led government assumed power at the centre in 2014, new attacks against JU began, as BJP's political master, the Rashtriya Swayamsevak Sangh (RSS)-backed goons, assaulted the students of JU and tried to vilify its image. For instance, in 2016, when the RSS attacked Jawaharlal Nehru University (JNU), the JU students stood firmly in solidarity. The RSS in West Bengal could not tolerate that; the RSS-BJP members took out a march to JU, tried to enter the campus and created a ruckus to 'teach a lesson' to JU students. Similarly, intolerance and provocation by the BJP were witnessed in 2019; during the hard-fought anti- Citizenship (Amendment) Act, 2019 (CAA) struggle

[2] Under TMC rule, student organizations like the SFI were prohibited from entering students' union rooms. TMC goons occupied the union rooms at Calcutta University (CU) and several CU-affiliated colleges. The SFI activists and sympathizers were even stopped from sitting for exams. In the case of JU, TMC could not capture the leadership in the same way, but they tried to create an environment of terror. In a few instances, the TMC tried to bribe the students before the elections, and even stop the students from exercising their democratic right to cast vote.

in the country, JU students strongly supported the constitutional rights of the citizens. At that time, the then BJP MP, Babul Supriyo, visited JU and faced students' opposition; he manhandled students and openly incited the local goons to enter JU and vandalize the students' union room.

JU students never failed to protect the democratic culture of the university. Despite strong resistance from the TMC government, the students forced the government to conduct students' union elections six times between 2011 and 2020. No right-wing force, whether the student wing of the Hindutva fascistic RSS or the authoritarian TMC, could secure even minimal representation at JU in these six elections. It was always the left organizations that were elected to the students' unions.[3]

Post-2011, the TMC-backed goons created a ruckus around the college elections. This resulted in the killing of a police constable by the TMC in February 2013 at the Horimohon Ghosh College in the Garden Reach area. Citing this incident, the students' union elections in colleges and universities across West Bengal were stalled. The JU elections, held in March every year, were also cancelled due to the state government's decision. During this period, SFI and other leftist students' organizations organized a civil disobedience movement against curtailing the students' democratic right to have students' union elections. We lost our beloved Comrade Sudipto Gupta in that movement due to police brutality.[4] On that April evening, Comrade Sudipto's blood-

[3] At JU, in the tradition of vibrant student politics, several students' organizations co-exist. The SFI, All India Students' Federation (AISF), All India Democratic Students' Organisation (AIDSO), and All India Students' Association (AISA) are part of an organized left students' movement. The Forum for Arts Students (FAS) and We the Independent (WTI) are independent student groups with liberal and secular outlooks.

[4] Martyred comrade Sudipto Gupta was killed in police custody in 2013 when he, along with other protesting students, was detained in a police bus by the West Bengal police after a demonstration in Kolkata demanding the restoration of students' union elections. See: Sulagna Sengupta, 'SFI Student Leader Sudipto Gupta Beaten To Death, Shows Post Mortem Report,' *The*

soaked corpse reinvigorated all students with a determination that had never been witnessed before. In 2014, the students of JU gave a befitting response to the killers of Sudipto by electing his comrades to the students' union.

We remember 2014 as a year of struggle and victory; we fought for gender justice and exposed the university authority and the state government for their apathy on sexual harassment.

THE HOK KOLOROB MOVEMENT[5]

Crimes against women under the TMC regime had hit new heights. The safety of women and girls in public spaces had been trampled upon by anti-social forces associated with the ruling party. From Kamduni to Madhyamgram, from rural colleges to urban university campuses, female students faced grotesque sexual violence. Unfortunately, the female students at JU, too, were not spared from these horrific acts. In this climate of emboldened misogyny, our university campus witnessed an ugly incident on 28 August 2014. A second-year student complained of being molested by male students who were residents on campus. She was dragged into the Old Boys' Hostel at JU during the university's festival – 'Sanskriti'. They molested her, and when her friends tried to extricate her from the situation, they were beaten up by a dozen men who were residents of the hostel.

On 1 September, the survivor and her father brought the incident to the notice of the VC in charge, Prof. Abhijit Chakraborty. To their shock and dismay, however, the VC asked them to 'cool off' for a few days, and he did not establish an enquiry committee

Indian Express, 4 April 2013, http://archive.indianexpress.com/news/sfi-student-leader-sudipto-gupta-beaten-to-death-shows-postmortem-report/1097459/.

[5] In 2015, I wrote a piece, 'Why I Refused the Medal,' for a progressive online journal, *Vikalp*, in which I narrated our struggle at JU. Substantial portions of that article have been used in this piece with changes and additions. See https://vikalp.ind.in/2015/01/why-irefused-meda/.

to investigate the matter. The survivor's father then filed a police complaint on 2 September, and the next day he sent a formal letter to the administration of JU. We, too, approached Prof. Abhijit Chakraborty, demanding justice. His response reflected the tone of the TMC administration ruling the state. He wanted to suppress the complaint and refused any dialogue with the students or the victim's family. The incident and the response of the VC resulted in a massive outrage amongst the students. We began a demonstration at the university on 3 September 2014. After 100 hours of sit-in protests by the students, there was no response from either the VC or the university's Executive Council (EC), the highest decision-making body. The protest immediately attracted wide support, and students from across India participated in the campaign in solidarity with JU students using the hashtag Hok Kolorob (Let there be clamour!) – a slogan raised at JU during the protest.

The Arts Faculty Students' Union (AFSU) had pressed for a transparent and impartial investigation into the incident from the very beginning. However, certain members of the Internal Complaints Cell (ICC) made concerted attempts to downplay the incident while at the same time demeaning the survivor with constant taunts about her character and clothes. In fact, two university professors went to the survivor's home asking her questions regarding the 'dress' she wore during the incident. We repeatedly raised questions regarding the effectiveness of the ICC and its role since the movement began. The ICC is not elected; its student members come from the respective unions of the three faculty councils – Arts, Science, and Engineering and Technology – and are merely nominated to the body. The other members are teachers, researchers, and official staff representatives come from their respective unions/associations. But every member of the ICC is nominated by the VC. Due to this nominating process, during the 2014 case, the administration used the opportunity for their benefit and they made a selection of members to the committee by keeping the members' respective associations hidden. We raised questions about the ICC because of its non-transparency in selecting its members, and its role during the 2014 case. It was shocking to find out how a certain member of the ICC went to great lengths to malign the survivor and derail the investigation. These were 'loyal' faculty members bent on helping the university authorities to suppress the voice of the complainant. Their response was aligned with CM Mamata Banerjee's theory of 'rape' as a '*choto ghotona*' (petty matter).[6]

The irony is that the survivor herself was a panel candidate for the Trinamool Congress Chattro Parishad (TMCP) in the 2014 AFSU election. Despite that, the ruling establishment did not take up her cause when the incident happened; instead, they resorted to maligning the character of an individual belonging to their own organization. It was the students belonging to the opposite of the political spectrum who fought against the injustice and demanded a transparent inquiry. The progressive students went on a hunger strike.

As the then General Secretary of AFSU, I resigned from ICC. Although other student representatives were part of the ICC, I was the lone representative to have submitted my resignation from the committee, citing my disagreement with the way in which the ICC functioned. However, it did not mean a withdrawal from the struggle. The resignation from the committee did not mean that our movement ceased. It instead represented a principled position adhering to the larger resistance. The tide of the students' movement was rising at JU. On 16 September 2014, the EC decided to dismiss the investigation into the incident; the students

[6] I cite here two incidents of gangrape in West Bengal. In February 2012 on Park Street, Kolkata a thirty-eight-year-old woman was gangraped in a moving car, and in June 2013 a twenty-year old woman was gangraped and murdered in Kamduni at North 24 Paraganas. Both these incidents created shock and anguish amongst the people of West Bengal; and subsequently, people raised questions about the role and actions of the state administration. However, the first woman Chief Minister of West Bengal chose to respond to this outburst by attributing the incidents as 'cooked up' by the Left opposition parties, and a 'petty matter'.

responded by staging an indefinite sit-in demonstration in front of Aurobindo Bhavan (the university's administrative building).

As the non-violent protest against the VC's indifference and attempted suppression of the complaint gained ground, the authorities handed over the campus to the custody of the local constabulary. Despite widespread objection by the teaching faculty and students, a show of force by the police was seen on campus.

On 17 September at 2:00 am, the VC unleashed the combined might of the local police and thugs on the student protesters. Brutal treatment and molestation accompanied arrests made by the police. After this incident, as students at JU, we came together under the banner of a united student movement. Our movement began with the aim of achieving five demands: (i) The removal of Prof. Abhijit Chakraborty as VC, (ii) An independent judicial enquiry into the molestation incident of 28 August, (iii) An independent judicial enquiry into the brutal police action against peaceful student protesters during the early hours of 17 September, (iv) The immediate reconstitution of ICC in such a way to function democratically and transparently, and (v) The end of campus surveillance by the police.

On 20 September, a huge demonstration made its way through the city's streets. We received support from the wider society. Large segments of the masses and the students from other institutions joined us; they were outraged by the official indifference and incitement of sexual violence and rising police brutality, which had, by now, become routine in West Bengal. Our procession led us to the Governor of West Bengal who also happened to be the Chancellor of our University. We described our ordeal in detail and placed our demands before him, seeking his intervention.

Continued indifference by the authorities and the state government's contempt towards our movement were expressed through counter-demonstrations organized by the TMC outside our university. The government even went so far as to reward Prof. Abhijit Chakraborty with the position of permanent VC for the next four years. The order, announced in October, was signed by the chancellor even though we had urged him to remove Prof. Abhijit Chakraborty from his position as the interim VC.

On 17 October, a large mass of students held a symbolic hunger strike. Between 30-31 October, the students held a referendum on the five-point charter of demands first in the Art's Faculty and followed by similar referendums in the Engineering and Science Faculties. There was an overwhelming show of support for the removal of the VC (97 per cent) and the other demands. In this context, I should point out that we had been boycotting classes since the police action on 17 September. However, after several days of completely boycotting the classes, we decided to return to class and resume our academic engagements. But simultaneously, we continued with the movement. We did not respond to rollcalls as a sign of protest. We were unwilling to allow the university authorities to claim that 'normalcy' had returned to the campus. As long as the VC remained *in situ* (on-site), how could we forget his gross, notorious actions against the student community? We took our end-of-semester examinations. Even when writing the examinations, we protested in a novel way. We signed a separate sheet during the examinations, a rallying call, demanding the VC's resignation.

Meanwhile, the university's annual Convocation Day was approaching. On the eve of the Convocation, the students held a General Body meeting, and we decided to boycott the event. On the night of 23 December, I learned that I was to be awarded the Best Graduate Medal the next day at the Convocation. I decided to decline the medal as a participant in the united students' movement. The following day, 24 December, I attended the Convocation, went on stage when my name was called, and politely told the chancellor I could not accept the award in the presence of the VC who had refused to listen to a student who had been molested and instead summoned the police to beat, molest, and arrest peaceful student protestors. We would not accept that the Governor, who was also the university's chancellor, showed egregious audacity by appearing on the convocation stage with the VC, who was complicit with the goons in criminally thrashing the students. Yes, I turned down my university's Best Graduate of the Year Medal. It was an ideological decision as an activist in one of the most significant, mature, and constructive student movements to have emerged in India in recent years. My decision resulted from our collective resistance to authoritarian violence and patriarchy. It was rooted in a conscious programme adopted by most of my fellow students. I wasn't alone. A range of graduate and postgraduate students – 100 of us – refused the medals, degrees, and certificates at the Convocation. Some of our alumni respectfully returned their medals as a sign of protest and solidarity with us.

The chancellor asked me to leave the venue. My sole intention was to publicly reiterate to the university's higher authorities that we were firmly committed to achieving our demands. Sadly, some misinterpreted my public gesture, and I faced unpleasant criticism. My political conviction and that of my comrades was also vilified since we were part of the largest left organization in the country.

Our peaceful boycott was successful despite the stray abuse faced by some of us for taking this step, an act of conviction in our movement born in desperate times. We were able to convey to the public at large that we could not accept awards in the presence of a VC who was destroying our university.

In a sense, our movement was entering a critical stage. For the past three months, we had held varied forms of protest yet remained peaceful. The VC had criminalized us, called us names, called in the police, and accused us of carrying sharp weapons. We were unarmed. Our only weapon was the united movement composed of us – the students. On 5 January 2015, a General Body Meeting (GBM) of JU students was held. A solemn decision was reached. Twelve friends began a fast-unto-death. The education minister offered to meet them five days later at his office in Bikash Bhavan. Our friends were taken there in an ambulance as some of them were already showing signs of physical deterioration. The Minister did not make any firm commitment. Over the weekend, two friends were hospitalized, and others fell sick. Under these circumstances, on 12 January, the education minister came to JU to meet us.

Within thirty minutes of his arrival, the West Bengal CM also arrived. After meeting the students, she suddenly announced that the VC had agreed to resign. We were overjoyed. This had been our principal demand. The determination to remove him had started our movement. We saw the CM's announcement as a gesture of defeat: the government had been forced by the united resistance of the students to capitulate to our first demand. At the same time, the CM's propensity for drama was a sober reminder that the Chancellor is the only authority, by law, empowered to remove the VC formally. This prompted many questions: How can the CM interfere so blatantly in the functioning of a supposedly autonomous institution? Did her gimmick not give away the fact that Prof. Abhijit Chakraborty had been installed as VC by her government? Did they not reinstate him because we refused to accept him? How long can we put up with the brutal and anti-democratic interference in running schools, colleges, and universities by the TMC hooligan-driven autocratic state government? How can we accept the new draconian law controlling higher education in West Bengal, which has effectively done away with the internal democratic structure of institutions, including the democratic representation of students in the highest decision-making bodies?

Today, the Executive Council of JU is bereft of even elected faculty members. Selection, rather than election, is the rule. Students and non-teaching staff have no representation, democratic or otherwise. This is entirely unacceptable to us. We must continue to fight the gross authoritarianism breeding on our campuses. Thus, when the CM announced the VC's resignation, we analyzed it thoroughly; we then let everyone know that, even as JU students agitated for months demanding the VC's resignation, it must be done by following all democratic procedures and within the rules of the university and not by the whims and fancies of the CM.

We must prevent our campus from turning into a prison camp, a detention centre of the Guantanamo Bay variety. The other main demands are yet to be met. We must continue to fight for them and against the combined forces of patriarchy, autocracy, and right-wing violence. Only a united student movement can help us to achieve these aims. We are fighting to save our university, an open space that, in the past, had made us happy. It is not owned by the state government, the TMC, or the police. However, the broader dimensions of our struggle are not just confined to restoring democracy within our university. We want campus democracy in every educational institution along with freedoms for ordinary people.

HOK KOLOROB TAUGHT US MANY LESSONS

The ruling establishment tried branding this movement as a movement of 'outsiders'. Yes, the movement, indeed, proved to be a source of inspiration for the masses outside the confines of the university. The idea of Hok Kolorob was not confined within the walls of JU. It had, in fact, become part of the people's day to day experience. The people of West Bengal had suffered immensely since TMC assumed power in the state government and this suffering is continuing. When JU students began the movement against the autocratic functioning of the VC in the university and the semi-fascist tyranny of the state government, the larger sections of the people of West Bengal could relate to the movement of the JU students. Students, teachers, researchers, non-teaching staff, lab assistants, school students, guardians, and alumni all took part in the rain-soaked procession of 20 September 2014, and we were joined by thousands of people who were not associated with the university. The rally was historic. That rally followed two previous rallies held in solidarity with JU on 17 and 18 September that witnessed about five thousand and ten thousand participants, respectively.

The ruling class always targeted JU with narratives such as, 'In JU they don't study, they only do politics'. I remember that even during those tumultuous times when we had decided to boycott the classes as a form of protest, even then, we had not boycotted academics. The professors had cooperated with us and actively supported us in setting up alternative classrooms – on the playground, in the green zone, and so on – as a form of protest. The narrative by the ruling class directed against the university was because JU was never an ideal example of 'obedience' – the students consistently disappointed the ruling clan with their questions and protests. The tradition of JU bears testimony to the fact that it has never bowed down in insipid obedience to the authorities. So, the attack was not a new thing for us. However, the scathing attacks against the university and students' politics accelerated during the movement. Nevertheless, we received unconditional solidarity from various sections of people, both within and outside the state.

When we saw blatant apathy from all institutions of the ruling establishment, including the Nabanna (Office of the Chief Minister) or the Raj Bhavan (Office and residence of the Governor), despite protests from almost all sections of society, we realized we had to turn all platforms into protest platforms. Hok Kolorob, therefore, became a symbol of the new thrust and inspiration of the entire student movement. Without the Hok Kolorob experiences, I probably would never have known that one could sit for examinations, even while boycotting classes. I would not have learned that classes can commence under the shade of a tree. Without Hok Kolorob, I would never have known that one could stay awake at night, for months on end, with fellow students, guarding the campus.

Refusing our medals was a historic moment for us. It became

our biggest weapon. Despite having earned the distinction of 'the best graduate' of that academic session, a student refusing the honour of being awarded the same was an extraordinary way to register a protest against injustice symbolically.

It was Hok Kolorob that taught us that one could firmly reject a university authority that betrays the students. When others wonder how we could refuse to take medals from the Chancellor, JU's struggle provides them with the answer. We heard from our elders that General Carriappa, who was determined to wipe out every communist on campus, once asked, 'Is there a communist here?' in one such JU convocation, and a student replied – 'Yes, here I am!'. This unending legacy of determined struggle was what enabled the united students of all three faculties – the Arts, Science, and Engineering – to create and participate in the Hok Kolorob movement.

The Hok Kolorob movement succeeded in shining a light on gender sensitization and triumphed in taking its practices to new heights. At a time when women were brutally tortured in many ways throughout the state and the entire country, the movement taught us how to engage caringly and diligently in dealing with the question of gender equality. Hok Kolorob also paved the way for a new journey towards a united students' movement.

During the movement, more than six left, ultra-left, and independent student organizations came together, putting aside their ideological differences, to support the entire student community to strengthen this movement. It taught everyone a lesson. These organizations contested students' union elections against each other. But they came together and created strong barricades against the right-wing fascistic forces whenever required. This proves that ideological thinking, debates, and discussions have taken centre stage in shaping a united movement.

THE IMPACT OF THE UNITED MOVEMENT

The Hok Kolorob movement influenced campus politics in several ways. This movement thoroughly impacted the 2015 students' union elections. The JU students' mandate was once again against the TMC and the BJP. Even though there were differences in viewpoints amongst the students, those did not create a roadblock in resisting the regional right-wing parties like the TMC or the Hindutva fascistic BJP. We knew that unity was the key to defeating them. In the 2015 elections, the SFI ran against the independent students' organizations. The students voted in favour of independent student organizations in the election, and the SFI was defeated. However, this did not make SFI withdraw support from student protests against the right-wing, held by the leadership of the newly elected union. Although there were contestations amongst the students' organizations in the student elections, the Jadavpur students held firm in opposition to right-wing fundamentalism, communalism, and authoritarianism.

The fight for Gender Justice did not end with Hok Kolorob – it had just begun. Against a growing atmosphere of hostility towards women, society needs the strength of ideologically committed people who treat women as human beings and not objects.

At JU, the students' union, on the one hand, agitated for the installation of sanitary napkin vending machines on the campus premises; on the other hand, the union continuously organized protest demonstrations to create a committee for gender sensitization through transparent elections. Although ICC exists at JU, its members are not elected, and the committee is ineffective. We have protested to create a committee with psychologists and doctors elected by the students, teachers, researchers, staff, and university authorities.

The Hok Kolorob movement originated in an ideologically sickened society that unleashes violence against women. Even after the demonstrations, several serious discriminatory attitudes persist towards women. These problems reflect the years of societal practice of various forms of oppression of women. The only proper cure for these problems is gender sensitization. Therefore, the union has embarked on a continuous fight to establish an effective committee for gender sensitization on campus.

Since educational institutions are a primary source of developing one's character and consciousness, it becomes imperative to begin the process of sensitization on the campus itself. In the AFSU elections 2020, we demanded the creation of a gender sensitization cell with elected student representatives and the establishment of a separate course whose goal is to raise consciousness and awareness about daily discriminatory and divisive practices. As its most important demand, the SFI-run AFSU has agitated to establish an abuse-free campus. To facilitate this, the union demanded the creation of a phone application – Abuse Locating Application and Awareness Programme (ALAAP) – for raising awareness and registering a complaint against gender-based harassment as well as against discrimination on the campus on an immediate basis if one so wishes to.

CONCLUSION

From the struggle against British Imperialism to the protests against the post-independent undemocratic structure of the Indian state to the agitations against the violent right-wing fascistic forces of today – the history of JU is replete with many examples of united movements. JU means standing in the first row; JU means fighting incessantly against injustice. JU means accepting many existing traditions, thoughts, and beliefs while setting alternative examples to enrich our culture. JU is the human wall of collective harmony against all discriminatory practices and a pledge to isolate them. JU is an icon of reason against irrationality. Our belief system and its practical demonstrations are why JU still dares to shout out loud – '*Jaan thakte harbona, Fascibad manbona*' (As long as we are alive, we cannot be defeated, we won't tolerate fascism). The legacy of perseverance, harmony, and rationality has been constant throughout the history of JU. Wherever there is torture, misconduct, protest, and dissent, JU will always hear the cries of the victims and will, in turn, always respond, with millions of reverberating voices – 'Yes, we are present!'

#NoColour - Support FTII Movement

Satarupa Chakraborty

An interview with Ameya Vivek Gore[1]

The Film and Television Institute of India (FTII) was established by the Government of India in 1960 in Pune on the premises of the stellar film company *Prabhat*. The name and influence of the iconic film studio slowly became associated with FTII, and the institute became the most reputed film school in the country, subsequently drawing national and international recognition in establishing new standards in filmmaking.

In 2015, FTII was in the media spotlight due to a controversy that erupted with the appointment of Mr Gajendra Chauhan as the institute's chairperson.

Since the shift of power in the centre in 2014 – the United Progressive Alliance (UPA)-II government was replaced by the Bharatiya Janata Party (BJP)-led National Democratic Alliance (NDA) – the country witnessed several protests by the students.

FTII was one of the first institutes targeted when BJP assumed governmental control. Students called for a strike and boycotted classes for over five months. The students' outrage came as a response to the non-transparent appointment of Mr Gajendra Chauhan as the head of FTII. The institute's legacy was so precious

[1] Conducted on 8 September 2020 and updated in May 2022.

to the students that they wouldn't be silenced by the BJP's attempts to change the essence of the FTII.

Protests at the institute immediately garnered support from students' unions and various progressive organizations across the country. They drew support from many veteran filmmakers and FTII alumni in protest against the political appointment of Mr Gajendra Chauhan.

Ameya Vivek Gore, a student from FTII, who was one of the key participants in the movement and braved police actions, spoke to Satarupa Chakraborty. This interview covers a range of topics beginning with an understanding of FTII's political legacy. Ameya also recounts the targeting of students by the authorities and how the students resisted the assaults.

FTII had appointed a range of people as chairpersons in the past. Why did the students oppose the appointment of Mr Gajendra Chauhan as the chairperson in 2015?

On 9 June 2015, Mr Gajendra Chauhan was appointed as the Chairperson of FTII. As the news spread, the students were very upset. Within a day, we decided to go on a strike. The students gathered near the wisdom tree, and the discussion about the agitation began there. From that day forward, there was no looking back. I joined the strike from the beginning; there was never a question of not joining it.

Selection for the chairperson or any leadership position at FTII has to be based on their wisdom, credentials, and expertise. They should not be appointed on the basis of their political affiliation or connections. Therefore, we used #NoColour and #SupportFTII as a slogan for the movement. When we say, 'No Colour', we mean that no one should be appointed because they are close to someone from the ruling party. It does not mean that they should not have any ideology. Everyone believes in something and has some kind of ideology. We believe that in a place like a film school, the chairperson needs to have a vision that allows for and encourages honest expression and exploration by the students while making films.

Even if a chairperson has an ideology, this should not create a roadblock for him or the students. It was the manner in which Chauhan's appointment happened that created the apprehension as to why such a person was chosen for the institute without having similar credentials as his predecessors.

Since Chauhan's appointment was political, would you have preferred if an 'apolitical' person was selected as chairperson?

FTII has always been a political space. We have always discussed and debated what is happening in society and politics. However, FTII is not political in the same way as, for example, Jawaharlal Nehru University (JNU) is political. We approach politics from a different point of view. For instance, we are more fascinated by or interested in the 'politics of image'. For students at JNU, their entry point in understanding fascism may be predominantly from a socio-political or historical point of view. For us, the entry point in understanding fascism is from films. For example, when I think about fascism, I recollect the film *Triumph des Willens* (Triumph of the Will). It is an outright propaganda film by a German director cum producer named Leni Riefenstahl. It was made during the time of Nazi Germany. When I teach filmmaking courses, I show this film to my students. For me, how the shots have been arranged, or the scenes have been depicted, or 'how the desire has been stoked and created' – are all political. For me, that is politics. I get to see how Hitler is portrayed as 'the supreme figure' who is all-powerful, and the little boys are juxtaposed with him, creating an impression that the boys will also aspire to be like Hitler one day.

Before Mr Chauhan, the director and screenwriter Saeed Akhtar Mirza was the chairperson of the FTII Society. One can clearly see that he has an ideology, and it is reflected in his work. His films are very nuanced in their political understanding. So, it's certainly not about having an 'apolitical' chairperson. However, we knew that anyone appointed to this position should have a broad vision, allowing students to explore what they are all about and how they relate to one another and the world around them.

As it is widely known, FTII has a great legacy – what does it mean? What was the vision for creating a film institute like this?

In FTII's legacy, *Prabhat* is a crucial factor.[2] So, it is partly about *Prabhat* – FTII's history and legacy have a lot to do with where it is geographically located. But there is another part of its history and legacy that is important to know in order to understand the institute's vision. FTII (formerly known as the Film Institute of India) was founded in 1960. Indira Gandhi first headed the Ministry of Information and Broadcasting (I&B Ministry) from 1964 to 1966. During her second tenure in 1971, the institute received full support of I&B Ministry. Later, when she visited the Soviet Union in 1976, she was deeply inspired by the film school she saw there. At that time, the Indian political leadership wanted to create a film school that made films about India. These leaders felt that a film school was essential for nation-building; that it was vital to train people with the necessary technical skills so that a full-fledged film industry could develop, and people from all socio-economic classes could find representation there. They wanted the institute to be a place where people could find their voices. It is essential that anyone heading the institute understands this vision and advances it, adapting it to the current times.

[2] 'The present-day FTII campus was initially land bought by the Prabhat Film Company way back in the year 1933. The company was founded in Kolhapur in 1929 and moved to Pune four years later. A stellar and pioneering film company of its time, it produced several important and iconic films such as *Shejari, Sant Dnyaneshwar*, and *Sairandhri*, which was the only colour film made by Prabhat. Such was the legacy of this iconic studio that, at the time, it was the biggest film studio in Asia! The productions made by the Prabhat Film Company in its heyday included forty-five films made in both Marathi and Hindi languages.' https://ftii.ac.in/p/about-ftii.

What type of films did FTII originally make and what kind of films are made today?

FTII productions tried to capture some of the very basic realities of our country, poverty and inequality, for example. A lot of those films were rather preachy and simplistic. Film language and aesthetics were still taking root in the country. As the process was very technology-intensive, a transformation in cinema was not possible overnight. When Ritwik Ghatak began teaching at FTII, the trend started to change. We have heard several interesting incidents about his 'innovative' teaching methods. Ritwik Ghatak's films are profoundly political and, at the same time, incredible works of art. He directly or indirectly influenced a range of students; they started internalizing his approach to filmmaking. It started evolving into a medium of personal and political expression. There were other, less charismatic, teachers as well. People in various departments, at different levels, dedicated their entire lives to the institute – that's how legacies are built. Due to such people, a range of students got excellent training. When such people are appointed, the outcomes may be something that can have a lifelong impact on individuals, on institutions, on the industry, and on society and its people. That's why teachers and institutional leaders are crucial to institution building and filmmaking.

You mentioned that FTII is a political space. Does it have a history of political movements led by its students? Can you reflect on the students' participation in raising their demands in earlier movements before your movement began in 2015?

In 2009, a committee was set up by the administration whose objective was making FTII profitable. Even though the institute was not being overtly privatized, the students understood the effects this would have on the institute. At that time, Mr U. R. Ananthamurthy was the chairperson of the FTII Society (during the UPA-II regime). The students called for a strike to resist the privatization of the institute. I was new to the institute back then and enjoyed my days off instead of participating in the protest. The strike continued for about three days. The students were protesting against future fee hikes to ensure that a film-school education remained affordable for Indian students across different classes. At that time, Mr U.R. Anantamurthy supported the demands of the strike, and the proposed changes were rolled back. We have heard from former students that around the year 2000, there was another big strike against a similar attempt by private entrepreneurs trying to take over FTII. The students protested and resisted that attempt too. The students, time and again, have taken political actions against any move by the administration or the government that hurts the interests of FTII. And the interests of FTII include the rights of its workers too. The FTII student body has consistently supported the institute's staff members, mess workers, lights boys, and electricians. When a mess worker required financial help to pay for surgery of a family member, the students would often chip in to help them out. This culture was something I was always proud of as a student – it is something I will always remember fondly.

You mentioned that you did not participate in the students' strike in 2009. What motivated you to join the strike in 2015?

By 2015, I understood the ethos of FTII. It was not a completely rosy picture as several problems existed on campus. But FTII had become like family to me. That's why I had no second thoughts about joining the strike in 2015. Chauhan's appointment was simply unacceptable to us; a chairperson's appointment is not something that is easily reversed. Striking seemed to be the only option for the students to register their opposition to the appointment. Students at FTII were not protesting against a political party, i.e., BJP. The protest was against this particular appointment.

At that point in time, a lot of issues pertaining to students' rights were percolating at other national universities and institutes as well. The FTII Students' Body had always expressed solidarity with other student bodies, which took a strong stance in these matters. However, a lot of students at FTII, including me, were not overtly political. Therefore, when we started the strike, it was primarily focused on the question of Chauhan's appointment. In the beginning, for many FTII students, it was more a question of 'legacy' than a political issue. How could this person, whose credentials were that of a B-grade actor, become the chairperson of our prestigious institute? This sentiment was powerful. Due to this, it was relatively easy to mobilize the students to join the strike. Everyone participated on their own. I, too, did the same. However, some of our senior students saw a much greater threat here. The Chairperson would have the powers to appoint the dean, the director, and people in other important positions. He could take major administrative and academic decisions that could completely change the fabric of the institution. With time, this became clearer to the rest of us as well.

FTII is both an institute for film and for television. Television captures the attention of a larger audience and their imagination. The viewership of television is higher. In that way, television has a vital role to play in society. Do you not think that Mr Gajendra Chauhan was a known figure in the television industry, if not cinema? In this sense, can you elaborate on why his appointment was resisted by focussing on his credentials in films, yet neglecting his role on television?

FTII offers courses in film as well as television. At the time, even students specializing in television completely supported the movement, and actively joined the protests. There are court cases still pending against a few of the students who majored in television. To be honest, we do not think it is right to say that Mr Gajendra Chauhan has impressive television credentials. Another important distinction is that when we say that the chairperson should have credentials, it is not necessary for them to be a film practitioner as such. For instance, U.R. Ananthamurthy and R.K. Laxman had been chairpersons of FTII, but they were not hard-core film practitioners. However, they had certain credibility and respect (due to their work in their own fields) within and outside FTII. Mr Ananatamurthy understood the importance of an affordable film education for all classes, which is why he listened to the students' demands. So, it is about standing up for what is right. It is about having a vision of what's in the best interests of the students. It is about understanding the issues of India and its people. It is about interacting with society and thereby having an inclusive worldview. Take R.K. Laxman, for example. His life's journey was so full of unique experiences and accomplishments. He understood the people of this country and what their needs were. Even if the person being appointed was not a film practitioner, if he had the kind of experience and insight of an R.K. Laxman, we would have welcomed him with open arms. Just because Mr Gajendra Chauhan played the role of Yudhishthir in the *Mahabharata* serial it didn't prove his credentials to lead an institute like FTII. This became quite evident when Chauhan began to give interviews to the T.V. channels. Everyone understood that this person did not have the intellectual imagination required to run a film institute. He said in an interview, '*Jo chal jata hein, wo acha cinema hai*' (A good movie is one that is a commercial success). If someone has this sort of superficial and commercialized view of cinema, how do you expect him to run an institution with the type of vision we have been discussing? There were some other appointments to the FTII Society, apart from the chairperson, which never came to light. The only credential these people had, was that they were connected to the ruling party or their ideology. I have interacted personally with some of them. I felt that their understanding of cinema and politics was very dangerous.

Together, these people could have been very dangerous for FTII's future, as none of them had any vision. Not just Mr Gajendra Chauhan, but Anupam Kher, Chauhan's successor, was highly unsuccessful as chairperson. Kher joined FTII as Chairperson and quit soon afterwards. He could not run the institute for even a year. He was rarely present at FTII as he was busy with his own activities. Sadly, the government's focus doesn't appear to be the betterment of the institute. When Kher was appointed, his affiliation with the BJP was quite clear. However, we did not protest against his appointment, as he had better credentials and a large body of work to his credit. But ultimately, he could not and did not contribute anything to the institute. If there is the political will, the government can do a lot for the advancement of FTII in particular and Indian cinema in general. But that certainly doesn't seem to be a priority for them.

The government and its defenders always put forth the argument that FTII needs efficiency in order to justify the administrator they select. How do you view the argument of efficiency vis-à-vis the development of the institution?

At the time, FTII was already having various problems; they were complex issues, including administrative delays, a lack of technology, and student indiscipline, to name a few. Also, the digital revolution was kicking in big time, which is why important changes in the course structure were necessary. In a situation like that, we needed someone who was not only competent but also extremely patient and had a very clear vision of cinema and its future. We needed someone who could handle the situation delicately, understanding all the nuances. People representing the government have always argued that the person appointed should be a very efficient administrator. They seem to forget that efficiency cannot be the only measure of success, especially in an art school. Basing success on only efficiency is akin to saying that Nazism was good because the trains ran on time. The reason they make such arguments and actually send people (whom they consider efficient) to the institutes is not to develop the institutions but to discipline everybody. This has become a trend, particularly in educational institutions where they want an obedient student population and faculty; they make everybody fall into line. But they have no idea why the line is being formed or why it is even needed. One of us jokingly said in an interview at that time, 'Why don't you appoint someone with military experience as the Chairperson, if discipline is all that matters to you?' More importantly, what the process really needed was to be democratic and transparent. The Ministry of Information and Broadcasting had simply selected Mr Chauhan because he was close to the ruling party, while ignoring many other towering personalities. We wanted to ensure these criteria were not used in the future, no matter who came to power.

I came across many references to the 'Wisdom Tree' during the FTII movement. This name is fascinating. Does this particular area in the institute have any spatial historic significance around which the movement was built?

There is an old mango tree at the institute outside the main theatre area where all the screenings happen. Film legends, including Ritwik Ghatak, used to sit under it and discuss films at length. The discussions were so intense that it symbolically became a place where one had an epiphany of wisdom. So, people started calling it the 'Wisdom Tree'. Over time, this became the name to which people would relate to and identify the space. I have heard that, in earlier years, a newcomer to the institute could not immediately go there and participate; it was like one had to earn their place under the 'Wisdom Tree'.

The location of the tree is at a crossroad. It's a place where people coming from different directions can meet. Sitting under the tree, you can see people coming from all directions. It was the main site where we gathered during the movement. There was a romanticism about the place, and it also kept the movement going.

How long did the movement continue?

The movement against Chauhan's appointment was quite a

long one, lasting from 150 to 160 days. It was the longest movement ever at FTII. In our experience, it is tough to sustain a strike for so long, but we managed.

I read that there were some open classes around the Wisdom Tree during the agitation. How do such classes contribute to the academic culture of the institute and the movement?

I was one of the members who was assigned to take the lead in organizing the classes. Since I spoke Marathi, I could contact people in Pune to come and organize sessions. I had a lot of fun attending many of them. Most of the open classes were not on films – they were sharing sessions. Mr Arvind Gupta came and gave a session on the scientific learning toys that he had developed. A Pune-based artist, Sangram, did a session on origami. The renowned photographer Dayanita Singh gave a lesson on photography. Dr Kumar Saptarshi spoke on Satyagraha (holding on to the truth) and how he viewed Satyagraha in today's context. It was exciting to learn about these various fields, we were thrilled. Those classes helped keep the momentum going. However, due to the nature of our areas of study, such classes were very difficult to continue after the strike.

What was the core demand of the movement? How did you pursue the demand?

Before Mr Gajendra Chauhan was formally installed as chairperson, we heard the official announcement of his appointment. The FTII students' body had several rounds of meetings with the then director of the institute, Mr D.J. Narayan, who was very friendly to the students. Later, we also tried to have discussions with the officials of the I&B Ministry. The procedure of appointing the chairman of the institute was very loose and partly ad-hoc. In every meeting, we demanded an overall change in that process. We wanted more transparency to ensure that political appointments did not happen in the future. That was the most critical part in our charter of demands, which we stressed time and again. What was the administration's reaction to this movement? The I&B Ministry did not seem to be responding to our demands. They would hold discussions, but not budge at all. Director D.J. Narayan, who was usually sensitive to student issues, was transferred in the middle of the strike and a temporary director was sent in his place (a director is usually an Indian Information Service officer.) The media was trying to create its own narrative. They ran headlines like 'FTII vs Gajendra Chauhan', instead of explaining the nuances of the issue. The administration accused the students' movement of damaging the institute's public image. We continued to have meetings with the new FTII director.

In conjunction with this struggle, another issue developed. The students of the 2008 batch became guinea pigs during the digital transformation of the institute. As a result, this batch suffered considerably. New equipment was introduced without the students having any training on how to use it. The swine flu epidemic, at that time, made matters worse. Their course completion was delayed. In fact, the batch that came after them, the 2009 class, completed their courses before them. This issue was a critical problem facing the 2008 batch students. In the middle of the strike, members of the administration decided to shift the blame for the strike on the 2008 batch, mainly because these students represented the most senior members on campus. The administration assumed that the situation would automatically be resolved if they removed the 2008 batch from campus.

Was there any punitive action against the 2008 batch of students or on any of you by the administration? What led to the filing of charges against you? How did this action impact you?

Half of the 2008 batch had passed out before the strike, while the other half was staying on campus. They had been given extra time to finish their projects before the strike's commencement.

But in the middle of the strike, the administration gave notice that all 2008 batch members would have to leave the campus within the ten days. Later, they would be given a few days to return and finish their projects. Before this notice was issued, these students had already been granted the extension, yet this sudden decision was taken by the newly appointed director. Some of the student body members went to his office to ask the basis on which this decision was taken. According to the normal process, this decision can only be taken in consultation with the academic council. The process was not being followed. He assured us that he would look into the matter and try to resolve it. The next day however, a fresh notice was sent out, announcing that he would implement the previous decision that we had opposed. We felt betrayed. We needed to send a message loud and clear to the administration that they could not flout norms and take the students for granted. We returned to his office for another meeting. The entire meeting was recorded on video this time. Throughout the whole session, we all spoke calmly, displaying no agitation. However, the administration suddenly called security and then the police. Though there was no physical confrontation from our side, the police came and started forcibly removing us from the director's office. They started a lathi-charge. Due to the police lathi-charge, a glass window in the office was broken. The administration then filed charges against us for destroying public property, along with several other offences. A couple of days later, at midnight, the police arrived on campus. Although many students were present at the meeting, only thirty-five of us were targeted with a First Information Report (FIR). Most of the targeted students had been prominently visible in the protest. They handpicked the students who they thought were more important to be eliminated. Of the thirty-five targeted, five of us were arrested that night. We were immediately granted bail, but the case is still pending and active. It has, to some extent, affected us personally and professionally. For instance, it is a hassle to get a passport now. I must now apply annually to renew my passport instead of the usual ten years. Apart from that, the unpredictability of the court proceedings is also draining at times. We have kind of gotten used to this but having a case hanging over our heads is never a pleasant feeling.

Were you prepared to face this kind of action? How did this action impact you?

I admit that I did not imagine that going to a meeting would bring about such harsh consequences. I was not really prepared for this at the time. I wasn't ready to have false charges filed against me. Now that it has happened, we have accepted it with courage. When people ask me, 'you went to the institute to study, why did you get involved with politics?' I reject this type of thinking. My reason is simple: educational institutions are established not only for studying. I believe that learning is incomplete if a value system is not infused into universities and institutes of higher learning. Although I was not prepared for such consequences, I don't regret my actions. All of my activities were part and parcel of the struggle and my education. The administration and the ministry wanted to teach us a lesson and set an example. That is why they filed charges against us. Was there any positive outcome from the struggle? After our protest, the director put his decision against the 2008 batch of students on hold. A committee was set up to examine the issues facing the 2008 batch. They were eventually given more time for submissions.

We continued our discussions about FTII issues with the ministry. Unfortunately, nothing positive ever came from those meetings. We had meetings with the Joint Secretary and other officials in the ministry, but it turned out to be just a farce. They could not defend their appointment of Mr Gajendra Chauhan. Ostensibly, they met with us just to show they were concerned; in actuality, their hands were tied. But some tangible things did happen, which never came out in the media. For instance, Mr Gajendra Chauhan remained chairperson, but it was decided that he would not interfere in academic matters. Normally, the chairperson is the head of the governing council, which deals with the administrative aspects of the institute, as well as the academic council that deals with academic matters. For the first time, a distinction between the governing council and the academic council was made, and it was decided that Mr Gajendra Chauhan would not head the academic council. This was a significant and positive outcome of our struggle. Although Mr Gajendra Chouhan continued as chairperson for a while longer, his tenure ended soon after and he did not make any major decisions during his time. Amongst the FTII society members, a few are selected to be part of the governing council. Due to our struggle, most of the members against whom we were protesting were not selected for the governing council.

Another positive outcome of the protest was that the government and administration felt the need to think ten times before making any anti-student decision. Our protests brought about constant media attention to FTII. The governing council also feared a Right to Information (RTI) request. We developed a network within and outside Pune that allowed us to highlight all legitimate issues and created a platform to unite people with the demands of our movements. The students' unity and perseverance brought about this type of strength.

When did the students decide to end the strike? What compelled the students to end it?

In October of 2015, we called off the strike. The administration did what is done historically to break progressive movements. First, they would tell us that they would set up a committee to address the issues, but it was just a formality. Some representatives from the I&B Ministry delegation would tell us that they were in agreement with our demands but were powerless to do anything. It had become a prestige issue for the government. Removing Mr Gajendra Chauhan would have meant that they were taking a step backwards. It would have meant that students from all over the country could rise up and have their demands met. They did not want to set that kind of example. They had the whole State machinery behind them, and they had already pressed charges against us. There was also pressure from students at FTII about how much longer the strike would continue, as classes were not happening. As a last resort, we called a hunger strike, in which a few students were forcibly hospitalized. We did everything we could to push our demands. In the end, however, the students were getting more and more frustrated. We were worried that the administration would try to trigger the students into making a mistake so that they could take disciplinary action and possibly file more legal complaints against us. Our struggle had been non-violent and we were committed to this. As we wanted to avoid any physical altercation, we finally decided to call off the strike.

What do you think were the challenges of the movement?

It is not easy to continue a strike for 150 days, particularly when fighting with an adamant government and administration. Many people were left with a feeling of failure. But when I look back, I feel that it was certainly not a complete failure. Probably with the experience that we have now, we would have dealt with things differently. However, that was our journey, and it was essential for all of us. This movement has inspired many people, both within and outside FTII. However, understanding why we didn't achieve all the demands of the movement is also very important. It was such a big movement, which went on for over five months at one of India's biggest institutions where students are selected after rigorous screening and a national entrance exam. For five long months, all these students unanimously stood up for a cause. Our demands were clear and just and we never resorted to violence. Yet reversing Chauhan's appointment could not be achieved. It is a critical failure. It shows where we are as a country. It speaks to the nature of the ruling party. This failure is significant, but it must be viewed from the point of view of who is ruling today and how they are ruling. It is also significant for future students to reflect on and think about new and innovative forms of protest.

What, according to you, would have been a more successful outcome of the movement?

The removal of Mr Gajendra Chauhan would have been significant. Ideally, with such a large-scale opposition from the students at the institute, he should have resigned. As mentioned before, we were also asking for a more transparent process. The I&B Ministry nominates people to the FTII Society, but the nomination process was very hazy at that point in time. We were, therefore, asking for a concrete and transparent process in appointing the chairperson. These two were the most important and essential demands. The movement would have been a total success had these two demands been met.

What, in your opinion, would have made the movement stronger? Were there any disagreements amongst the students during the movement? How did you resolve them?

In retrospect, I think a much bigger churning is needed inside the institute and outside within the larger student community. In the throes of the moment, developments sometimes restricted our flexibility to respond as we might have wanted, and we couldn't extricate ourselves from a tight spot. Questioning our strategy and tactics continuously strengthens our thoughts and outcomes, and this process needs to be undertaken more thoroughly. Developing a teacher-student relationship within an institute is very important. In FTII, this relationship has to be made stronger. Besides, a movement is not possible without uniting the students. But this unity does not get forged overnight. It is a continuous process. When a movement doesn't have goals, it tends to become a mob if the agitation continues for too long. I am proud that FTII's movement, despite lasting for so long, never became a mob. We were constantly debating and discussing amongst ourselves. We had our differences and sometimes the discussion got frustrating. But most often, we could reach a consensus. We rarely had to call for a vote to resolve our differences.

What did the movement mean to you personally?

The movement was instrumental in impacting my personal journey, starting out as an ignorant student to developing a political opinion. For example, before the 2014 Lok Sabha (the lower house of India's bicameral Parliament) elections my friends and I would have discussions on whether to support Narendra Modi or Rahul Gandhi to be the Prime Minister of India. In these discussions, I would often find myself confused, as I did not understand the nuances of politics. Now, when I have such a discussion with my friends, I say that I am not interested in a match between the Undertaker and the Rock (WWE Wrestlers). I feel that personality-based politics is no different from a wrestling match. I believe that if someone wants to do something for the country, he or she should work for the people. And this can also be done without getting involved in electoral politics. When someone is interested in contributing constructively to the people and society in any way, there are many ways to do it. A discussion about whether we should have Modi or Rahul Gandhi as the prime minister is a highly superficial exercise, in my opinion. I have reached this point primarily because of the strike; my perspective on politics has completely changed. The movement transformed me tremendously, so much so that it influenced my work as a filmmaker. I have realized that everything I make is political on some level. Now, I have become more responsible in that process. I met so many people from different backgrounds during the strike. Most of the time, without a thorough engagement, we do not realize that most of our friends are from the same class or caste background. During the movement, I got to know what diversity is – I got to know people from Dalit organizations, and from left and right organizations. I dealt with the All India Students' Association (AISA), Akhil Bharatiya Vidyarthi Parishad (ABVP), and several others. I remember that I had a naive view about everyone, including those from the ABVP. I used to engage with them, and I found that not all of them are insensitive people on a personal level. I used to believe that everyone should get equal space to express themselves in a protest. If an ABVP member wanted to come and talk at the protest that we had organized, I thought that they should be given that space and engage in a dialogue. But one incident, during the movement, opened my eyes to their politics. One day during the strike, some ABVP members from outside FTII came near the institute's gate and tried to stage a counter-protest to disrupt the ongoing movement. It was a shock to me. It was okay if they did not want to join the movement and instead ally themselves with the government. But to come to the FTII gate and make attempts to disrupt the movement was something that was truly shocking. The next day, we stood close to the gate where ABVP was supposed to stage another protest against us. Several paintings had been made by FTII students, faculty members, artists, and others who visited the institute during the strike. We carried all these paintings to the gate and placed them in such a way as to leave very little space for ABVP members to stand. When the ABVP cadres arrived, they were puzzled. Soon after, a few ABVP members approached us at the gate. During the early days of the movement, I remember feeling intimidated by some of them. I remember there was an ABVP member who had come to our campus. I was talking to him, trying to explain the situation in detail. He casually asked me where I parked my motorbike. I wondered whether they would note down my bike's number and follow me. But on that day, when the same person came towards me, I looked him in the eye, and said, 'welcome to our campus', with a handshake. They did not expect this, and they stepped back. Due to the heavy presence of the media near the gate, they chose not to destroy our paintings. Otherwise, they would have risked public sentiment turning completely against them had the media covered their violent actions. They still tried their best to protest, but it was a complete flop, as our paintings covered them, so hardly anyone noticed them. After some time, they started shouting '*Bharat mata ki jai*' (Hail Mother India). We, too, shouted '*Bharat mata ki jai*', which further left them perplexed. We live in a time when anybody who criticizes the government's moves is labelled a leftist, or a Maoist, or an urban Naxal, or an anti-national. We shouted this slogan to counter their narrative of associating individuals and movements in those terms. My experience on that day was so fulfilling when I realized how much confidence and courage I had gained. I cannot think of another way to have achieved this.

Emergence of Ambedkar Periyar Study Circle at the Indian Institute of Technology Madras and the Ensuing Struggle

Abhinav Surya

The Indian Institute of Technology Madras (IIT-M) is one of the first three Indian Institutes of Technology (IITs) in India, which was established in 1959 with an agreement, signed in Bonn, between India and Germany. Located in Madras city (now Chennai) in the state of Tamil Nadu, IIT-M received wide recognition and even the title – 'Institute of National Importance'. Today, the institute is one of the premier public institutions of higher education and learning in the country, which has sixteen academic departments along with a few advanced research centres that accommodate around 8000 students along with about 550 teaching faculty.[1]

While the institute is considered to have attracted the best minds of the country, this could not make IIT-M an institute that would reflect modern progressive values. Rather, it has been an institute that is largely dominated by conservative ideals and values. For instance, with the institute's support and endorsement,

[1] 'About IIT Madras,' Indian Institute of Technology Madras, https://www.iitm.ac.in/the-institute/about-iit-madras/overview.

regular religious and spiritual events are held, with an emphasis on one religion, Hinduism. And there was hardly any resistance to such activities on campus.

Under the guise that IIT-M was a 'peaceful' and 'apolitical' campus, the technologically savvy and brilliant minds from across the nation worked or studied in the institute without much reflection on the issues that affected society or questioned the administration.

However, the discourse began to change when a section of ideologically progressive students began to question the status quo. Slowly, they identified the need to have platforms, which could serve as the ones to continue discussions about various social, political, and economic issues, and organize meetings to discuss the literature by various social reformers such as Dr Bhim Rao Ambedkar and Erode Venkatappa Ramasamy, popularly known as Periyar. With discussions and debates being initiated by a section of students, the discourse within the campus gradually changed, which stood as a counterpoint to the dominant, conservative culture at IIT-M. The formation of Ambedkar Periyar Study Circle (APSC) and the ensuing struggle was the outcome of progressive politics, which slowly spread throughout the campus.

RISE OF PROGRESSIVE POLITICS AT IIT-M

Since its inception, IIT-M has witnessed very few students' struggles. The students' protests were largely limited to issues centred on specific problems within IIT-M. From the recent past, we could only remember the agitation of 2012 when the students protested the disruption by the administration of the institute's culture, and in early 2013, for serving poor quality food in the hostel mess.[2]

[2] The interaction between the old and the new students was considered as part of the institute's culture. The administration during 2012 allotted separate hostels for the first year UG students, which was considered by the IIT-M

Hardly any of these struggles were ideologically driven and aligned with a larger social cause. However, that changed in June 2013 when a struggle ensued based on an ideological position. The post-graduate students organized a massive protest march against the proposed fee hike and the low stipends for the scholars. The struggle focused not only on the issues faced by students and scholars in the institute as an isolated case but also raised questions against neoliberalism and the privatization of education. Such a struggle stood out in the history of the institute as the spirit of student movements was generally lacking at IIT-M. A small group of students, who were members of Quest, a student organization, challenged the conservative ideological discourse, which was dominant at the institute. Quest attempted to promote discussions on scientific temper and rationality between 2013 and 2015. However, apart from that, the ideological space was largely dominated by right-wing groups such as Dhruva, Vivekananda Study Circle, the International Society for Krishna Consciousness (ISKCON), etc. In fact, they received the liberal support and patronage of the administration.

In 2013, a student-run organization, the Extra Mural Lectures team (which is funded by the institute), organized a lecture by Ms Teesta Setalvad. The lecture offered a much-needed boost for the subdued progressive voices of the institute. Setalvad's lecture focused primarily on the state of communal harmony in the nation. However, blinded by the so-called 'Modi Wave', a section of Hindutva fanatics jeered and bullied her even though there was no provocation from the organizer's side. The speaker calmly countered their mindless arguments with facts and logic. This incident awakened the progressive students on campus who felt the lack of a strong platform where progressive ideas were discussed without the fear of being bullied.

This event led to the emergence of two progressive student

students as a disruptive action on the peaceful culture of the 'insti' (local slang for 'institute') life.

organizations – ChintaBAR (an independent student organization) and the APSC to create safe spaces for discussion. It marked the beginning of the first major penetration of progressive ideology into the conservative campus of IIT-M. Incidentally, both these groups began their activities on Ambedkar Jayanti Day (14 April) 2014, following which more coordinated efforts began. A series of activities including lectures, debates, panel discussions, movie screenings, poster pastings, pamphlet distribution, etc. started on campus. Through these activities, we started raising questions on the status of oppression, which exists in various forms in our society.

These students' groups raised opposition to the stigma of the IIT-M administration, which put restrictions on the non-vegetarian food at the mess – an attack on India's diverse food culture. The groups' discussions ranged from strong opposition to the anti-people measures of the Bharatiya Janata Party (BJP)-led National Democratic Alliance (NDA) government such as the imposition of the Hindi language, relaxing regulations against corporations by diluting labor laws, undertaking anti-farmer measures, etc. and created space for politicization of the students. We also initiated discussions on other larger national and international issues such as the turmoil in Kashmir or issues on global imperialism like the Israeli-Palestinian conflict, etc. The events and activities of these organizations slowly and steadily dented the walls of the fort that the conservatives had built over the years. The agenda put forward by these groups was fairly well received by the students of IIT-M. Even as the administration tried to restrict the activities of these groups by placing unfair restrictions on them, the progressive voices only grew in strength. These groups offered courage and a platform to the progressive minds of the institute, who had remained passive for a long time due to the strong conservative culture that gripped the campus, and which shamed any display of alternative politics on campus.

The conservative face of a large group of students and

the majority of the administration was laid bare by their ugly opposition to the event Celebrating Love, organized by ChintaBAR, in support of the famous Kiss of Love protests in 2014 against the moral policing by the Hindutva fundamentalists.[3] The participants voiced slogans, such as, 'Love is not immoral, moral policing is!', while a section of right-wing students openly supported the moral policing that existed at the institute and in our society. The administration, on the other hand, issued veiled threats to the academic life of the organizers of the event. These events initiated a large discussion, both on campus and in the state, and also exposed the soft-Hindutva sections within the campus. The next big dent, and a serious one this time, came when students belonging to these progressive groups exposed the shameful casteist face of IIT-M's administration. Under the Right to Information (RTI) 2005, the students revealed an application filed on 29 December 2014, which disclosed that only 6 per cent of the MS-PhD scholars recruited by the institute from 2008 to 2015 had been from the Scheduled Caste/Scheduled Tribe (SC/ST) category as opposed to over 64 per cent coming from the general category (primarily from the forward castes, the so-called upper caste). It also revealed that an overwhelming 464 of the 536 (about 86 per cent of the total) teaching faculty members at IIT-M were from the 'General Category'. Only eleven members of the teaching faculty, comprising only 2 per cent were from the SC category and only two members were from the ST category. The figures revealed through the RTI became widely known, and they drew the attention of people outside IIT-M. Many academicians as well as others from across the country raised strong criticisms about the recruitment policies of IIT-M. This act naturally created huge discomfort for the IIT-M administration. Further, it also

[3] Jonathan Ananda, 'It's Just Celebration and Expression of Love, Say IIT-Madras Students,' *The New Indian Express*, 15 November 2014, https://www.newindianexpress.com/cities/chennai/2014/nov/15/Its-Just-Celebration-and-Expression-of-Love-Say-IIT-Madras-Students-682674.html.

irked the Hindutva groups who were already enraged by the vocal opposition of the progressive students who were registering their voice against the anti-people policies of the BJP-led government under Prime Minister Narendra Modi.

Following this, the administration and the Hindutva students' groups began building a false narrative against the progressive student groups by claiming that these students were 'damaging the institute's image'. The authority made an attempt to curtail the rise of the progressive politics by proposing a set of 'Guidelines' for activities of student organizations at IIT-M. This proposal was put in front of the Students' Affairs Council (SAC), a legislative body of the students' representatives. The progressive students actively participated in the discussions on the proposed 'Guidelines'. We exposed the anti-student stance of the right-wing groups and the administration. Further, we ensured that the guidelines passed by SAC did not become highly regressive. However, the original draft of the meeting was altered by the administration. Instead, in the modified draft-Guidelines, they included a set of restrictive rules, among which included that student organizations' activities would be monitored by a teaching faculty appointed by the dean. Such rules in the draft-Guidelines were never discussed democratically; in fact, the student representatives were not aware of them.

DEMOCRATIC STRUGGLE FOR DISSENT

The biggest blow to the right-wing politics came on the occasion of the first anniversary of APSC, when it organized a lecture on the 'Contemporary Relevance of Dr Ambedkar' on 14 April 2015 (on Dr Babasaheb Bhimrao Ramji Ambedkar's birthday). At a time when the Hindutva forces were making consistent attempts to appropriate the name of Dr Ambedkar, APSC distributed a pamphlet, which clearly detailed Dr Ambedkar's ideology. The pamphlet quoted Ambedkar's writings; it exposed how the Hindutva groups and the Modi government were going against everything for which Babasaheb stood. They brutally attacked the minorities and oppressed classes of the country through their policies and actions, which were against the basic principles of social justice. When the pamphlet quoted remarks by Dr Ambedkar from his book *Annihilation of Caste*, such as, 'You must destroy the religion of the shrutis and the smritis', the right-wing students became aggressive.[4] After realizing that they stood completely exposed in their agenda to appropriate Ambedkar, the Hindutva groups began to draw up nasty plans to put down the progressive students' activities.

The enraged students, with their loyalty to the ideology of the Hindutva politics, wrote an anonymous letter to the Ministry of Human Resource Development (MHRD) complaining about the activities of APSC.[5] The hastily written letter alleged that 'One student group, "Ambedkar Periyar", is trying to dealign the ST/SC students and trying to make them protest against the MHRD and Central government. They are creating hatred among the students in the name of caste and trying to polarize the ST/SC students. They are also trying to create hatred against the Honorable Prime Minister and Hindus'. The anonymous complaint letter received a prompt response from the MHRD. Prisca Mathew, the Under Secretary to the Government of India, wrote a letter to the director of IIT-M on 15 May 2015. The MHRD's letter requested 'comments' from the director of IIT-M simply on the basis of this anonymous letter.[6] Perhaps the anonymous letter was a warning bell, which

[4] B.R.Ambedkar, 'The Annihilation of Caste' Southern Asian Institute, Columbia University, https://ccnmtl.columbia.edu/projects/mmt/ambedkar/web/.

[5] The letter sent in the name of 'Students, IIT-M' seemed to have been received by the MHRD on 14 April 2015, the same day on which Ambedkar Jayanti was commemorated. See the contents of the letter here: https://www.t5eiitm.org/wp-content/ploads/2015/05/11393130_925796720844639_6415538406934770993_n.jpg

[6] The 'subject' of the letter was: 'Distribution of controversial posters and pamphlets on the campus of IIT Madras and creating an atmosphere of hatred (sic) among the students by one of the student groups namely

echoed in the hearts of the Hindutva leadership at the centre. Therefore, it became necessary to secure the right-wing ideological fort of IIT-M from any rational and progressive thinking.

The intervention by the central government provided an opportunity for IIT-M's administration to crack down on the progressive students' politics, which questioned the establishment, and the Brahminical ideology and practices. IIT-M's Dean of Students sent an e-mail on 22 May 2015, 'derecognizing' APSC based on the letter received from the MHRD.[7] Ironically, while the MHRD complaint letter reflected deep fear among the right-wing camp, their bigotry was exposed, the reason stated by IIT-M to 'derecognize' APSC was 'because of the misuse of the privileges'.

This intervention was followed by huge protests that began at IIT-M and drew solidarity from across the country. The IIT-M administration's partnership with the Hindutva camp to crack down upon progressive politics on the campus attracted widespread criticism from all over the country. National TV channel debates were busy branding APSC as another group of 'anti-national' students, following those at Jawaharlal Nehru University (JNU). They went even further by identifying names of APSC members, accusing this group of attempts to turn IIT-M into the 'JNU of southern India'. But the people of Tamil Nadu were not fooled; the narrative, which the BJP-ruled government wanted to establish by using the national television channels, was a failure in Tamil Nadu. Social reformists and leaders such as Ambedkar and Periyar are icons in Tamil Nadu, which is known as the 'land of social justice' due to the assertion of the rights by the people

Ambedkar-Periyar.' See the contents of the letter: Scroll Staff, 'Banned IIT-Madras student group responds to charges of 'spreading hatred' against Modi government,' Scroll.in, 29 May 2015, https://scroll.in/article/730961/banned-iit-madras-student-group-responds-to-charges-of-spreading-hatred-against-modi-government.

7 Mayank Jain, 'As rationalist forum is derecognied by IIT Madras, students claim Hindutva groups thrive unhindered,' Scroll.in, 30 May 2015, https://scroll.in/article/731040/as-rationalist-forum-is-derecognised-byiit-madras-students-claim-hindutva-groups-thrive-unhindered.

of the oppressed communities. Within the state, therefore, all major political organizations, except the Rashtriya Swayamsevak Sangh-Bharatiya Janata Party (RSS-BJP), and the All India Anna Dravida Munnetra Kazhagam (AIADMK) erupted against the ban of APSC. The national parties such as the Communist Party of India (Marxist) (CPI(M)), Communist Party of India (CPI), Indian National Congress (INC) etc., as well as the regional parties such as, Dravida Munnetra Kazhagam (DMK), Viduthalai Chiruthaigal Katchi (VCK), Marumalarchi Dravida Munnetra Kazhagam (MDMK) etc. were all united in criticizing the IIT-M administration and the central government for their attempts to push the Hindutva agenda by restricting progressive politics on campus. In addition, the National Commission for Scheduled Castes (NCSC) sought a detailed report on the incident at IIT-M campus. The main entrance of the campus was surrounded by the protesters against the ban on APSC. The spirit of the protest was such that even though a huge battalion of police was deployed around the main gate of IIT-M for a week, the protest continued.

The support did not only come from the political forces. Academicians across the nation voiced, in unison, their opposition to the ban on APSC and against the undemocratic and unconstitutional decision by the IIT-M authority. Renowned activist and fearless writer Anand Teltumbde extended solidarity through a Facebook post in which he said:

> I congratulate you for challenging the undemocratic action by the IIT Madras authorities at the behest of their political bosses ... Needless to say India is with you in your fight against such highhandedness of the spineless authorities of a hallowed institution as IIT Madras.[8]

[8] Apoorva Puranik, 'Student solidarity: IIT-B gets its version of banned Chennai group,' *Hindustan Times*, 02 June 2015, https://www.hindustantimes.com/mumbai/student-solidarity-iit-b-gets-its-version-of-banned-chennai-group/story-6uYPOZU0oEYLApBisU2SQK.html.

A plethora of academicians wrote to the director of IIT-M to register their protest against the ban. Retired JNU professor Dr Chaman Lal, English Dalit poet S. Chandramohan, and several other scholars voiced their opposition to the Hindutva brigade's cowardly act. Writer Arundhati Roy hailed the courage of progressive students at IIT-M and stated that APSC faced the wrath of the right-wing as 'they have made the connection between corporate globalization and the perpetuation of caste'.[9] The biggest voice of support from the academic fraternity arrived when the noted American mathematician, David Bryant Mumford, in his letter to the IIT-M Director, wrote:

> I was deeply shocked that Ambedkar Periyar Study Circle was 'derecognised'. I believe campuses must allow open discussion of divisive issues even when it offends some people so that all aspects of an issue are out in the open. Today's youth are tomorrow's leaders and one wants them to think deeply about the direction in which we are all headed.[10]

The overwhelming support from politicians and academicians offered huge encouragement to the progressive students at IIT-M. Right from the beginning, the MHRD and IIT-M authorities were aware that their actions were completely autocratic; from the MHRD acting on a notorious anonymous letter full of hatred

[9] Arundhati Roy's statement, in full, as reported, 'It is because they have seen through this charade and put their finger on the most dangerous possible place. They have made the connection between corporate globalisation and the perpetuation of caste. There is hardly anything more threatening to this present ruling establishment than doing what APSC did – celebrating both Bhagat Singh and Ambedkar. This is what has brought them into the line of fire. This is what is sought to be quashed. The APSC derecognition is a recognition of a kind.' See: Ilangovan Rajasekaran, 'Derecognising dissent,' *Frontline*, 26 June 2015, https://frontline.thehindu.com/the-nation/derecognising-dissent/article7294361.ece.

[10] David Mumford, ' 'All men are created equal'?,' David Mumford Archive for Reprints, Notes, Talks, and Blog, 16 June 2015, https://www.dam.brown.edu/people/mumford/blog/2015/AllMen.html.

towards the SCs, STs and Ambedkar, to the IIT-M administration citing a set of ambiguous and regressive rules imposed without consulting the student representatives, to banning APSC, both of these institutions did not adhere to the democratic procedure. APSC members countered the IIT-M administration not just politically, but also by pointing out the violations of procedures and processes by the administration. APSC exposed the bias of the authority towards the right-wing organizations. While the right-wing organizations violated the administration's 'guidelines', the administration did not take action against them and, in fact, was tolerant of the events of the right-wing, promoting unscientific ideas such as creationism, which were detrimental to the vision and idea of a modern society. The sequence of events made clear that, in fact, there was a nexus between the IIT-M administration and the Hindutva forces in power.

The students, however, fought all these attacks with courage. The APSC members had to endure personal and psychological torture unleashed on them by their Supervisors and Professors. Many APSC members also faced the Hindutva groups' vile abuses on the internet through their organized cyber trolls.

The MHRD and the IIT-M administration expected to get away with their unethical and undemocratic actions. But they failed to foresee the resilience of a small group of ideologically driven progressive students. Ultimately, the IIT-M administration had to concede. The ban on APSC was lifted. The regressive rules on student organizations were suspended. It was a major victory for the emerging progressive voices of the institute and the nation.

THE FUTURE OF STUDENTS' MOVEMENT IN IIT-M

Following this episode, IIT-M did not give up on any of its efforts to curtail progressive students' politics. Some of the regressive rules, such as the ban on the distribution of pamphlets, restrictions on poster pasting, and the administration-monitored activities of the students' organization, were still retained. The frequency of suspending students' activities increased with the authorities citing frivolous reasons. However, all these attempts could not stop the growth of the voices for change. Post APSC-protest, spontaneous student's movements multiplied several folds. Support increased for progressive activities. Even though conservative ideas dominate the discourse amongst the students at IIT-M due to its very composition, the progressive politics have turned into a force with which to be reckoned. Any anti-people and anti-student measures by the government incite a definitive resistance from a large group of students at IIT-M. Notably, another progressive students' group, ChintaBAR, organized protests against the authoritarian crackdown of the central government at JNU and the BJP-led government's brutality in the Kashmir valley, which received massive and unprecedented support from the students. APSC's protest march condemning the institutional murder of Rohith Vemula, the united campaign against the neoliberal onslaught on Education, and ChintaBAR's rebellious Beef Party against the Hindutva's politics of food fascism are some of the prominent struggles in the recent past. All these protests received immense students' support and were successful in exposing the anti-student positions and character of the right-wing groups, which operate within IIT-M, as they stood on the opposite side every time the students raised a voice for their rights. While the progressive student organizations are relentless in their efforts to expose the link between the everyday struggles faced by the student community to the larger neoliberal agenda of the state, the right-wing students' groups stand in support of the ruling party's positions. As a result of the protests for APSC, the progressive students have created a much wider space for political agitation. It is a huge achievement that the students of IIT-M are no longer hesitant to come out in support of campaigns against fee hikes or demands for a better quality of hostel life or even to extend solidarity with other movements.

Even though the progress has been slow, it is as remarkable as the progress of the left-leaning students' movement at other campuses around the country, for it has attained such a high level in the span of just a few years on a campus, which had established an unchallenged monopoly of right-wing ideology that enjoyed abundant administrative support. The APSC Struggle and the struggle that followed to reverse the decision of the administration should be viewed as a victorious battle for the right to freedom of speech on campus. It can be viewed as the culmination of the dialectical struggle between IIT-M's history of perpetuating conservatism and the rising new current for change. It offered a new beginning by setting new cultural standards. Student struggles, including various activities such as protest marches, political discussions, poster pasting, and pamphlet distribution on social, economic, and political issues, were no longer seen as completely alien to IITs, especially at IIT-M. While the struggle continues for organized student politics to have representation on campus, protest marches, political actions like candle-light vigils, signature campaigns, and other acts of resistance, which were rare on the campus, have now become regular phenomena. This shows that an understanding has developed among students about the need for organized struggle to address the issues arising from time to time.

The way forward is to unite the progressive students of the campus and transform the discrete movements and activities into an organized political movement of the students. It is the only way to politicize the 'apolitical' IITs that otherwise were dominated by social-elite ideology, i.e., to maintain the status quo. Progressive politics face not just the task of countering right-wing ideology but also the task of recovering the best minds of the nation from the individualistic culture of IITs, which prevented students from thinking about social issues and forced them to merely be careerist machines focused primarily on grooming themselves to sell their labour power on the capitalist market. In this process, coordination among the progressive political organizations of all IITs and the democratic and progressive student movements of the nation is extremely crucial.

The foundation has been laid. The APSC struggle has etched itself in the history of IIT-M and will inspire students for years to come. The challenge of scripting a progressive future for IITs, to turn them into institutes of socially aware technical scholars, has been greatly boosted by the student struggles of this decade. As Lenin says, 'We are surrounded on all sides by enemies, and we have to advance almost constantly under their fire'.[11] Neoliberalism operates in the cultural space of IITs by promoting individualism and soft-Hindutva, and we can never relax in our duty to win over the students by elevating their issues and politicizing them.

[11] Vladimir Ilyich Lenin, 'What Is To Be Done? Burning Questions Of Our Movement,' Marxists.org, https://www.marxists.org/archive/lenin/works/1901/witbd/i.htm.

Why JNU is Under Attack: The Stand With JNU Movement and After

Subin Dennis

> This is not a JNU struggle alone now; this has become a much wider struggle. What you are fighting to defend is much wider – secularism, democracy, the right to free expression. All the constitutional rights, which are given to the citizens of this country, are under attack. This attack has concentrated against you in JNU because you represent the most advanced, organized, and conscious sections of the democratic students of India.
>
> Prakash Karat, Polit Bureau member of the Communist Party of India (Marxist), and former President of JNUSU, speaking at JNU's Freedom Square, 15 February 2016

On 12 February 2016, at around noon, we received news that Kanhaiya Kumar, the President of the Jawaharlal Nehru University Students' Union (JNUSU), had been arrested by the police and charged with sedition.

There were already reports that hostels were being raided by the police, looking for people accused of having raised 'anti-India slogans' during a public programme three days earlier, on 9 February.

The 9 February programme, organized by a small group of students, was in memory of two people. One of them was Afzal Guru, a surrendered militant in Kashmir who was convicted of the attacks on the Indian Parliament that took place on 13 December 2001. He was hanged in 2013 after being sentenced to death by the Supreme Court 'to satisfy the collective conscience of the society' (the court's own words) and not because there was sufficient evidence to justify the hanging. The second one was Maqbool Bhat, a separatist leader in Kashmir who was hanged in 1984.

The organizers said they were holding the programme against 'the judicial killing' of Afzal Guru and Maqbool Bhat. Akhil Bharatiya Vidyarthi Parishad (ABVP) tried to disrupt the programme. This prompted many students to reach the venue to defend the programme organizers' freedom of expression, although they may not have agreed with the opinions expressed at the programme.

Soon, allegations were made by some media outlets that 'anti-national slogans' had been raised during this programme. To compound the issue, the TV channel Zee News aired doctored videos, which 'showed' that slogans like 'India down, down' and 'Pakistan long live' were raised on the campus after the programme. Indeed, masked participants (they were suspected of being from outside JNU) had raised anti-India slogans that called for the country's break-up. In response, the JNUSU and all major Left organizations on campus issued statements condemning such communally charged, divisive slogans. Later investigation showed that those who raised these slogans were not Jawaharlal Nehru University (JNU) students but outsiders. Their identities remain unknown.

The interest of the corporate media or the Rashtriya Swayamsevak Sangh (RSS)-led Sangh Parivar was not to establish the truth, but to paint the students of JNU as 'anti-national' so that a crackdown could be initiated against the student movement. RSS, Bharatiya Janata Party (BJP) and ABVP, and their media allies orchestrated a massive campaign demanding a crackdown on JNU and against the so-called 'anti-national' activities taking place at the university. They alleged that Kanhaiya Kumar, the JNUSU President, was among those who led the anti-India sloganeering calling for the secession of Kashmir. This sounded implausible because raising such slogans would go contrary to the political positions of Kanhaiya's organization, All India Students' Federation (AISF). But that didn't deter the RSS-BJP-ABVP, the corporate media, or the State machinery acting at the behest of the Sangh Parivar from making these wild allegations.

The arrest of the JNUSU President was the beginning of a frontal assault on the university's student movement, which had successfully resisted the commercialization and communalization of education for more than forty years. Precisely because of the politics championed by the JNU students' movement, the university has been a target of attack by the RSS-BJP, who were waiting to create an opportunity to begin a crackdown on ideological grounds and on behalf of those who wanted to privatize higher education. In fact, way back in 2002, some leaders of the Vishva Hindu Parishad (VHP), the religious wing of the RSS, had demanded that JNU should be closed down. Following the incidents of 9 February 2016, there was a call to shut down JNU from some campaigners of the RSS-BJP-ABVP.

On 12 February, the Delhi Police reached the campus gates. A new VC – Mamidala Jagadesh Kumar, known to be close to RSS – had been appointed just a week before, on 9 February. Along with the registrar, who is also known to have RSS links, Jagadesh Kumar gave blanket permission for the Delhi police to enter the campus, pick up as many students as they wanted, and remain on campus that day. This was the background for the JNUSU President's arrest.

There was a shadow of uncertainty on the campus in the first few hours after Kanhaiya's arrest on charges of sedition based on a draconian law. The top leaders of the major student organizations on the campus went underground since it wasn't clear who the police were planning to arrest and charge with sedition. The Jawaharlal Nehru Teacher's Association (JNUTA) swung into action. Its office-bearers went to meet the VC, demanding an end to the police terror on the campus. At around 4:00 pm, the JNUTA announced that there would be a press conference at 6 pm, and subsequently, a march in defence of JNU's democratic ethos. The press conference was held in the evening. Although it was called on such short notice, the #SaveJNU March that followed turned out to be the largest JNU had seen in years – more than a thousand students and teachers marched to demand an end to police raj, the release of the JNUSU President, and an end to the witch-hunt of innocent students.

With this march, the most significant movement JNU had seen in several decades – #StandWithJNU – was launched. The immediate aims of the movement were realized after a few weeks of intense agitation. But the JNU administration soon changed its tactics, deploying direct methods to alter the character of the university.

In this article, we examine why JNU is under attack from the Hindutva forces and examine the Stand With JNU movement itself. We conclude by briefly discussing the broad contours of the continuing attacks on the university, and some lessons that could be learned from the experience of these attacks and the resistance against them.

WHY DOES THE RIGHT-WING HATE JNU?

JNU, New Delhi, which was set up in 1969, is considered a stronghold of the Left, particularly when it comes to its student movement. It has been an important part of the fight against neoliberal economic policies and communalism.

The JNU student movement, right from its inception in the early 1970s, has been a bulwark of resistance against right-wing economic policies. The university's student movement has been led by JNUSU, a body in which all JNU students are members by default. JNUSU is led by representatives who are elected every year. JNUSU has been led by left-wing organizations during the vast majority of the fifty-one years of its existence. It is the vision and organized action of these organizations that lie behind the politics championed by the JNU student movement.

The JNU students' movement has fought to ensure that students from all backgrounds, particularly those from socially marginalized and economically deprived backgrounds, can come and study at the university. There are mainly two ways that have been central in achieving this democratic right: First, the fees, both tuition and other fees such as hostel fees, have been kept low; and second, the implementation of affirmative action, which includes reservations and deprivation points, or extra marks in the entrance examinations, for students hailing from socially and economically backward sections and those from poor regions.

JNU has had a progressive admission policy from 1973 onwards. This was the result of a struggle by the Union of 1972-73 led by V.C. Koshy of Students' Federation of India (SFI). The Union advocated an admission policy that would enable students from socio-economically deprived backgrounds and those from backward regions to come and study at the university. The struggle forced the administration to provide deprivation points in the entrance examination to candidates, based on socio-economic and regional backwardness.[1]

The Union fought and ensured that fees would be kept low and that scholarships would be provided to students who were most in

[1] A situation arose in the 1980s when the deprivation points system was withdrawn. The university was closed *sine die* in 1983 as part of efforts to repress the student movement. There were no student admissions for a year, and the admission policy was scrapped. Later in 1993-94, the deprivation points system was partially restored and was in place till recently. But as part of the intensified attack on the university from 2016 onwards, the administration completely scrapped the deprivation point system in the case of research degrees.

need of them. The Union repeatedly fought off attempts to raise fees, so that even as most other educational institutions, including public educational institutions, have seen fees rise sharply in recent decades, JNU has, so far, avoided such a fate.

An important part of JNU's progressive legacy is its academics, which is known both for its high standards and for its social commitment. By and large, most teachers of JNU, particularly those in the social sciences and humanities departments, which account for the bulk of the students, maintain a progressive outlook. They uphold a commitment towards reason, and towards the principles of secularism and democracy – principles that have been foundational for India as a republic. Through their research, writings, and lectures, many faculty members challenge the Washington Consensus and the communal politics of the Sangh Parivar. Many JNU teachers and alumni have played, and continue to play, key roles in providing the intellectual arsenal to fight imperialism, neoliberal economic policies, and the Hindu supremacist politics of the RSS-BJP.

DEMOCRATIC ETHOS

Over the last five decades, the university community, led by the Left student movement and supported by progressive academics, has striven to inculcate a democratic ethos on the campus.

At the centre of such efforts has been the JNUSU itself. A culture of democratic debates was ingrained into the activities of the Union right from its inception. Extensive discussions preceded the formation of the Union in 1971.

Unlike most of the students' unions elsewhere in the country, the JNUSU was created by the students themselves, without any intervention by the university administration. The students wrote the Union's constitution and forced the administration to recognize the Union. Elections are held by an Election Committee, elected and led by students. All these elements, a first in the history of

India's student movement, gave the Union a unique autonomous character.

General Body Meetings (GBMs) held at various levels – university, school, and centre (department) – form a vital part of the practice of democracy in JNU. GBMs are held as and when necessary to take stock of the situation or the work of the Union, and to decide how to move forward. Contentious issues are often debated at University General Body Meetings (UGBMs). UGBM is the highest decision-making body with regard to the affairs of the Union, and the UGBM's decision is binding on the JNUSU Council, which forms the leadership of the Union.[2] Many UGBMs go on throughout the night, ending early in the morning.

Lively discussions and debates are a central feature of campus life at JNU. Debates on a range of topics from politics and economics to science, philosophy, and literature occur wherever students congregate – classrooms, other spaces in the academic complex, in the many canteens and eateries that dot the campus, hostel rooms, hostel dining halls, and so on. Precisely because students tend to discuss a lot of politics at the eateries, one of the ways in which the administration has cracked down on the student movement in recent years has been by preventing eateries, which used to remain open late into the night, from doing so any longer. The students' union and various students' organizations issue pamphlets on multiple topics, and copies of the pamphlets are kept in the hostel dining halls for students to read while having dinner. Posters in response to developments on campus or elsewhere in the world can be seen on the walls of the school buildings and hostels. Large, colourful graffiti, with themes ranging from Palestine to anti-caste movements, used to adorn the walls of the school buildings until recently. This graffiti used to be made by student organizations during summer vacations, and remained on the walls throughout

[2] The JNUSU Council forms the elected leadership of the Union. It consists of school-level councillors and four university-level office-bearers – President, Vice-President, General Secretary, and Joint Secretary.

the year. The graffiti used to be among the first things that caught the eye of first-time visitors to the JNU campus. Unfortunately, in a drive initiated in July 2019, the right-wing administration removed most of the graffiti.

Public meetings organized by various student organizations and the Union itself constitute an important element of university life. Many public meetings are held in the dining halls of hostels, at night after dinner (because it is more convenient for most students who are engaged with classes and other academic events during the day). Academics, activists, political leaders and other experts in various fields deliver lectures at such public meetings and answer questions from the participating students. Unsurprisingly, the administration has put up roadblocks to how meetings are conducted by refusing permission to hold such programmes in various hostel dining halls in recent years.

Students are exposed to ideas that help them understand the world through the many conversations in and outside classrooms. They learn to question the status quo, and resist tendencies and forces that try to take society backwards. The engaged citizenry produced by the democratic atmosphere at JNU is something that Hindutva forces fear. It is an atmosphere in which right-wing ideas choke.

Therefore, when the right-wing assault on the university began, it was clear that it was JNU's democratic ethos itself, constructed through years of democratic practice, that was under attack.

RESISTANCE TO HINDUTVA

In the second half of the 1990s, when the BJP came to power for the first time in India, there were resonances of the violent assertion of its new authority on the JNU campus as well, with the ABVP indulging in violence against students and teachers. But at the same time, there was push-back from the students. There was a rise in the number of cases of sexual harassment and assault against women. Students responded by rising in massive numbers against the hideous politics of the ABVP. They fought to set up a committee to deal with cases of harassment and to sensitize students and others on gender issues. The campaign was won by establishing the Gender Sensitization Committee against Sexual Harassment (GSCASH) in 1999. In India, it was the first time that such a body was set up at an educational institution. During the tenure of the BJP-led government of 1999-2004, there were attempts to introduce obscurantism and pseudo-science into the curriculum. The students, led by the Union, fought and forced the administration to withdraw the move. There was a massive tide of protest from JNU when more than 2,000 Muslims were massacred with the full backing of the State machinery in BJP-ruled Gujarat in 2002. Fact-finding teams of JNU students and teachers visited Gujarat, collected relief funds and material, and extended legal aid to the victims of the pogrom.

The determined opposition of the university's students towards Hindutva made the JNU student movement a target of attack for the RSS and its affiliated organizations. During the late 1990s and early 2000s, various Hindutva leaders began demanding that the university should be shut down, that it should – for example – be converted into a management institute.

Such calls took a more concrete form when the BJP returned to power in 2014 with a majority on its own in the Lok Sabha (the lower house of the Indian Parliament). Narendra Modi, who was the Chief Minister of Gujarat when his state machinery presided over the Gujarat pogrom of 2002, became the Prime Minister.

THE RUN-UP TO THE ATTACK ON JNU

A few developments were notable during the months preceding the attack on JNU, which began in February 2016.

The first was the Occupy UGC movement, which began in October 2015, against the decision of the University Grants

Commission (UGC) to withdraw the 'non-NET' fellowships for MPhil and PhD scholars in the central universities of India. Students camped out day and night at the UGC headquarters in Delhi, demanding the withdrawal of the decision, enhancement of fellowships, and the expansion of the fellowships to all universities in India. Since the UGC decision adversely affected the research scholars in all central universities, the movement impacted several campuses across the country. JNU, with its more established student movement, played a leading role in galvanizing research scholars into action. The struggle was a partial success, with the government being forced to withdraw the decision to scrap the fellowship. For the right-wing, this was another signal that curbing the student movement was essential for the privatization of education.

Around this time, the November 2015 issue of the RSS mouthpiece *Panchajanya* carried a cover story on JNU. One of the articles in the magazine claimed that JNU was home to a 'huge anti-national block, which has the aim of disintegrating India'. The cover article alleged, falsely of course, that 'JNU routinely hosts anti-national activities' and that 'pro-Naxal students' unions' openly celebrated the killing of seventy-five Central Reserve Police Force (CRPF) personnel in an ambush by Maoists in Dantewada, Chhattisgarh in 2010. *Panchajanya* was blowing the conch for an all-out attack on JNU.

The third development was the death of Rohith Vemula, an Ambedkarite activist at Univeristy of Hyderabad (UoH), on 17 January 2016 and the subsequent student uprising that came to be known as the Justice for Rohith movement. Rohith and his fellow activists of the Ambedkar Students' Association (ASA) were targeted by the ABVP, with even a Union Minister – Bandaru Dattatreya of the BJP, who was the Union Minister of State for Labour & Employment – pitching in by writing a letter to Smriti Irani, the Union Minister of Human Resource Development. ASA had protested the violent attack by the ABVP during a screening of *Muzaffarnagar Baaqi Hai*, a documentary on the Muzaffarnagar riots, at Delhi University (DU). Dattatreya used appalling words to refer to ASA in his letter, dated 17 August 2015. 'Hyderabad University ... has in the recent past, become a den of casteist, extremist, and anti-national politics', he wrote. The letter was forwarded to Appa Rao Podile, the university's VC. The university had already stopped Rohith's monthly stipend of Rs 25,000 in July. In September, Rohith and four other students – all Dalits – were suspended. They moved out of the hostel on 3 January 2016 and began a hunger strike. Rohith died by suicide on 17 January after writing a suicide note that exposed the brutality of the system, which reduced the value of a person 'to his immediate identity and nearest possibility'. Massive protests erupted on campuses and streets across India against the discrimination faced by Dalits in educational institutions, demanding punishment for those responsible for Rohith's death, and demanding a law, the Rohith Act, against social discrimination in educational institutions.

Ever since BJP came to power in 2014, significant student movements had already taken place at higher educational institutions such as the Indian Institute of Technology–Madras against the 'de-recognition' of the Ambedkar-Periyar Study Circle and at the Film and Television Institute of India (FTII) in Pune against the appointment of Mr Gajendra Chauhan, whose only 'qualification' was his fealty to the sangh parivar, as the institute's chairman.

With the Occupy UGC and the Justice for Rohith movements causing a further dent in the popularity of the RSS-BJP among the youth and the marginalized sections, something had to be done to arrest the slide. Attacking JNU by portraying it as a hub of 'anti-nationals' was the perfect ploy to divert attention from the Sangh Parivar's grisly politics and the BJP government's policy debacles. JNU had, in any case, been on the radar of the Hindutva forces for decades, and this was the perfect time to initiate the attack that they had been eagerly wanting to launch.

In January 2016, M. Jagadesh Kumar, a professor with RSS links, was appointed JNU's VC. His mandate was clear: destroy the student movement, and change the character of the university to suit the pro-corporate, pro-Hindutva politics of the RSS-BJP. If the very university is to be destroyed in this effort, so be it. A full-blown assault on the university began the very next month.

THE STAND WITH JNU MOVEMENT

In the weeks following 12 February 2016, students and teachers mobilized in large numbers and devised creative ways to send their message out to the wider world.

On the evening of 13 February, thousands of students, teachers, and alumni joined a public meeting at JNU in solidarity with the university community. Several prominent former student leaders of the university and other political leaders were among those who addressed the gathering. On 14 February, more than 3,000 students, teachers, and alumni formed a human chain that stretched for two kilometres on the JNU campus.

Large public gatherings with speeches and cultural programmes took place almost every day; they were held at the university's administration block during the weeks that followed. The venue soon became known as Freedom Square or Azaadi Chowk. This name came from the association of the word *Azaadi* (Freedom) with the movement. The word had been popularized earlier by the women's movement in India, as well as by movements against oppression and human rights violations in Kashmir. The term became more popular among students in Delhi during the movement against sexual assault triggered by the horrific gang-rape of a young woman in New Delhi on 16 December 2012. Around the time of the arrest of Kanhaiya Kumar, videos of him raising the slogan, calling for freedom from hunger, freedom from the politics of the Sangh Parivar, freedom from feudalism, freedom from capitalism, and so on, had gone viral. The slogan became even more popular during the Stand With JNU movement.

But there was more to the word Azaadi. It was common for JNU students to raise slogans such as '*Kerala maange azaadi, Manipur maange azaadi, Bengal maange azaadi*' (Kerala demands freedom, Manipur demands freedom, Bengal demands freedom) and so on. The commonly understood meaning of all these was not as calls for secession of these states but that the people of every state in India were demanding freedom from oppression, exploitation, hunger, and for greater federalism. But at the same time, some people were indeed in favour of the secession of Kashmir, some north-eastern states and so on. While these demands did not have the support of the majority of students, including those from the leading sections of the student movement on campus, there was still space for such views to be expressed on the campus.

But a new situation had arisen with the massive campaign by corporate media and the vast organizational machinery of the RSS and its affiliated organizations all over India. The campaign had managed to build up intense hostility towards JNU among large sections of people in the country. Within Delhi, many autorickshaw drivers refused rides for JNU students. Students of the university who stayed in its immediate vicinity faced hostility from their landlords and neighbours. There was even an incident of a DU student being detained by the police for carrying a flag of the SFI in his bag. The university could no longer be considered a safe space where all kinds of opinions could be expressed freely.

It was announced that a 'JNU Solidarity March' would be held outside the campus, from Mandi House to Janatar Mantar, on 18 February. In the run-up to the march, there were apprehensions that right-wing hoodlums might attack the march. As we reached the main gate of the campus to go out for the march, a school bus passed in front of the gate, and school children shouted at us, denouncing JNU students as 'agents of Pakistan'. Such was the effect of the ferocious campaign against JNU.

But students and teachers were undeterred. An unprecedented

number of people from the JNU community and others joined the march, with well above 10,000 people participating, including students, teachers, alumni, and others from various walks of life. The march concluded with a public meeting where several leaders from various political parties and organizations spoke. The programme concluded peacefully.

Earlier on 15 February, JNU teachers, students, journalists and even bystanders had been beaten up by RSS-backed lawyers when they came to the court at Patiala House Court Complex for the hearing of Kanhaiya Kumar's case. When Kanhaiya was brought into the courtroom in the same court complex on 17 February, he was also attacked by Sangh-backed lawyers, who kicked, dragged, and punched him. The police did not intervene, and the hooligans managed to leave without being stopped.

In response to the right-wing's use of 'nationalism' defined in narrow, chauvinistic terms to justify the crackdown on JNU, the university's teachers took the lead in organizing lectures on nationalism at Freedom Square. The series of twenty-six lectures, which ran from 17 February to 17 March, explored the varied concepts of nationalism and what it means when the nation refers to all its people rather than just a geographical territory as the right-wing often does. (A compilation of these lectures was later published as a book, *What the Nation Really Needs to Know: The JNU Nationalism Lectures*, 2016.) Another round of lectures, titled 'Azaadi: The Many Meanings of Freedom', was also held from 21 March to 9 April.

There were also marches and programmes at JNU and on the streets of Delhi in solidarity with, and as part of, the Justice for Rohith movement.

Umar Khalid and Anirban Bhattacharya, two leading organizers of the 9 February programme, had gone underground after the crackdown on JNU began. They surrendered to the police on 23 February and were sent to Tihar jail. With his Muslim family background, Umar was particularly targeted by the extreme right, which accused him of being a 'terrorist'. Secular, democratic voices within the university and outside rallied against the jailing of the two and against the hate speech directed at Umar.

Kanhaiya was granted interim bail by the Delhi High Court on 2 March and returned to the campus the next day. That evening, amid an electric atmosphere in Freedom Square, he gave a speech in front of thousands of students, teachers, and others, with the speech being telecast live by several television channels. Apart from energizing the gathering, Kanhaiya used the stage to clarify a crucial point – that the *azaadi* that he (and by extension, the student movement) was talking about was not 'freedom from India', but 'freedom within India' – freedom from hunger, feudalism, capitalism, caste oppression, and communalism.

It was clear that much of the populace in the rest of India who were keenly watching the developments in JNU had failed to grasp the importance of the need to protect the freedom to express opinions that would be deeply unpopular in most parts of the country. The support for the demand for the secession of Kashmir, for instance, was not an opinion shared by the majority of JNU students; but most of those in the university who disagreed with that demand did not believe that everybody who held a pro-secession opinion should be jailed. However, a large section of people outside the campus were suspicious that JNU students, in general, supported secessionism. But Kanhaiya dispelled such doubts with a few simple words, and in this sense, it held an important message for the rest of India. Further, with the thrust of the rest of the speech, he turned the tables on the Sangh Parivar.

On 17 March, Umar and Anirban were released on bail, and also addressed the thousands who gathered at Freedom Square to welcome them back.

While the immediate aim of freeing the jailed student activists was thus achieved, the struggle continued against the false charges and disciplinary action that the JNU administration sought to take against various students.

THE AFTERMATH

The right-wing attack on JNU and the resistance against it resulted in the ABVP becoming more isolated than it had previously been. The attempt to discredit and rein in the student movement by accusing it of being 'anti-national' failed.

However, in the subsequent months and years, the RSS-backed JNU administration adopted a more direct approach to achieve its aims.

It was recognized that the basic 'problem' was that students from all backgrounds are coming to the university, learning about the world and about various approaches to understand society, and thus developing a critical attitude towards right-wing politics. If students from socially and economically deprived backgrounds join the university, they are even more likely to end up being critics of ruling class policies. Hence, to curb the student movement, the attack must be directed at the root of the 'problem' itself.

Thus, the JNU administration cut seats in the MPhil and PhD research programmes of the university; if there were fewer students, there would be fewer people to criticize the Hindutva forces and the government run by them. More than a thousand seats were cut in 2017, the first year this measure was put into place. In addition, undeserving, incompetent pro-RSS candidates were recruited to faculty positions, flouting norms and overlooking deserving candidates. With RSS acolytes who could remain university teachers for decades, the curriculum could be changed to reflect pro-market, pro-Hindutva politics, thus inflicting long-term damage on academic standards and the very character of the university.

The Sangh Parivar believes that it is a 'problem' that many students spend a considerable period on campus, acquiring the capacity to think critically and the capacity to act politically based on such thinking. Therefore, the goal is to reduce the students' stay on campus to shorter periods. The MPhil/PhD programme –

which used to be an integrated one and allowed MPhil. students to proceed to PhD automatically if they scored a minimum stipulated grade on their MPhil – has now been split into two. Thus, there was now less likelihood that MPhil students would continue into PhD programmes.[3] Likewise, the progression of students who have completed their Master's degrees to MPhil has been impeded by a change in the way the entrance examination is held. While the question papers were earlier set by JNU teachers and hence had some connection with what was taught as part of the university's Master's programmes, they are now set by the National Testing Agency. This agency has notoriously drafted sub-par question papers, consisting of questions lifted from sub-standard websites. The result is that the percentage of JNU students progressing from the Master's programme to the MPhil programme at the university has gone down. The administration and the RSS are hoping that this would weaken the student movement by depriving it of activists. But so far, this has not worked, with newer students also being inexorably drawn into the struggle against the right-wing, realizing that there is no other way to prevent the destruction of the university.

The VC has also made it a habit to get decisions taken in important bodies such as the Academic Council and the Executive Council by denying space for debate and discussion in these fora. The VC or his henchmen would read out their agenda in the meetings of such councils, and then unilaterally declare their proposals passed, often without even bothering to let those who oppose the proposals speak.

Those who dare to participate in strike actions are being subjected to ruthless punishment by the JNU administration. Hefty fines and suspensions are the most common methods being used to deter students and teachers from putting up a fight against the administration riding roughshod over the university community.

[3] The MPhil/PhD integrated programme in JNU was later scrapped in 2017 for the academic year 2018-19.

In spite of such repression, the JNU student movement continues to fight to keep education affordable to all students. The latest fee hike attempt was in 2019, which the JNU administration was forced to roll back due to a massive student movement that right-wing forces led by ABVP tried – violently, and yet unsuccessfully – to crush.

IN LIEU OF A CONCLUSION

The experience of the attacks on JNU in 2016 hold some valuable lessons for the democratic movement.

The first lesson is the need to recognize certain limitations of the JNU establishment that existed before the take-over by the forces of Hindutva; these limitations made it easier for the far right to attack and damage the university.

Two main issues are pertinent here. First, the previous JNU establishment did not bother to fill faculty posts reserved for Scheduled Castes (SC), Scheduled Tribes (ST), and Other Backward Classes (OBC). Vacancies in several faculty positions, particularly reserved posts, remained unfilled for many years, which itself is sufficient reason to criticize the attitude of the establishment. And now the existence of so many unfilled posts has provided the opportunity for the right-wing to recruit incompetent pro-Sangh candidates, often from specializations or fields other than those required for the posts, and overlooking many competent and suitable candidates. (Lest this be seen as the Sangh Parivar being more committed to social justice, it has to be pointed out that even now, many reserved category faculty positions remain unfilled and that reservations are not being fulfilled in PhD programmes.)

Second, the JNU VC had been given overbearing powers at the inception of the university, without much democratic accountability towards other sections of the university community. That blind trust in the VC could create problems, in the long run, was something that had been pointed out right at the beginning when the JNU Bill to set up the university was being discussed by the Parliament in the mid-1960s.[4] This turned out to be prophetic. When the university had relatively liberal VCs, their administrative powers appeared somewhat benign, although students often found that the means to exert democratic pressure on the VC were limited if he/she was adamant. But when the VC is somebody who has been sent with the express mandate of changing the character of the university by riding roughshod over all democratic bodies, the VC's wide-ranging powers enable him/her to act in a dictatorial manner.

The second, and perhaps more important lesson, is that the concept of the 'safe space' is no longer viable. Many students and teachers at JNU used to think of the university as an island, vastly different from the rest of the country, and which might continue to remain so. (There is even a Facebook page – The Island Diaries – which provide updates about the developments at JNU.) The idea that JNU could exist as a progressive space in the midst of a vast ocean of reaction without the ocean impinging upon the island was always dubious. But from 2016 onwards, it became clear, beyond all doubt, that the island mentality was no longer tenable. JNU, or any other supposedly safe space, such as the state of Kerala for instance, can protect itself only by taking progressive politics outside their own borders, and by replicating elsewhere many of the conditions that have made the existence of progressive spaces possible. In other words, these 'safe havens' themselves cannot

[4] '[Lok Sabha MP] Bakar Ali Mirza pointed out to Jha [V.S. Jha, eminent scholar and member of the Education Commission, who had been invited by a joint committee of parliament to which the JNU Bill was sent in 1965 to discuss and give final shape to it] that this blind trust in the post of VC could create problems in the long run. Jha partially agreed with this, however he insisted the VC be given a reasonable amount of control over the appointment of faculty and not be put under restraint. Reiterating his request for trust being reposed in the VC, Jha argued that instead of leaving the appointments to some ambiguous committees, it would be far more reasonable to trust a responsible VC.' See: Rakesh Batabyal, *JNU: The Making of a University* (Noida: Harper Collins, 2014), p. 37.

be protected without progressive politics spreading outside the confines to which they have been restricted now.

A corollary to this proposition is that the current wave of attacks on JNU may not cease until and unless the far right, which is ruling the country, and which has infiltrated all State institutions, is ousted from State power.

As far as JNU is concerned, the students and teachers are carrying on their struggle to save the university, despite the unrelenting assaults they have been facing since February 2016. This refusal to surrender continues to inspire those who dream of a more democratic and egalitarian world.

Struggles for Education as a Right

The Struggle for Hostel Facilities in Undivided Andhra Pradesh

Pindiga Ambedkar

An Interview with Kadigalla Bhaskar[1]

Education is the best tool for the transformation of society and also for generating economic mobility. Higher education is important for the growth of a country and for both social and material prosperity. Enrolment in higher education has been increasing worldwide; there has also been a steady increase in students' enrolment in higher education in India. According to the All India Survey on Higher Education Report (AISHE Report), 2018-19, a total number of 3,73,99,388 students enrolled in higher education in India, with a majority of them, 2,98,29,075 (79.8 per cent) enrolled in undergraduate programs in the academic year 2014-15.[2]

According to the Ministry of Human Resource Development (MHRD)'s Educational Statistics report in 2018, about 26,05,97,000 students were in pursuit of an education (Class I-XII). To avail oneself of quality education, good educational institutions are

[1] Conducted on 30 November 2018 and updated in May 2022.

[2] Ministry of Human Resource Development, All India Survey on Higher Education 2018-19, (New Delhi: PMSB Department of Higher Education, 2019), T-43, https://ruralindiaonline.org/en/library/resource/all-india-survey-on-higher-education-2018-19/.

important. Access to good living accommodations is required for good education to be possible.

Of the students who migrate to towns and cities for an education, a majority of them look for living accommodations in the institutions' hostels. Due to a lack of university-sponsored accommodations, the students are forced to live in rented or paying-guest accommodations near educational institutes. Around a major educational institution, a range of activities develop: landlords provide rented accommodations to students, coaching centres open up to prepare students for competitive exams, small eateries to cater to the needs of the students, etc. However, due to their inability to afford the rented accommodations near the campuses, many of the students end up travelling considerable distances between their living accommodations and the university, thereby spending most of their precious time – sometimes close to five hours a day – for travel in the highly polluted city.

Nearly thirty lakh (three million) students seek admission to various undergraduate programmes every year. The issues of affordability, quality, and equity of education must be taken into account to understand how these thirty-lakh probable undergraduate students will pursue their education. Lack of proper living accommodations is a hurdle, and even if accommodations are available, the quality of life in these hostels, run by private or government agencies, is inferior. Such conditions cause tremendous hardship and pressure on the students. This is an all-Indian phenomenon that continues to the present. The available data from the AISHE Report, 2018-2019 indicates that 22,95,190 students reside in 29,133 hostels. The majority of the students are without living accommodations. The existing hostels are poorly maintained, and there is insufficient staff to care for the students.[3]

To address the problems of the hostels, the Students' Federation of India (SFI) has led heroic struggles for students' hostels. One

[3] Ibid.

such struggle is the movement for improving the conditions of the Welfare Hostels in united Andhra Pradesh. These hostels date back to the freedom movement. Different caste groups started hostels in cities and towns where their community's students could live. The students pursued their education in different schools and colleges while staying in these hostels.

There were many welfare hostels in united Andhra Pradesh for the Other Backward Classes (OBC), which were privately managed, and until the mid-1970s, their maintenance was subsidized by the government. Welfare hostels played a vital role in the education of the Scheduled Castes (SCs) and Scheduled Tribes (STs). Most of the agricultural labourers were from these communities, and they continue to be from these social groups – the students who lived in the welfare hostels mostly hailed from this socio-economic background. Thousands of workers used to migrate from one place to another, beginning with sowing and ending with harvesting. Due to the migration of workers, their children's education suffered greatly.

The Internal Emergency, imposed in 1975, gave enormous power to the State machinery, especially the bureaucracy. In Andhra Pradesh, people-oriented bureaucrats such as S.R. Sankaran, an officer in the Indian Administrative Service (IAS) initiated the takeover of privately run community hostels by the government and also increased their number. Forty new school hostels were established in seventeen districts for Scheduled Castes and the government took over 1,400 hostels. The welfare students' hostels grew over the years. Currently, there are 5,243 hostels for the SCs, the STs, and the Backward Classes in the combined states of Telangana and Andhra Pradesh.[4] In addition to these, there are residential schools built on the model of the central government-run Jawahar Navodaya Vidyalaya (JNV) (schools, particularly in rural areas). They are administered by the SCs, STs, and OBCs

[4] In the states of Andhra-Telangana OBCs are classified as BCs.

departments of the state governments of Andhra and Telangana.

The Government of India adopted neoliberal policies in the 1990s. As a result of these policies, the welfare benefits and schemes for the citizens were reduced. The quality of education in the states suffered the most. For a decade and a half, the hostels in Andhra Pradesh were neglected and were on the verge of being closed down. The SFI state leadership addressed this issue rigorously. The students began a movement in 2005 that grew massively within the state. They started with a survey covering 4,027 hostels in 960 blocks spread across the state. The students undertook the survey in order to understand the local problems in the hostels. The SFI activists spent seventeen days in each district and a total of 421 days in various districts across the state. The survey was the foundation for the SFI's cycle rally, covering all twenty-three districts of united Andhra Pradesh. The rally covered a total of 25,777 km on bicycles, one of the longest cycle rallies witnessed in the united Andhra Pradesh.

With meticulous planning and execution, the agitating students continued the protests for a year, demanding more hostels. Around 3,167 SFI activists took part in the cycle rally. Ninety-eight of them were arrested on charges of protesting in the state capital, Hyderabad, and their cases continue to this day. Before the agitation, the government did not cover the entire cost of the daily food allowance, a student was provided with only twelve rupees per day. Due to the agitation, the government was forced to increase the daily amount from twelve rupees to eighteen rupees, sufficient for the students to get two basic meals daily. The movement garnered wide public support and subsequently grew tremendously. As a result of the movement, the government was forced to accept the demands of the students, many hostels were built, funds allocation increased significantly, and vacant posts in the hostel departments were filled.

The movement for hostels in united Andhra Pradesh had a

tremendous impact. While today students are fighting the brutal assaults of neoliberal policies across India, a struggle such as the hostel struggle in united Andhra Pradesh still inspires the students. When many educational institutions fail to provide basic hostel facilities to the students, it is imperative to question the policy makers and organize students to fight for their rights. A movement that brought primary students' demands to light and demonstrated a courageous fight to confront the neoliberal onslaught on education may guide generations of students on how to build a mass movement.

Kadigalla Bhaskar, the former state secretary of SFI, Andhra Pradesh, spoke with Pindiga Ambedkar of the Tricontinental Research on how they built the movement and led it to a conclusion marked by a massive victory.

What is the background of the movement?

The government hostels started running officially in the united Andhra Pradesh in 1972. Before 1972, the hostels were run privately. The government provided the funds, but the hostels were privately managed. Therefore, although the government-run hostels started in 1972, the government-sponsored hostels and their expansion did not happen until the Emergency of 1975 when progressive IAS officers like S. R. Sankaran, Gopal Rao, and others – who played an important role – pushed the government to take over the hostels as well as expand them. However, over time, the conditions of the hostels worsened. The infrastructure was abysmal. Even the conditions of hostels in the towns and cities were very poor.

The movement began by focusing on the crisis of hostels and other related issues in Andhra Pradesh. Initially, we dealt with the problem of hostels locally. Then we released a booklet regarding the social welfare hostels, which was the first step in beginning the movement. We started with the history of how the hostels were started. Thereafter, we conducted a survey from June 2005 to December 2006 to learn about the problems that the students faced during their university attendance.

The survey revealed that sufficient funds were not being allotted to the hostels. There was no mechanism to increase the fund allotments based on changes in commodity prices, and there was a lack of monitoring of the functioning of the hostels.

There were about 8,04,987 students residing in 5,263 hostels. The students began and ended their days confronting the hostels' problems. For the women students, the conditions were even worse; they had to wake up at 3:30 in the morning to take a bath. Students didn't have space for washing their clothes, they were given poor quality food; and there was a considerable lack of tutors. We exposed these micro-level problems only after we conducted the survey. An agitation thus began under the leadership of the SFI on the hostel issues, which was considered the most significant movement to improve the hostels.

What were the critical issues on which the movement was built?

Our primary focus was on the issue of the hostel mess charges. We demanded that the mess charges' rates (i.e., the government allowance of food) be proportionately increased based on the rise of inflation. As there were insufficient tutors for the students staying in the hostels, we raised the demand for additional tutors. We wanted to strengthen the welfare hostel system so that the students from downtrodden backgrounds could study effectively.

What were the challenges that triggered the agitation?

After 1995, the students faced severe challenges regarding their hostels; the government neglected the issue so much so that the hostels were destroyed in ten years. In fact, the students feared that they might even be closed down. Usually, hostels were attached to the schools. Students from different villages used to stay in the hostel and study in the school. Over the years, the number of government-run schools increased. But there wasn't a subsequent increase in the number of hostels. In addition, the government's allowances for food and cosmetic charges (which includes basic necessities such as soap, etc.) and other rules regarding the welfare hostels were not being appropriately implemented. There was large-scale corruption throughout the system. The government-stipulated uniforms, textbooks, and proper menus were not provided to the students. The students did not receive their textbooks until the middle of the academic year. It became increasingly difficult for a student to study amid these challenges.

What strategies were adopted to campaign on the issues, and how did SFI build the movement?

To reach the students, we worked for more than a year. In the beginning, we began the *cycle yatra* (cycle rally). We visited most of the social welfare hostels in the state of united Andhra Pradesh. We visited nearly 3,000 hostels.

We formed teams in every district. Team members were assigned to visit the hostels, eat food from the hostel mess, spend the night in the hostel with the residents, and inquire about their problems. We collected information about their conditions from about 3,000 hostels. Our comrades summarized the findings. Based on the findings, we prepared a memorandum concretely raising issues and connected those with our greater demands. We submitted the memorandum to the government. Our *cycle yatra* covered twenty-three districts in the state, and we protested in front of the district collectors' offices in all twenty-three district headquarters. At the block level, we organized relay hunger strikes.

As the movement was gaining strength and advancing towards its goal, we escalated the protest. We called for a hunger strike and started it at the state capital, Hyderabad, near Comrade Sundarayya park, with one representative from each district. The hunger strike continued for six days. We received immense public support for our movement. Leaders from across the political spectrum came and expressed their solidarity with the movement. Even different civil society organizations came.

We called for a march towards the state secretariat in Hyderabad, which was joined by thousands of students. Most leaders, including me, were on hunger strike, but we continued marching. When we reached the Himayatnagar area, the police charged toward us with lathis drawn. The Congress government ruled the state during the agitation. The government deployed a massive police force, cracking down on the protestors severely injuring several protesters. Ninety-eight student leaders from all the districts were sent to the police remand. We were in jail for two days and later were released on bail. The case is still pending. The police arrested us for the 'crime' of protesting at the state capital and participating in and leading the march.

Was the movement successful? What are the concrete achievements?

It was undoubtedly a successful movement. Following the movement, the government-allotted funds for the mess allowances for the students were increased. For instance, cosmetic allowances used to be ten rupees per month for boys and young men and twenty rupees per month for girls and young women. It increased substantially. The cosmetic allowances are now 100 rupees for boys and 180 rupees for girls. Mess allowances used to be twelve rupees per day per student. It increased to eighteen rupees per day. Post-matric students received only two meals a day. We agitated for the post-matric students also who resided in the hostel facilities attached to their colleges. One of our core demands was increasing the number of residential schools and the number of hostels. This was also attained. Vacant warden posts have been filled with new recruits. It was also the same time when the fee reimbursement scheme was introduced.

Due to our movement, there was a positive response from

the political parties. Usually, most political parties tend to neglect the hostel issues of the students; however, the SFI-led movement created sufficient pressure for even the political parties to react and extend support to the movement.

Was this movement decentralized? How did you educate the students about their rights?

We provided guidelines, which were released from the SFI state-centre, and those would then be taken to the district levels. It was a highly decentralized movement, and evidently, around 50,000 students across the state participated in the movement, which had its base at the local levels.

We published booklets and pamphlets that were distributed to the students. Those documents included information regarding the government rules, etc. In the first booklet, we highlighted the rights of the hostel students as per the government rules; we listed the types of facilities that the government needed to provide to students.

Were there ever any attacks on hostels by right-wing groups?

Recently, in the Sangareddy district, at a degree college's social welfare hostel, members of Akhil Bharatiya Vidyarthi Parishad (ABVP) instigated an attack. They were celebrating Chatrapati Shivaji's birthday. They demanded that the social welfare hostel students, who were Ambedkarites, participate in the celebrations. The students refused. ABVP members hired some goons to attack the students. We went there, addressed the students, and lodged a police complaint.

I have been associated with the Osmania University (OU) students' movement since 1997. Between 1997-2000, we could not even enter the university's premises due to large-scale violence perpetrated by the ABVP. They used to resort to violence whenever a threat countered their politics. After 2000, the ABVP became weak. Before 2000, the Dalit student organizations were not visible by name. In 2001, the SC, ST, and progressive students' unions formed a joint platform. They moved jointly against the ABVP. The ABVP comprised of the students from the dominant 'upper castes'. However, during the 2000s, the number of SC students at OU increased. Dalit consciousness spread, and there was a confluence of Left and Dalit ideology. After that, the ABVP's power was thoroughly diluted. The ABVP leaders were corrupt and getting involved in businesses. Now, they do not have the strength to attack anymore. But sometimes, they attack by taking help from outsiders.

Students' Struggle for Social Justice at Tata Institute of Social Sciences

Sandeep Mahato, Gaurav Gharde,
Aravindhan Nagarajan

The Tata Institute of Social Sciences (TISS) is a university with over 4,500 students and over 250 faculty spread across four campuses – Mumbai, Guwahati, Tuljapur, and Hyderabad.[1] It began as a Graduate School of Social Work – set up by Sir Dorabji Tata in 1936. Later, in 1944, the institution was named TISS. In the entirety of TISS's history, 1964 is considered its 'landmark' year when the university was declared 'deemed-to-be a University under Section 3 of the University Grants Commission Act (UGC), 1956'. A deemed public university receives a majority of its funding and aid from the UGC and the Central Government of India. However, a deemed public university is unlike a centrally-funded public university, and it doesn't receive the funding and infrastructural benefits in the same way as the other universities. Amid the continuous threats of fund cuts, TISS was able to retain its position as a prestigious Indian university through its academic

[1] The analysis of budgetary spending, fees, and expenditures mentioned in this essay, are based on an earlier article published by one of the authors. See: Aravindhan Nagarajan, 'TISS Students Strike: Privatisation of Education Threatens Social Justice,' *Economic and Political Weekly*, 'Engage' Vol. 53, Issue No. 8 (2018), https://www.epw.in/engage/article/tiss-students-strike-privatisation-education-threatens-social-justice

strength and commitment to the underprivileged.

With a high ranking awarded by the National Assessment and Accreditation Council (NAAC) at par with the professional and vocational courses, TISS had a vision for inclusive education. As a university, it has encouraged diversity, and it is known for providing quality higher education. It has been committed to the principles of social justice and implemented affirmative actions. TISS has always taken pride in its history, and the university was established with a vision to create: 'An institution of excellence in higher education that continually responds to changing social realities through the development and application of knowledge; towards creating a people-centred, ecologically sustainable and just society, which promotes and protects dignity, equality, social justice, and human rights for all'.[2]

Through its various departments, TISS worked at the level of policy and governance with the Government of India and state governments. It is one of the few institutes that offer interdisciplinary courses in the social sciences, and it has contributed to the traditional social sciences' disciplines as well. With the increased privatization of higher education in India, the Central deemed-to-be-Universities were one of the first institutes of higher education to face funding cuts from the UGC. TISS resorted to collecting the fees from students and increased its fees annually, discussed later in the article. Until recently, the students from socially and economically deprived communities were, to a certain extent, given freeship and fee waivers. However, things changed when the Government of India stopped providing funds to post-matric scholarships intended for the Scheduled Castes (SC) and Scheduled Tribes (ST) students. The ill-effects of non-implementation of the policy were felt at TISS.

On 21 February 2018, students at TISS Mumbai began a strike against the withdrawal of financial support for students and rising

[2] 'About TISS,' Tata Institute of Social Sciences, https://www.tiss.edu/about-tiss/overview/.

fees. This protest followed closely on the heels of another protest in 2017 by TISS students to raise a charter of demands on the issue of fee hikes and their effects on the Government of India-Post Matric Scholarship (GoI-PMS) students. While a partial rollback in fee hikes for some students was achieved in 2017, the situation remained unresolved, leading to the prevailing situation in 2018.

Several meetings were held between student groups, the students' union, and the TISS administration regarding the demands of the students. The students' focus was on the demand to maintain the system of freeship for students from marginalized backgrounds. However, the university administration gave no assurances about maintaining the system of fee waivers. The last straw for the students was the insistence of the administration (in February 2018) that the students enrolled between 2017 and 2019 and new enrolees henceforth should pay the entire fees upfront every semester. The students began protests across the four TISS campuses as a response to this. The students formed coordinating groups within the TISS Mumbai campus as well as on the other campuses of the university. This initiative was the first step to carry out the protests in an organized manner. The protests included hunger strikes by the students at TISS Hyderabad and Guwahati demanding the scrapping of fee hikes and the need for basic infrastructure at their respective campuses. The 2018 strike and subsequent protests at TISS became the largest student action seen at the university, with students from across all four TISS campuses participating for well over three months.

Why did the students across TISS campuses protest for several months? The answer lies in the manner in which privatization of higher education in India has eroded the practical achievement of social justice, thus, becoming a challenge for the students from the disadvantaged sections to pursue higher education. Therefore, the students rallied against the current TISS administration's assaults against them. At the heart of the protests was the students' long-standing demand, across all four campuses, to maintain the system of freeship for students availing themselves of the GoI-PMS scheme, and the demand to stop the annual rise of fees charged by the institute.

REDUCTION OF PUBLIC FUNDING AND WITHDRAWAL OF FEE-WAIVERS

Students at institutes such as TISS face a dual assault with privatization policies. First is the burden of funding cuts from UGC. TISS receives non-planned expenditures from UGC of around fifty crore rupees annually. The release of these funds has not been timely, resulting in arrears, and in 2016 the Ministry of Human Resource Development (MHRD) decided to cut this funding by 5 per cent annually so that today's funding is half of 2016 levels.[3] Independent centres initiated and sponsored by the UGC were also under threat. Since the end of the twelfth five-year plan in 2017, the UGC has been sending out notices about withdrawing its funding to both the Women Studies and the Social Exclusion and Inclusive Policy centres at different universities.[4] As a university with these departments, TISS has felt the immediate threat of such notices by the UGC, with these departments on the verge of closure.

The second assault came from the non-release of funds for the GoI-PMS scheme by the central government. The GoI-PMS is an umbrella scheme for post-matric education and the only one of its kind, which offered scholarships to 5.5 million students in 2016-17.[5] The scheme was introduced in 1944 for students from

[3] Anubhuti Vishnoi, 'Modi government releases funds for TISS after 5% cut,' *The Economic Times*, 3 June 2015, https://economictimes.indiatimes.com/industry/services/education/modi-government-releases-funds-for-tiss-after-5-cut/articleshow/47521478.cms?from=mdr.

[4] Mridula Chari, '35 staff at Mumbai's TISS are fired because of UGC funding ambiguity,' Scroll.in, 26 May 2017, https://scroll.in/article/832881/35-staff-at-mumbais-tiss-are-fired-because-of-ugc-funding-ambiguity.

[5] Protiva Kundu, 'Shrinking Education Budget Has Hit Scholarships For

SC and ST backgrounds; it was further extended for the non-creamy layer Other Backward Caste (NC-OBC) students in 2006-07. This scholarship scheme for the categories mentioned above is given to the students whose family income is less than Rs 2.5 lakhs and less than Rs 1 lakh (for some categories) per annum. Students granted scholarships under this scheme get a tuition fee waiver and a monthly scholarship amount to cover dining and hostel charges. Education, a democratic right, has historically been denied through the yoke of caste and class inequalities. Through this scholarship, students from SC, ST, and OBC backgrounds can access higher education in India. As a part of the scheme, the students from across different states apply to their respective state governments to avail themselves of this scholarship to pay their fees. Over the past decade, it has also been one of the most underfunded and inadequate schemes supported by the central government. Through the systematic fund cuts, the GoI-PMS scheme has been severely affected.

At TISS, until 2014, students eligible for the GoI-PMS were admitted by paying a nominal fee of Rs 4,500. There was also financial support provided to students in the form of a fee waiver. The TISS administration undertook this with the expectation of funds being released from the Central government for GoI-PMS students. In 2014, the scholarship amount to students began to be paid through the direct benefit transfer mechanism. Before 2014, the scholarship money for the students was directly released by the state governments to the institute. Since 2014, this money was transferred to students' accounts, after which the institute entered into a legal agreement with the concerned students to ensure that the received amount was paid to the college.

Post-2014, the TISS administration discontinued this waiver of upfront fee payments for NC-OBC students. In 2016-17, it

Students From Deprived Communities,' IndiaSpend, 30 January 2020, https://www.indiaspend.com/shrinking-education-budget-has-hit-scholarships-for-students-from-deprived-communities/.

discontinued the waiver for SC and ST students who would avail themselves of the GoI-PMS scheme. A family that earns less than eight thousand rupees a month had to spend more than eighty thousand rupees annually in fees for their children's admission. Therefore, this has had a severely crippling effect on many students from low-income backgrounds from applying to TISS.

One such student is Ramesh Singh. Hailing from a low-income family in Bihar, Ramesh is a GoI-PMS scholar. Ramesh enrolled in the Social Work programme at TISS, following his elder brother's footsteps, who had studied at the institute five years ago, availing himself of the same GoI-PMS scheme and the fee waiver provided to him by TISS. Ramesh and his brother were the first in the family to be admitted into institutes of higher education. Ramesh's family has an annual income of less than one lakh rupees. For a family with a yearly income of around one lakh per annum (this is the annual income cut-off for NC-OBC students), the admission fee for a single person at TISS currently is approximately 80,000 to 120,000 rupees per annum.

In 2013-14, the fees (including the dining hall, hostel facility, and electricity charges) were Rs 18,000 per semester. In 2014-15, it was increased by Rs 2,000, making the total fees Rs 20,000. It was further increased by Rs 4,000 in 2015-16 – bringing the fee total to Rs 24,000; and again in 2016-2017, the fees were increased by Rs 7,000, resulting in a total fee for one semester of Rs 31,000.[6] This shows the gradual progression of fee hikes at TISS. In fact, the fees charged at TISS today are far higher than most of the deemed universities (including those whose funding was cut).

With the subsequent fee hike, it is unaffordable for low-income families to support their children's education in an expensive city like Mumbai. For students such as Ramesh, the dream to study and be first-generation learners is shot down because students like

[6] The data of the subsequent increase of fees in TISS from 2013 to 2017 has been gathered from the various prospectus released by the TISS between 2013 and 2016.

him cannot afford the costs of university education without the fee waiver provided by TISS and the successful implementation of the GoI-PMS scheme.

INCREASING FEES AND 'CRYING WOLF'

The increase in fees theoretically increases the institute's 'expenditure' on students. However, in actuality, the burden of fee hikes, the non-release of GoI-PMS funds by the central government, and the university's withdrawal of the fee-waiver policy fall directly on the students. The TISS administration argued that continuing with the fee waiver for GoI-PMS students implied incurring more significant deficits. The TISS administration exacerbated the situation using a disingenuous combination of statistics and policy.

Let us examine how TISS would calculate its deficit on the GoI-PMS scholarship funding. They define deficit as the difference between fees charged by the institute for a student and the money received by it from the students through the GoI-PMS payments. So far, so good. But each time the fee increases, the university's claim on the expenditure deficit for GoI-PMS students also increases. Even if the university receives a higher amount of money from the GoI-PMS payments, the deficit will still increase because the fees have increased.

To provide a concrete example of this problem, let us examine budgetary allocations and expenditures under the GoI-PMS scheme. The amount allocated in the central budget for 2018-19 was Rs 3,000 crores, which is a reduction from Rs 3,347.99 crores allocated in 2017-18. In the 2018-19 budget, the planned expenditure allocated by the central government for GoI-PMS students belonging to the SC category was only Rs 3,000 crores. To make matters worse, until February 2018, the arrears reported by the Ministry of Social Justice and Empowerment for the GoI-

PMS for the SC category was Rs 6,824.51 crores. By March 2018, the cumulative deficit faced by state governments to implement the GoI-PMS scheme was over Rs 6,000 crores.[7] This arrear is being carried forward, and funds will be released to the state governments. The states with the highest arrears in this scheme are Tamil Nadu (Rs 1,547.56 crores), Uttar Pradesh (Rs 1,490.30 crores), Maharashtra (Rs 1,433.92 crores), and Punjab (Rs 835.24 crores).[8] In the absence of central funding, different state governments either provide inadequate funding or do not provide funding for GoI-PMS students.

As they continue to raise fees, the deficit will only increase with no end in sight. And this deficit is overcome by charging the students higher fees. This completes the privatization playbook: the central government reduces funding, which implies students don't get the funds transferred to them by state governments, the university charges higher fees from students and then withdraws the policies such as fee waivers. What follows from these policies is the dismantling of public sector utilities and services, which in turn crushes the dream of students to pursue higher education and eliminates this dream from the students of marginalized backgrounds for generations to come.

While the current government under the Bharatiya Janata Party (BJP) extended the privatization agenda of universities in a much more forceful manner, the process was not started by the BJP-led government alone. It is a process that has continued for several decades before the BJP's rule. It began in the 1990s when the governments led by Congress adopted neoliberal policies. BJP accelerated this process further with greater privatization of education. The essence of the privatization playbook is to provide higher education for only the privileged and the elite. The end

7 Aravindhan Nagarajan, 'TISS Students Strike: Privatisation of Education Threatens Social Justice,' *Economic and Political Weekly* 'Engage' Vol. 53, Issue No. 8 (2018), https://www.epw.in/engage/article/tiss-students-strike-privatisation-education-threatens-social-justice.

8 Ibid.

game of these policies is to fuel the rise of self-financing courses and private universities, with no commitment to the constitutional principles of social justice!

The students understood the effects of this playbook, which posed a direct assault on the principles of social justice. We understood that this increased privatization would hit students from marginalized communities the hardest. The students who have been fighting know the importance of reservations, which have ensured greater diversity and representation of communities from marginalized backgrounds in higher education. The increase in representation of students from diverse backgrounds was only possible through affirmative action. The ruling forces of our country are eroding this hard-earned right by making higher education unaffordable and out of reach for these students.

As the GoI-PMS scheme applies to all post-Graduate students across the country, the questions raised by the students of TISS were the questions that represented the issues of the entire community of students across India.

THE FIGHT AGAINST PRIVATIZATION

TISS students responded to this reactionary playbook through a united fight. Across different political worldviews, the Left, the Ambedkarite, the Adivasi, and the Queer organizations came together. Our alumni and faculty supported us. The solidarity poured in from across the country. The Ambedkarite and Left organizations along with the various students' unions, extended their support for the TISS movement. Ironically, the Akhil Bharatiya Vidyarthi Parishad (ABVP), supported the TISS students.[9] However, this was a token support: we were urged by ABVP to resort to letter-writing instead of protests. The protests continued with help from several quarters, but the TISS

[9] On the 24 February 2018 a statement was issued to this effect by Ashish Chauhan, the National Secretary of the ABVP through its office in Mumbai.

administration resorted to intimidating the students who were leading the movement.

The students stood firm throughout the agitation. We won a partial battle by ensuring a limited rollback of the 2018-20 batches fees and an option to pay fees in instalments for the GoI-PMS scheme availing students. But the fee hike was not reversed. The students who participated in the struggle were vilified by the administration and penalized with disciplinary actions. Many students, in fact, were served show-cause notices and had to wage prolonged legal battles against cases filed by the TISS administration. Despite this, the student groups at TISS continued to fight against the increase in fees and consistently highlighted the importance of continuing schemes such as GoI-PMS. The TISS struggle successfully brought the debate on the significance of such government scholarships to the centre stage of Indian higher education. TISS students with different political persuasions put aside their differences and came together. They picketed the university's main entrance to offer solidarity to each other and the many others who would join the university in the future. They made their demands heard through slogans until their voices were hoarse. The demand that this movement took up was the basic truth that quality education with dignity is a fundamental right – to learn and be part of a university space that represents a better future.

The students' protests at TISS are a story about the hopes and aspirations of students from across the country. It is a story of students who recognize the policies of privatization at play and the scarring effects they can have on the first-generation learners and students who come from marginalized backgrounds. It is also a struggle that offers hope for students across the country by recognizing the challenge and fighting back. This struggle has proven that we must stake our claim in the present and for our future.

Fees Must Fall Movement, JNU

Satarupa Chakraborty

An interview with Aishe Ghosh[1]

Jawaharlal Nehru University, is considered to be one of the most politically vibrant campuses in India. The role played by the Jawaharlal Nehru University Students' Union (JNUSU) has been historically very significant. This is so because student politics drive the critical agendas at the university with regard to the policies and decisions in various statutory bodies. The JNUSU led many important struggles: fighting the Emergency under Mrs Indira Gandhi, fighting to adopt a progressive admission policy, fighting to institutionalize the Gender Sensitization Committee against Sexual Harassment (GSCASH) and fighting to implement the reservation policy. As a result of the continuous struggles, the university community has been able to preserve an inherently democratic and inclusive structure.

Since 2016, however, there has been a continuous onslaught by the State on the university. The students and the teachers are collectively fighting a difficult battle to save the university. Aishe Ghosh, the JNUSU President, emerged as an important leader in this fight at Jawaharlal Nehru University (JNU) and Indian higher education in general. She emerged as a symbol of resistance,

[1] Conducted on 26 January 2020 and updated in May 2022.

leading the Fees Must Fall movement, which had worldwide recognition. She survived brutal physical attacks by the hoodlums of Rashtriya Swayamsevak Sangh (RSS) and its student wing. Ghosh kept the spirit of the movement alive with the slogan – 'Not an inch back' – demanding a complete rollback of the fee hike. She speaks to Satarupa Chakraborty of Tricontinental Research about her journey since the 2019 JNUSU election, the Fees Must Fall movement and the present state of the student movement in India.

JNUSU ELECTION AND THE ROLE OF THE JNU AUTHORITY

What transpired during the JNUSU election in 2019?

In 2019, conducting the JNUSU election itself was a protest against the administration's onslaught on the well-celebrated democratic culture and practice at JNU. Two students filed petitions against the Election Committee (EC), alleging violations in the election procedure. They were members of the ABVP and this was done with the intention to stall the JNUSU election as per the administration's dictate.

The administration chose to target the students-led EC, assuming that the EC members were apolitical students and that it would be easy to break them so that the election itself became null and void. But they failed. The EC did not give up, and instead, the members stood strong. The EC impartially follows all legal procedures in conducting the elections; it is one of the most transparent bodies on campus. As a result, the Delhi High Court ruled in favour of EC and the students. The petitions by the administration-backed students were disposed of, and the Delhi High Court, in its judgment on 17 September 2019, directed the EC to declare the JNUSU results.

It was not easy for the students. We underwent mental, physical, and financial harassment due to the administration's attack. The administration thought their attack against us would exhaust the students so that they would think twice before conducting and contesting elections in the future. They wanted to generate fear in us. Except, they forgot we contest elections not because we gain anything personally but because we are committed to representing the students' voice. The students valued this commitment. The united-Left slate of candidates won all central panel seats with a thumping majority, and thus, it marked a massive defeat, once again, for the Akhil Bharatiya Vidyarthi Parishad (ABVP), on the historically progressive campus.

What followed after the election?

The JNU administration, despite the Delhi High Court directive, did not notify JNUSU of the results, which is the official procedure after the EC declares the results. The JNU administration had excluded the students' union representatives from representing in the statutory bodies of the university and, thus, from the decision-making process. This meant that the administration did not want us at the statutory committee meetings where important decisions were made. The administration's intention was evident when the 152nd Academic Council (AC) meeting was held on 15 October 2019 without inviting the JNUSU officeholders. We staged a protest; our slogan was 'No AC without JNUSU'. What shocked us was that certain centre (department) chairpersons who are members of the Academic Council but had been critical of the VC and the present administration were also not invited to the meeting. Such is the twisted 'democracy' practised by the VC of JNU, where members are not invited to voice their opinion inside the decision-making institutions.

The administration's reason for keeping critical voices out of the meeting was to ensure that there was no opposition to their new regressive hostel manual, which proposed a massive fee hike and other unacceptable rules to the students. Our protest began with a call that the draft hostel manual must be rejected.

FIGHT FOR THE RIGHT TO UNIONIZE

The JNU administration has used various methods to curtail the democratic space on campus. Would you describe the assault by the administration against the students and the union, as well as the struggles of the union to defend and extend campus democracy?

On 15 October 2019, the JNU administration posted a notice signed by the Dean of Students, Umesh Kadam, that stated: 'The JNUSU Office shall be double locked and sealed by 5:00 pm on 16/10/2019'. The notice justified this atrocious move by saying that there had been 'misuse of University property'. The JNUSU office is a symbol of the JNU student community's right to representation and to unionize. These rights are embodied in the existence of JNUSU. The students saw the notice from the administration as an attack on the student body. It showed an absolute disregard for the democratic mandate of the union, as well as for the judgment of the Delhi High Court to acknowledge the election and, therefore, the union's leadership. The intention behind the administration's move was clear: to delegitimize the union. In the past few years, many of our public spaces on campus were slowly taken away. These spaces allowed us to hold democratic debates and discussions. JNU's popular spaces like dhabas [cafes] or the mess halls, where public discussions used to happen, were restricted by the administration. Now, the mess halls are mainly used by the RSS-affiliated political groups.

The JNUSU office remained one of the last spaces where we could organize our meetings and discussions. Therefore, the students resisted these authoritarian measures completely. JNUSU called on students to come to a demonstration on 16 October, at which the administration's notification was burnt. The students then occupied the JNUSU office with a sit-in. We ensured that the administration officials who came, along with the security guards, to double lock the JNUSU office were sent back unsuccessful. The sit-in continued for a few days, and they could not lock the JNUSU office. Instead, in protest, students closed the office of the dean of students.[2] Failing to lock the JNUSU office, the administration instead put a lock on the gate of Parthasarathy Rocks, popularly known as PSR, at JNU, a place where students would gather.

How do you view this specific move by the JNU administration vis-à-vis the right of students to unionize? Why do the administration and the right-wing governments perceive the existence of the students' union as a threat?

The administration's notice to lock down the union room was a symbolic gesture to delegitimize the students' voices. It is actually not the first time the current administration has unleashed an attack on the students' union – the union has been under attack for the past few years. First, they stopped union office bearers from attending the statutory committee meetings in violation of the statutes. Then they stopped the union councillors from attending the school-level Board of Studies meetings. Their attempt to sabotage the union reached such a level that they prevented the notification of the election results, an election held by the union for their leadership. The previous union leadership worked on the day-to-day issues of the students and resisted all anti-student moves by the administration without the administration even recognizing the union's leadership.

The authority refused to issue a receipt of letters from the union; and would not recognize that members are elected to the students' union through a fair, democratic process. The current pressure on the union by the administration appears to have the aims of delegitimizing the union and then slowly eliminating unionization

[2] JNUSU later put up a sarcastic poster at the Dean of Student's office mimicking the language of the administration's notices of threats and intimidation. The poster said: 'Notice: This office has been double-locked because the behaviour of the Dean of Students is unbecoming of a JNU official. You can collect the keys after providing an explanation for your action at the JNUSU office. Sd/- Competent Authority, JNUSU'.

itself. However, the students and the union have fought back every time. The union's legitimacy comes from the students; it does not come from any recognition by the administration. The union has raised students' demands continuously, even without the administration's recognition.

The administration wants to delegitimize the union because they know very well that as long as the students have their union, there will be resistance whenever they try to implement anti-student policies. We agitated against fee hikes for ninety days during the 2019 movement. They could have easily implemented the fee hike if there wasn't a union. As a result of having a students' union that fights against anti-student policies, both union members and the student population have confidence in each other. The union's role, therefore, is crucial. Even if students expressed anger about the fee hike, those criticisms would not have been effective without an organized presence like the union. Thus, unionization is very important to maintain and extend the rights of the students.

The administration is threatened by the fact that the union makes us strong. The right-wing government has been attacking the unions within the larger context, regardless of whether students, teachers, or staff are involved. The JNU administration has not only failed to invite the students' union to key meetings but has also not invited the Teachers' Association and the JNU Staff Association to meetings where they are ordinarily represented. This is an attack on all unions, on all forms of collective power.

FIGHT FOR DEMOCRATIC SPACE

Why did the administration lock up the Parthasarathy Rocks (PSR), where students gather? What does this space mean to the students? How did the students fight the undemocratic and authoritarian moves by the administration on scuttling democratic space within the university?

Places such as PSR have immense significance in a student's life.

In fact, such spaces are essential for a student's research. Pursuing research is not an easy task. We understand that to do good research, students need a good research environment. Physical spaces like PSR help students immensely in their research; students even acknowledge these spaces in their research papers. PSR is a place to hang out when someone feels too burdened. At other times, students simply visit the area, sit on the rocks surrounded by the lush greenery, and think deeply. Or sometimes, the students will reflect on what they have written in the draft chapters of their dissertation or thesis. It is an oasis on campus.

A decade ago, in 2009, the administration tried to rent out the PSR for commercial purposes. With the present administration's attitude toward students, we knew that the intention behind restricting PSR was not only to curtail the space for students – and therefore penalize students – but to extend its agenda of privatization.

However, JNUSU and the students resisted the administration's scheme to privatize PSR. We marched from Sabarmati Dhaba to PSR, broke the lock put up by the administration, and called for an all-night vigil to protect our PSR. Students came out in large numbers to defend their right to PSR; they ensured that the space, which belonged to them, remained free.

FEES MUST FALL MOVEMENT

How did the anti-fee hike movement begin?

On 3 October 2019, we received a circular from the administration. This circular said that an updated hostel manual was now available online. Students were given a few days to respond with their suggestions. We read the draft hostel manual and found many of the clauses extremely regressive. We started an email campaign requesting that students reply to the email address provided by the administration with their comments. We highlighted to the common students our objections to various clauses in the new draft hostel manual. The draft hostel manual suggested a dress code, curfew timing for the hostels etc. These were already in the earlier hostel manual, but they could not be implemented since the students had boycotted them for decades. As we knew the history of the present VC well, we decided that we should not take a risk and let these old – but not implemented – policies go unaddressed. Beginning with his tenure at JNU, this VC has tried to adopt regressive policies and then forcefully implement them. Such regressive rules are in practice in many universities. For several years, JNU resisted these policies due to its vibrant students' resistance. However, we could get a sense that the administration was eager to push these rules anew. For example, there were 24/7 reading rooms in various school buildings; they now wanted these reading rooms closed by 10:00 pm. One of the clauses in the draft manual said that students must return to their hostels as soon as the library closes. With this clause, the administration tried to restrict students' mobility and activities, making sure that the 24/7 reading room would close when the library closes, which is at 11:00 pm. The students understood that if they did not protest these policies, JNU would become a prison for students, just as many other universities had become.

What were the new clauses in the draft hostel manual compared to the existing manual?

The existing manual is – as opposed to the new draft – inclusive on many counts. The existing manual said that students from marginalized communities, students with disabilities, and women students, should get immediate room allotment in the hostel; this was omitted in the new draft. The current manual had a specific rate chart for fees, which held the administration to the rates that students would be charged; the new manual has no such chart and gives the administration the authority to increase the fees at its whim. The draft manual also included clauses such as service and utility charges, water and electricity bills, salaries of the contractual staff working in the hostel, and other charges.

How did the union build the movement?

The draft manual created an uproar among the student community. The union members met with the hostel presidents, and we decided to send emails to the Dean of Students (DoS). The last date to send the emails was 18 October at noon. An Inter-Hall Administration (IHA) meeting of students with the DoS was set to start at 3:00 pm. As we had raised our objections in the emails, we hoped that the administration would not proceed with the draft manual's problematic clauses. More than 3,000 students had sent emails to the DoS. The DoS postponed the IHA meeting from 18 October to 28 October as his office feared the students' protest. The present administration was not being honest and democratic. The new date, 28 October, was the day after Diwali. They knew that many students would go home for their holidays and thus would not be on campus for the meeting.

Even after several requests to invite the JNUSU representatives to the IHA meeting, the Dean did not invite the students' union representatives. Thus, despite the fact that our mobilization might not be huge, we held discussions with the hostel presidents and called for a protest to be held at the meeting's venue on 28 October. We had no choice but to confront the administration.

We entered the meeting hall with the hostel presidents. Our simple demand was to include the student representatives at the meeting. We wanted to have a fair discussion about the hostel manual. However, the administration, which has no respect for any democratic dialogue, adjourned the meeting without discussing the draft hostel manual. The meeting was then reconvened later in the afternoon without any prior notice to the committee members, which in itself was a violation. This meeting was a sham as there was no discussion. The administration showed a few slides, and the chair announced that the manual had been 'passed'. The meeting also 'passed' a motion to increase university fees by 10 per cent every year. After the fiasco of 28 October, we knew that we had to call for a university general strike. Hence the union called for a strike, with the central slogan – *Fees Must Fall and Education for All.*

The movement continued until the Delhi High Court intervened on our behalf on 24 January 2020.

What were the core demands of the anti-fee hike movement?

We demanded the revocation of the entire draft hostel manual. We demanded that education should be accessible to all. At JNU, students from various backgrounds came to pursue higher education with an admission fee of Rs. 283. With the proposed fee hike, there was a massive danger of changing the character of the university, where students from far-flung areas and deprived sections would not be able to attend. This administration had already scrapped JNU's well-celebrated admission policy, which granted deprivation points for women and students coming from backward regions. If the hostel fee increased, it would lead to a massive departure of students who would not be able to afford the new fees. Thus, our core demand was a complete rollback of the draft hostel manual.

As a part of the overall demand to roll back the draft hostel manual, one of the essential demands was to revoke the service and utility (water and electricity) charges. This was a very dangerous clause as students' fees were linked to the salary of the contractual workers. This meant that the administration was foregoing its responsibility of paying the salaries of workers and, in turn, was planning to meet these expenses from the students' fees. The addition of the service and utility charges attempted to privatize the university. As you increase these fees, it prices out poorer students, who can no longer afford higher education. Privatization has already seeped into various campuses where students are charged higher fees. Our movement highlighted the question of privatization of higher education and the need for the government to fund public education, rather than hand it over to the private sector. Even the Delhi High Court judge has acknowledged that the government has to fund education; it is the responsibility of the government to look for sources of funds rather than slapping the burden on the students.[3]

Did the political struggle by the students win any concrete victories?

Within a few days of the strike, the administration was pressured to withdraw two clauses from the draft hostel manual, the dress code and the curfew timing. After that, and again because of student pressure, the administration said they would provide discounts to any candidate from a below poverty line (BPL) class. But we were not satisfied. We demanded a complete rollback of the draft manual and that JNUSU should be involved in any decision-making that involved students. We decided to hold public protests. We marched outside the university with two main demands. First, lacking confidence in the VC, we called for his immediate removal. Second, we demanded that the draft hostel manual be scrapped. We made these demands to the Ministry of Human Resource Development (MHRD). As thousands of students came out into the streets, it forced the ministry to invite JNUSU for further deliberations. We explained the context of our demands to officials at the ministry. After several rounds of discussions, MHRD recommended that the university withdraw the service and utility charges. It suggested that the university and the University Grants Commission (UGC) bear the service and

[3] Justice Rajiv Shakdher, during the hearing, noted, 'Government cannot get out of education. Government has to fund public education. The burden of paying the salaries of contractual workers is not on the students. Someone has to find the funds'. See, Richa Banka, 'At JNU fee hearing, High Court's clear message to govt on funding education,' *Hindustan Times*, 24 January 2020, https://www.hindustantimes.com/india-news/at-jnu-fee-hearing-high-court-s-clear-message-to-govt-on-funding-education/story-P9afDI6CjB7O7ey8zYsq7M.html.

utility expenses. It also recommended that JNUSU be invited to discuss the manual. During the ninety days of our movement, we faced a great deal of repression: threats from the administration, negative media campaigns against us, and brutal attacks by the police. All of this was worth it. We felt that we had saved our educational system.

Could you talk about the solidarity you experienced from other campuses in India and from abroad?

Many institutions inside and outside India face similar problems of privatization and a general attack on education. The issue of fee hikes has been experienced almost everywhere in public education. So this meant that our JNU movement was part of a much larger dynamic. Many other students, students' unions, and movements could relate to our struggles. A range of colleges offered us solidarity as they continued with their own struggles – the Indian Institutes of Technology (IIT), the Institutes of Medical Science, and even a few colleges such as the Uttarakhand Ayurvedic Medical College.

We even received messages of solidarity from outside India. On 17 November 2019, Shaeera Kalla, former President, Students Representative Council, Wits University, South Africa, one of the leaders of the historic Fees Must Fall movement in that country, sent a note of solidarity with our struggle:

> President Aishe I send you love and strength. I know things must be very difficult, but I trust you are leading to the best of your ability. Please let me know what the best way to send our solidarity is, so that we can put our heads together and come up with something that assists the movement.
>
> As a first step, I am keen to write up a letter of solidarity. If you would like to be connected to media in South Africa, I can also arrange that.

Look forward to hearing more from you!
Yours in solidarity,
Shaeera.

Solidarity from across India and outside helped JNU students not feel isolated even though there were malicious campaigns against JNU during the movement.

The pro-privatization view argues that students of the so-called 'productive' educational institutions – the technology and medical schools, for instance – pay huge fees, as do students in private colleges; therefore, why should the JNU students or students who study humanities and social sciences in public institutions not pay a huge fee as well? They attempt to make humanities and social sciences students appear as a burden on the taxpayer. How do you respond to this?

When we worked on campus to defend our democratic spaces and the right of students to education, the corporate media ignored us. When we took our long marches and our strikes public, the corporate media vilified our protests. Questions were raised by pro-government and pro-privatization sections, such as why JNU students should only pay Rs 20 for room rent? Why shouldn't the 'nominal' increase laid out in the draft hostel manual be implemented? They argued that students at the IITs and the Indian Institutes of Management (IIMs), which are public institutions, are paying much higher fees, contributing more to society.

Our response to these questions is simple. We are not demanding that JNU students be given extra privileges – we are not saying that only we – JNU students – should have a lower fee structure. What we are saying is why should any student – even in the technology and management schools – pay enormous fees for their education? Once the students complete their courses and are employed, they become taxpayers and contribute to society in various manners. Therefore, when they are students, all their study-related expenses should be borne by the State. As students, we need to ask where the taxpayers' money should be invested? Should it be given away to big corporations, or should it be invested in education, health, and the basic needs of people in society? If the amount of money spent on the corporate giveaways were to be spent on IIT and IIM students, then all our education would be paid for, and we could concentrate on our studies rather than worry about the costs.

We do not want to see students distraught because they cannot afford to pay hostel fees or tuition fees. We have seen several deaths by suicide – which we call institutional murders – by students because they find themselves unable to cover their bills. Those who talk about the students at the IITs and the IIMs need to understand that these students are not happy about paying higher fees. Instead, they are forced to do so. One needs to look at the data on deaths by suicide at the IITs and the IIMs where the fees are high. Instead of framing the debate on State educational subsidies, we need to debate how the State should fund the totality of student expenses at our educational institutions. Why is the fellowship money not sufficiently increased? Why should students pay even a penny from their own pockets for their education?

The question of fees needs to be seen in an even wider context, along with the jobs crisis in our country. Students pay huge fees to secure their degrees from prestigious universities and research institutions and then face hurdles when it comes to finding a job. This has often led to significant anxiety and depression amongst students, with the ultimate and ghastly extreme being death by suicide. Burdened with loans, holding a degree, but jobless, this is a real crisis. If institutions or the State leave no other option for the students than to end their lives, these must be called institutional murders. Those who are posing these questions to the protesting students, are only adding weight to the system that is responsible for taking away students' lives.

Do you think that the anti-fee hike movement somehow generated a debate on campuses, which are often considered 'apolitical campuses'?

There were protests held on many campuses where there had been no previous history of such protests. Even though only ten or twenty students were on a march, their protests were only the beginning of a growing movement. These activities are preparing students to be ready to fight for their rights. The solidarity marches and solidarity statements set in motion a process on these campuses. It is evident that these campuses will no longer be silent.

You led a movement that lasted for over three months. There were ups and downs in the movement. What kept the movement alive and united over this period? What were the challenges you faced?

There were several challenges. Every night I used to think that maybe tomorrow would be better. But sometimes, the next day was even more challenging than the previous one. There were days when some 3,000 students would come for a demonstration or a march – but only a few would arrive the next day. There were times when some students would severely criticize the union. Despite all these challenges, we, in the union – and we, the students, stood together. We were clear on our goals, and we knew our unity could defeat the administration. There were agreements and disagreements. We cared about the disagreements, which were serious and important, and tried to solve those through dialogue. The hostels' presidents and the Student-Faculty Committee (SFC) representatives played an important role in the movement. We have had several General Body Meetings (GBMs) at a hostel level and at a centre level, along with meetings of all organizations on campus. Therefore, the decision-making process was decentralized. More and more students participated in the movement.

The administration was trying to divide us; there were continuous threats against us. They issued several notices threatening the students with severe punishment. But what kept us going was our ongoing dialogue, our protests, and our united resolutions. At times, the number of students participating dropped. We would review and analyze why the drop in numbers occurred. We were not deterred. With our analysis in hand, we would go out amongst the students again, propagate our ideas, earn their confidence, and move forward. Each day, in fact, was a learning opportunity, and we, as office holders, grew up with the movement. The good part is that every student, whether as hostel representatives, or those in class, or those that the VC intended to delegitimize, retained their vigour to fight back. Today, it is not only the students' union office holders who are recognized as leaders on campus; hostel presidents and class representatives are equally recognized. And this, in my opinion, is one of the essential successes of the movement, that new leaders were created.

Your union had to call for several boycotts – of classes, of examinations, and boycotts of registration. These are serious measures, and they relate directly to academics. One can imagine that teachers might not have agreed with such actions. What kind of response did you receive from the JNU Teachers' Association (JNUTA)?

The support we received from our teachers left me speechless. It has a lot to do with the JNU culture, where the teachers join hands with the students to fight any authoritarian action by the administration as well as to fight the State if it attacks the university. This goes back to the founding of JNU. Some teachers wrote emails to their students asking them to join the protests since these protests were about saving the educational system in general, and their education in particular. They suggested that learning could happen not only in their classrooms but also at the protest sites – sociology and political science – for instance, were being practised across the campus!

Our teachers were ready to provide students with extra classes to complete their syllabi and extend the examination schedule beyond its required dates. Except for a handful of teachers who sided with the administration, we received enormous support from our teachers, without which it would have been far more difficult for us to develop and sustain a successful movement. There were times when the teachers did not agree with our protest methods, but they never penalized us or intervened in the students' decisions. The JNUTA's role in the whole movement was exemplary. They not only issued solidarity statements but provided a physical presence and guidance at every moment of the movement's development. The teacher-student relationship at JNU will be preserved for a long time.

How do you see yourself as the leader of the movement? How did the movement contribute to you personally?

When I came to the campus, I saw a few comrades leading the union. At that time, I could not imagine myself in that position. But after I got elected, every single day was a learning experience. I have realized that it is a huge responsibility to be in the leadership of the union. But I knew that I had the support of the students and thus never felt alone. I grew up as an activist. No one can teach you how to be a good president; it is only through day-to-day experience that one learns the duties and responsibilities of a leader and can then deliver results. I can say for sure that the person I was before being elected to the post of president is not the same person I am today. I am sure that I will continue to grow as an activist and as a person by the time I complete my tenure as president. Each day I learn something new from the movement and the people around me.

What led to the 5 January 2020 physical attack on you and other students? What was the role of the administration and the Delhi police in the rampage?

Before I talk about the attack on this specific day, I want to go on record about how we have been treated throughout the movement. Our peaceful, long marches outside the university were brutally attacked by the Delhi Police, which works directly under the central government's Home Ministry. The administration has initiated actions against us without any preliminary enquiries. In fact, some students received hostel eviction notices. All these things were happening simultaneously as the state, and the administration repeatedly tried to break our movement. When those attacks did not succeed, the Akhil Bharatiya Vidyarthi Parishad (ABVP) members tried to divide the students. The JNUSU, after a unanimous mandate of the university general body meeting (UGBM), decided that the students would boycott the registration process unless the fee increase was withdrawn. The ABVP began to tell students to register with the increased fee. This disoriented some students. We all had come to the university to study. But we were forced to take to the streets because of the attacks on our education. For ABVP, the students' right to education was irrelevant. They preferred to countermand the students' mandate. Due to ABVP's inability to mobilize large number of students in favour of their politics, they started physical attacks on the protesting students and the union members leading the strikes.

On 5 January, masked Rashtriya Swayamsevak Sangh (RSS) workers from outside the campus attacked the students. It was an orchestrated attack by the members of ABVP-JNU and the RSS teachers at JNU. After the violence, we distributed a press release exposing the evidence that the ABVP-JNU leaders and the RSS teachers (who also hold administrative positions) were involved in organizing the mob attack on JNU students. It was an unprecedented attack.

The intention behind these attacks was two-fold: (a) to generate fear among the activists and (b) to change the discourse from fee hikes to violence. The ruling party-backed mainstream media immediately started broadcasting how the violence happened on campus with left-wing organizational leadership. They ignored the issue of the fee hikes and blamed the 'undisciplined' students for engaging in political action instead of registering for classes. They accused the JNUSU of unleashing violence against students who wanted to register and study. It was an attempt to defame and break the movement.

The violence could not have happened without the support of the administration and the Delhi Police. In fact, it was a well-coordinated strategy. A huge group of masked men were allowed to enter the campus with iron rods, hammers, and other weapons, as there were no security guards at the gates to stop them. Ironically, I had repeatedly asked the police officials for their intervention when the situation on campus was getting tense. But they did nothing. Moreover, the masked goons were given complete protection by the police as they were leaving the campus in a rally celebrating their victory. Can all this happen without orders from the top officials and the university authority?

What do these attacks mean personally for you? These masked goons beat you on 5 January. Rather than investigate the culprits, a First Information Report (FIR) was filed against you with the police that suggested that you were the culprit. A mural of you with your head in a bandage at Jamia Millia Islamia (JMI) has now been defaced. How has this attack impacted your sense of safety and security?

I was definitely traumatized by these acts. The attack of 5 January changed my life immensely. After the attack, I was severely injured – they beat me with iron rods – while in the hospital, I thought I would die. Since then, I have received dangerous threats and much abuse.

However, I feel I am not alone in this fight. Today, I have a voice that I must use to amplify the voices of all students. There is now public recognition of what I have been saying. Now people want to hear my voice. This gives me much strength and courage. I feel privileged by the extent of solidarity I have received because of the attack on me. I know that this is because I am the JNUSU president, and JNU is in Delhi. There are many such attacks, often more brutal, happening in other parts of the country every day. People are getting killed. The media pays no attention to them, nor does our society. If people in those struggles have the courage to continue fighting, despite the trauma inflicted on them, I, too, can continue the fight. We are inspiring each other in this difficult time. And I am certainly not alone.

You joined JNU just after the 9 February 2016 incident, when the Shut Down JNU campaign was launched – defaming the university; and the sedition laws against the JNUSU President and other students. Over the years, and after the Stand With JNU and Fees Must Fall movements, what has changed on the campus?

There is a commonality to the nature of the attack. But these two situations are very different. In 2016, the university was attacked, and then the movement began. This time, we were in a movement to defend the university when the attack occurred. The attack followed the movement. The 2016 and 2019-20 events are also different in terms of how public opinion was mobilized. After 9 February 2016, the right-wing propagandists succeeded in creating confusion amongst the people. Hatred was spread against the university as the media and the government consistently portrayed student leaders as anti-India; they still face sedition charges today. A specific section of the public succumbed to the right-wing media campaign. This time, despite their attempts, the right-wing and the corporate media were not entirely successful in spreading lies. Part of the reason was that the core issue of the 2019-2020 movement was to revoke the fee hike, which did not touch the broader questions of terrorism and nationalism. Thus, the government and the administration had to capitulate so that even a senior BJP leader and the former Human Resource Development Minister, Murli Manohar Joshi, called for the VC to be removed.

MOVEMENT IN DEFENCE OF THE INDIAN CONSTITUTION

The BJP government has put forward a spate of laws and policies, the CAA-NRC-NPR, that narrow the definition of citizenship and threaten minorities, mainly Muslims, with disenfranchisement. There is a widespread movement against this in the country of which students, youth, and women are in the lead. How do you connect yourself to that movement?

We, as students, first got connected to the movement when there was a massive crackdown on the students of JMI. JNUSU immediately called for protests at the Delhi Police Headquarters. It grew into a massive demonstration. Following this, the detained Jamia students were released within a few hours. Later, a committee was formed, of which I was a part, to take the protests against CAA, NRC, and NPR forward. After the crackdown on Jamia students, there was a larger demonstration of solidarity by students nationally. In fact, students at institutes and colleges, which do not have any history of protest, came out to support the students at Jamia and against the government's moves.

These protests indicated the volume of anger people had against the ruling government. I, as a youth, would not wish to live in a country where my fellow citizens are forced to live in a detention camp. It is atrocious how the government is trying to snatch away peoples' citizenship rights. The government worked hard to defame the protests, but they didn't succeed. Every day, huge masses of people participated in protests and raised their voices in a non-violent manner. These protests were democratic, colourful, and creative. The BJP is trying to polarize India today. They continue to make communal remarks by singling out Muslims and calling the protests 'Muslim' protests. Of course,

Muslims were protesting, but so were a wide range of people – a coalition of people who would like to maintain our Constitution. It is noteworthy that the Muslims are protesting under the slogan of saving the Indian Constitution and the secular fabric of the country. The fanatics, however, are raising sectarian and divisive slogans, such as '*Jai Shri Ram*' ('Victory to Lord Ram'). Everyone in the country, who understands what the Indian Constitution means to all of us, is protesting against the CAA, NRC, and NPR today. I am one of those people.

Struggles Against Neo-Liberal Assaults on Education

Against Profiteering in Education and For Democratic Rights: The Students' Movement in Kerala since the 1990s

P.M. Ranjith

The neoliberal economic policies that were set in motion during the mid-1980s and institutionalized by the beginning of the 1990s have brought about severe and far-reaching consequences in Indian society. The changes that took place in the higher education sector as a result of these policies were crucial. A significant marker of neoliberal policies was the retreat of the State from sectors like health, education, and public services. Government-funded efforts to expand higher education along with the universalization of primary education formed a crucial part of the nation-building process that the Indian state pursued after the end of colonial rule.

The Indian national movement had declared that 'the State shall provide for free and compulsory primary education' (Resolution passed by the Karachi Session of the Indian National Congress on 29-31 March 1931). The governments of independent India did not manage to put these words into action – illiteracy remained widespread, and there are not enough public schools in the country even today. Although governments set up many higher educational institutions, the numbers of such institutions were inadequate. Nevertheless, the concept of education as a commodity to be auctioned off to the highest paying bidders did not enjoy much currency during the first few decades after independence. The legacy of the Indian national movement, the prestige that socialism enjoyed in the post-World War II period, the emergence of welfare states in Western Europe, and the adoption of State interventionist policies by Third World countries provided the background to the policies of the Indian governments during this era. But all that turned upside down with India's adoption of the new economic policies of globalization. Education, particularly higher education, became a lucrative commodity for the newly opened up market instead of being a public service. The first victim of this change that the new economic policy imposed on the country was the professional education sector. However, subsequent experience showed that the impact of such policies went beyond professional education and widely influenced education as a whole.

This article aims to briefly describe the major changes in the higher education sector of Kerala during the last two decades with respect to privatization and attendant measures and the responses to such changes, including the resistance put up by the student movement.

BACKGROUND

The social, economic, and political conditions in Kerala are quite different when compared to those in other States in India. Land reforms from the 1960s onwards, progress in public education, and the resultant high literacy rates are characteristic features of Kerala.

While public education is strong in Kerala, educational institutions belonging to community and religious organizations have also been widespread in the State. Most of these are in the aided-sector – private educational institutions that receive financial aid from the government.

The enormous influence Left politics has in Kerala is a significant factor in determining the state's social and political life. The Left has come to power in the state government several times through parliamentary-democratic elections, while left-wing student and youth organizations are also strong in the state. The strongest voices of protest against privatization of higher education in Kerala have come from the left-wing student and youth movements.

ATTEMPTS TO PRIVATIZE HIGHER EDUCATION

A major push to privatize education in Kerala came during the early 1990s when neoliberal economic policies were being introduced in a big way in the country. The Congress-led United Democratic Front (UDF) government of 1991-1996 began efforts to privatize the higher education sector in the State. The first such experiments were in the cooperative sector, which was already strong in Kerala at the time. The UDF government tried to start private self-financed courses at the Cooperative Medical College in Pariyaram in the Kannur district. This initiative came from M.V. Raghavan, the Minister for Cooperation, and K. Karunakaran, the Chief Minister. Massive protests by the left-wing student and youth organizations erupted against this measure. On 25 November 1994, police fired on activists of the Students' Federation of India (SFI) and the Democratic Youth Federation of India (DYFI) who tried to wave black flags at M.V. Raghavan in Koothuparamba in the Kannur district. Five young activists – Babu, Madhu, Rajeevan, Roshan, and Shibulal – were killed, and several were injured. Massive agitations occurred all over the state following the Koothuparamba firing. Widespread discussions about the introduction of self-financed courses took place among the people. In the subsequent legislative assembly elections in 1996, the Congress-led alliance was defeated, and the Left Democratic Front (LDF) led by Chief Minister E.K. Nayanar came to power.

The new Left government took the principled stand that self-financed colleges should not be allowed. But the leading constituents of the ministry faced enormous pressure from alliance partners in the LDF. The management of private educational institutions tried to influence political parties that were part of LDF. The Education portfolio in the ministry was handled by P.J. Joseph, from the Kerala Congress (Joseph) party, which tended to uphold the interests, in this case, of elite sections among Christians in the south-central Kerala region. The great interest that Christian private managements had in starting self-financed colleges exerted significant influence on the positions of the Kerala Congress (Joseph). Community organizations, which had a considerable presence in the education sector, were already trying to start self-financed colleges. Kerala is a state with a large population of religious minorities, with Muslims and Christians making up almost forty-five per cent of the population. Compared to most other states in India, the religious minorities in Kerala have achieved greater social and economic progress, and have powerful political organizations which arguably at least represent the dominant sections among those communities.

During the tenure of the Nayanar government, several private managements sought permission from the education department to start self-financed colleges. As per the order of Minister P.J. Joseph, the Education Department gave Non-Objection Certificates (NOC) to twenty-one such engineering colleges. This was done without a cabinet decision, and it caused a major outcry in the LDF. The Left parties, including Communist Party of India (Marxist) (CPI(M)), and left-wing student and youth organizations called for protests. Following this, the Chief Minister called for a cabinet meeting, and the granting of the NOCs was cancelled. The private management went to Court against this step by the government. Meanwhile, the All-India Council of Technical Education (AICTE), the national body for the governance of technical educational institutions such as engineering colleges, gave recognition to ten out of twenty-one colleges to which the NOC was given initially. All these took place at a time when the tenure of the Nayanar government was about to end.

In the state assembly elections in 2001, the Congress-led UDF came to power, and A.K. Antony became the Chief Minister. The Congress-led ministry showed no restraint in allowing self-financed colleges. The Indian Union Muslim League, which handled the education portfolio, was enthusiastic about granting permission to such colleges in an unbridled fashion. In three years, nearly 500 self-financed engineering and medical colleges mushroomed in the state.

The policy that the UDF government announced at the time was, 'Two self-financed colleges for one government college'. According to this formula, every self-financed college had to set aside 50 per cent of their seats for students who would only have to pay the fee equivalent to that in government colleges. But the government did not take the initiative to sign a legally binding agreement with the management. As a result, the promised merit seats were widely scuttled in the state. Moreover, self-financed colleges turned out to be spaces where no organization, which stood for student rights, was allowed to function.

THE DEATH OF RAJANI S. ANAND

The death by suicide of Rajani S. Anand, a Dalit student, on 22 July 2004, was a major event that led to the heightening of the indignation in Kerala society against self-financed colleges. Rajani was a third-year bachelor's degree student in Computer Engineering at the self-financed college Institute of Human Resource Development, Adoor, in Pathanamthitta district. Having been forced to leave the college due to her inability to pay fees, she died after jumping from the top of the Office of the Commissioner for Entrance Examinations in Thiruvananthapuram. Rajani's father, a daily wage labourer, had tried to get a bank loan to pay his daughter's fees. But the efforts failed, as he didn't have enough property to provide as collateral for the loan. Rajani became the first victim of the self-financed education system.

Rajani's tragic death resulted in a surge of mass anger against the unjust system of profiteering self-financed colleges. Left student and youth organizations led massive protests all across the state. Police wielded brute force to repress the agitations, frequently resorting to the use of tear gas, water cannons, and grenades against the students. By 29 July, nearly 300 protestors were jailed, and cases were registered against about 15,000 people. The police said that 521 people had been arrested, and 124 cases registered. In response to just one instance – a march towards the Office of the Inspector General of Police at Kozhikode – cases were registered against 6,300 protestors.

There were incidents of even elected Members of the Kerala Legislative Assembly being manhandled. Pinarayi Vijayan, the CPI(M) state secretary, was also made an accused in a case. There were attacks by the police against the CPI(M)'s District Committee offices in Kannur, Kozhikode and Thrissur. The police laid siege to the CPI(M) Thrissur District Committee office for hours.

The protests following the death of Rajani S. Anand were the biggest student agitation the state had seen in the last twenty-five years. Following these protests, the government agreed to increase the scholarships for Scheduled Caste and Scheduled Tribe (SC/ST) students. But the Antony government did not agree to any fundamental change with regard to the self-financed colleges. The ire against the government on the self-financed colleges issue was one of the significant factors that led to the resignation of A.K. Antony from the office of Chief Minister. The UDF lost the assembly elections in 2006, and LDF came to power.

JUDICIAL INTERVENTION IN SELF-FINANCED COLLEGES

The massive student and youth agitations could not put an end to the profiteering by self-financed colleges. The Left government, which came to power in 2006, passed legislation to bring about some social control over the sector. But the law was questioned in court, and the Supreme Court struck it down. The 50:50 formula that was announced when A.K. Antony was Chief Minister was scuttled. Two private managements approached the High Court, and the court rejected the government's claim on 50 per cent seats.

Moreover, even for the 25 per cent of seats designated as 'government seats' (in which admission would be based on the merit list prepared on the basis of an entrance examination), the court fixed a fee of Rs. 1.5 lakh.

It can be seen that judicial interventions have helped private managements before as well. The most important case on the self-financed college issue is the T.M.A. Pai case. At the end of the legal battle between the Karnataka government and the T.M.A. Pai Foundation, an eleven-member bench delivered a verdict on 31 October 2002 that allowed minority communities to start their own educational institutions, and gave them full powers to admit students into those institutions. This verdict became the basis for other verdicts by the High Court in favour of the private self-financed colleges. The judicial intervention led to the striking down of the law passed by the Left government in 2006.

SEMESTERIZATION

Semesterization was one of the key reforms implemented in the recent past in Kerala's education sector at the graduation level. Following the model of many universities in the West, it entailed dividing the academic year into two – with examinations every six months – instead of once yearly. The Left government implemented the semester system as per the recommendations of the Kerala State Higher Education Council, which was then headed by the renowned historian K.N. Panikkar.

There were vocal protests when the semester system was implemented at Delhi University (DU), known to have some of India's best graduate (bachelor's degree) courses. Notably, teachers led these protests. But there was no significant protest against semesterization in Kerala. Even though the reform increased the burden on teachers and students, rigorous discussions among the academic community were missing.

Semesterization, without doubt, had a deleterious effect on student politics. Students were forced to keep aside the bulk of the academic year for preparation for examinations alone, to the detriment of even other knowledge-enhancing activities that are supposed to be part of academic life, not to mention extra-curricular activities. After nine years of experience with the semester system, the leaders of student organizations themselves admitted that the time spent on organizational activities had significantly decreased.

Political activity in Kerala's college campuses had already been subjected to unprecedented restrictions due to the implementation of the Lyngdoh Committee Recommendations (LCR). LCR put stiff restrictions on students' union elections in India, with several rules such as strict age limits for candidates and inordinate limits regarding the number of times a person can contest elections.[1]

[1] A pamphlet issued by the SFI's JNU unit on 11 August 2014 explained the problems with the LCR: 'The objective of the LCR, contrary to all pious statements, is to weaken the students' movement so as to pave the way for fee hikes, commercialization, privatization and centralization of higher education — a process that is already underway. LCR has put in place restrictions that are fundamentally undemocratic and exclusionary (particularly adversely affecting students from deprived sections). For instance, the clause that stipulates an age barrier of 22 years for BA students, 25 years for PG students and 28 years for MPhil/PhD students (30 years for JNU as per the relaxation granted), militates against students from deprived backgrounds who are often forced to enter higher education at a later age. The clause that prevents candidates from contesting more than once in the central panel and twice for councillor posts defies logic even as it serves to constrain

Semesterization adversely affected the vibrancy of campus politics even more.

THE STUDENT MOVEMENT IN THE ERA FOLLOWING THE ANTI-SELF-FINANCED COURSES STRUGGLES

Struggles against profiteering by self-financed colleges were something that the Left student organizations had been waging for more than a decade. The police firing in Koothuparamba in the Kannur district, which led to the death of five student and youth activists in November 1994, marked a historic moment in the fight against the commercialization of education in Kerala. But the fight against profiteering by self-financed colleges did not achieve its objectives.

The privatization policies of the Congress-led governments, and the interventions of the judiciary, cemented self-financed colleges as a concrete reality in Kerala. There was a kind of chaos in the state's higher education sector after the Supreme Court struck down the law enacted by the LDF government in 2006 to regulate self-financed colleges. It cannot be said that even public colleges and universities were completely free from this. More problems cropped up, such as the clamour of government-aided colleges for 'autonomy', and universities implementing measures aimed at privatization. The student community of Kerala responded to these with new energy and a sense of political purpose. Protests spread beyond the framework of organizations. Along with the defence of public education, other issues in higher education, such

---

the development of a mature leadership for the union. The eligibility criteria which prevents students who have been 'tried/convicted' for any criminal offence and those who have been 'subjected to any disciplinary action by the university authorities' only aids the college/university administrations to victimise student activists who have participated or led any kind of protests against unjust measures by the authorities. In short, the overarching framework of Lyngdoh curtails students' rights and has been damaging to our fight against anti-student college and university administrations and the neoliberal policies of the ruling classes'.

as social justice and gender justice, emerged as common issues in the student community.

FESTIVAL OF RESISTANCE

Calicut University, the biggest university in Kerala, witnessed a student movement in 2014-15, which lasted for more than 150 days. It was among the protests that garnered the most public attention in recent times. The movement was against the privatization attempts led by the VC, who was appointed by the Congress-led government of 2011-16. The VC tried to sell vast tracts of university-owned land for commercial purposes. Another effort was to clear the 'green belt' in the university and to use it to plant cash crops.

Moreover, several self-financed courses were also started at the university. The university levied high fees on the students for these courses. But the university authorities did not bother to build the necessary infrastructure for the students. The immediate trigger for the struggle was the University handing over the hostel meant for students who were admitted on the basis of merit to students of the private courses. The University's Department Students' Union began the agitation with the support of the SFI in October 2014. Hunger strikes, blockades, and police interventions, which took place several times, brought national attention to the struggle. Organizations of teachers and employees also lent support to the agitation. Leading figures in the fields of art, culture, and literature in Kerala came forward in solidarity with the struggle, which came to be known as the Festival of Resistance. Numerous cultural programmes and meetings took place at the struggle venue. Students of various universities abroad also sent messages expressing solidarity with the agitating students.

As the struggle intensified, things came to such a point that the university's VC could not enter the campus. Hundreds of students were injured in a lathi (baton) charge by the police and in attacks by Congress-Muslim League hoodlums. Several students had false charges slapped against them. But ultimately, the VC was forced to withdraw the proposal to sell the university's assets and land.

JISHNU PRANNOY CASE

The LDF came to power after the assembly elections in 2016, and CPI(M) leader Pinarayi Vijayan took oath as Chief Minister.

The death by suicide of Jishnu Prannoy, a student of Nehru College, Pambady in the Kottayam district, on 6 January 2017, created a massive wave of protest in the state. Jishnu had become *persona non grata* for the college's management after he organized students against the management's decision to ban student politics on campus. The management made a false allegation that Jishnu had copied in an exam, and preliminary investigations indicated that Jishnu killed himself after being deeply disturbed by the allegations. But subsequently, it became clear that before he died, Jishnu was beaten up at the college by goons hired by the college management. Following this, students led by SFI began a struggle. Massive agitations took place at the institutions owned by the Nehru Group. Protesters ransacked the management office at Jishnu's college. In response, the Left government swung into action, and the Nehru Group chairman himself was arrested. Subsequently, the case was transferred to the CBI as per the demand of Jishnu Prannoy's mother.

STRUGGLES FOR WOMEN'S MOBILITY

Kerala remains a conservative society as far as gender relations are concerned. Patriarchal restrictions on women's freedom and mobility are pervasive in the state. Some seemingly small but significant struggles have taken place in Kerala against rules that discriminate against women students and put shackles on their freedom and mobility.

The hostels for female students of colleges and universities in Kerala have been notorious for draconian rules, one of which has been the insistence that the hostel residents return to the hostel before dark, typically by 6:00 pm or 6:30 pm, or even earlier. On the other hand, men's hostels have much more relaxed rules, with residents allowed to return much later than their women counterparts.

The first major struggle in Kerala against such discriminatory 'curfews' began at the College of Engineering, Thiruvananthapuram (CET), in March 2015. A group of students at the college initiated the Break the Curfew movement, pointing out that the library was open until 8:00 pm and the computer lab was open until 9:00 pm, but the female students had to be back in the hostel before 6.30 pm. This meant that the women students were given easier projects that wouldn't require them to remain in the lab for too long, and thus they were excluded from teamwork. The agitating students organized online campaigns and protest demonstrations, wrote mass petitions, and stayed outside the hostel beyond the curfew times as part of the struggle. The college authorities were hostile to the demand.

In October 2015, the Committee on Gender Justice on Campuses, appointed by the Kerala State Higher Education Council, submitted its report. The report's recommendations said, 'Prevalent practices of Protectionism and surveillance should be stringently discouraged and the autonomy of women respected and secured'. Meanwhile, the UGC (Prevention, Prohibition and Redressal of Sexual Harassment of Women Employees and Students in Higher Educational Institutions) Regulations, 2015 also said, 'Concern for the safety of women students must not be cited to impose discriminatory rules for women in the hostels as compared to male students.'

But the UDF government took no action. The discriminatory rules stayed in place, and the movement appeared to fade away for the moment. Demands similar to those of the Break the Curfew movement were raised by students in various other colleges and university campuses across the state, but the system didn't budge.

The struggle was reborn in 2018-19 when a group of CET students formed a platform called Azadi.[2] The Azadi-led struggle against discriminatory curfew timings was also supported by SFI. Mass campaigns were held among the students, which raised awareness about the issue and won popular support for the cause of scrapping discriminatory rules. The students were met with character assassination attempts from people in positions of power in the college, along with threats of disciplinary action by authorities who were more interested in moral policing and patriarchal surveillance. But the students received support from T.K. Anandi, the Gender Advisor to the Government of Kerala.

The protest intensified from 18 February 2019 onwards, with several women students choosing to remain outside the Women's Hostel gates beyond the official curfew time. On the second day, about 100 women broke the curfew, and on the third day, about 600 women students protested outside the gates, defying the curfew rule. The authorities were finally forced to concede to the students' demand, a decision to extend the Women's Hostel's curfew to 9:30 pm – the same as the Men's Hostel's curfew – was made at a meeting attended by the College Principal, the Government's Gender Advisor, and the Higher Education Principal Secretary.

This triggered demands from women students in more colleges to end discriminatory curfews at their hostels. On 25 February, the struggle of the women students of Government Law College, Thiruvananthapuram, to extend the curfew time ended in victory. The same demand was also raised by women students of the Government College for Women, Thiruvananthapuram, and the Government Engineering College, Thrissur. In response, the LDF

[2] Discussions with Anjuradh T.R., who was a woman representative in the Students Union at CET during 2018-19 and chairperson of the Union during 2019-20, have been immensely helpful in writing about this struggle. While gratefully acknowledging her inputs, let me also make the obvious point that she is not responsible for any error that may appear in this article.

government issued an order on 7 April 2019, extending the curfew of all women's hostels under government colleges and government universities in Kerala to 9:30 pm, the same as the curfew time for men's hostels. This signalled a landmark victory in the struggle against gender-based discrimination on Kerala campuses.

The students at the forefront of the Azadi movement insist that the struggle didn't end there. The curfews were still too restrictive and need to change. Many more issues need to be addressed in the path toward gender justice on campuses.

CONCLUSION

Since the 1990s, the attempts by the ruling classes and the UDF governments they have propped up in Kerala to turn the education sector into an avenue for profit-making have intensified. In this regard, they have been firmly supported by the right-wing media, which has tried to manufacture consent in favour of more self-financed professional colleges and against organized student politics, which act as a bulwark against attempts to privatize and commercialize education. There were also judicial interventions to curtail campus democracy (reflected in, for instance, court verdicts that effectively prevented college students' union elections during the mid-2000s) and to neutralize the Left government's legislative attempts to prohibit profiteering by self-financed professional colleges.

Despite such challenges and setbacks, the student movement in Kerala, led by left-wing student organizations such as SFI, remains robust and vibrant.[3] Although the fight against self-financed colleges cannot be termed successful, the student movement created a dominant sentiment in Kerala society against unbridled profiteering by educational institutions. The student

[3] SFI is the largest student organization in Kerala, with about 15 lakh members. It has been winning elections to almost 90 per cent of students' unions in the colleges and universities of the state in the past two decades.

movement has been actively responding to incidents of caste atrocities across the country and amplifying voices against attacks on secularism and democracy under Bharatiya Janata Party rule. Recent years have also seen issues of gender justice and instances of caste discrimination on campuses and in society in general finding more salience than before in the discourses and struggles of the student movement.

Building Mass Movements: The Experience of Himachal Pradesh

Vikram Singh

The character of the students' movement in Himachal Pradesh University (HPU) in Shimla has been militant, and it has historically drawn mass support in waging battles against the state, and the state-appointed authorities within the university. The students have survived several attacks while fighting against the neoliberal policies of the state and for safeguarding the democratic rights of the students without surrendering to the power of the state. To cite from its history, in 2011, a staunch Rashtriya Swayamsevak Sangh *pracharak* (propagandist for RSS), Mr Arun Diwaker Nath Bajpayee, infamous for his authoritarian character and corruption, was appointed as the VC of HPU.

The following years were tough for the students. As soon as he assumed his office, the HPU authorities, hand and glove with the state government, came up with proposals for several fee hikes, up to ten times more than the existing fee structure. For instance, a private candidate (who could not attend regular classes) could appear for exams by paying Rs 100 as the examination fee. Such a fee structure provided opportunities to higher education for the female students, as well as those who belonged to disadvantaged socio-economic backgrounds. But in the new proposal, these fees were increased to Rs 1000, which was unaffordable for a large section of aspiring students. Similarly, the examination fee for the regular students was increased from Rs 200 to 2000, and the fee for a provisional certificate was hiked from Rs 500 to 1500.

In the tumultuous years between 2013 and 2014, by directly confronting the state government, the students registered the strongest resistance at HPU. Multiple struggles were fought during these years, igniting an enormous mass movement, one of the largest in the history of Himachal Pradesh. The history of the students' movement at Himachal Pradesh establishes the fact, time and again, that if students are organized to fight for a just cause, they can break the oppressors. This is evident in several movements of Himachal Pradesh which the students fought. I recollect a few instances from the past and wish to present a brief account from the historical movements before the readers.

The Left has limited strength in HPU. Nonetheless, the Students' Federation of India (SFI) operates there confidently. Movements by the students, inspired by the sacrifice of the student leaders and by the struggles to overcome daily hardships, directly challenge the general policy of privatization of education by the state and central governments. The struggles are many. The students once sent a former VC to prison for corruption in printing examination papers in 2002. They held a students' union election fighting against a ban on elections imposed for five-year by the Chief Minister – a result of the militant struggle that continued for two years and was won after a fast-unto-death hunger strike. They successfully ensured the daily mobilization of thousands of students across the state, making fundamental changes to the National Higher Education Mission (Rashtriya Uchchatar Shiksha Abhiyan – RUSA), which is otherwise a central government policy.

THE ANTI-RUSA MOVEMENT

In 2013, a planned attack was launched against the students when the authorities tried to implement RUSA. Through their struggle against RUSA, the students demonstrated their capability to intervene in the arena of policy-making effectively. When RUSA was implemented, higher education institutions were unable to understand the policy. It was implemented haphazardly, without any discussion with the key stakeholders. RUSA, for many reasons, adversely impacted higher education. After its implementation, the academic community criticized it, but without any consensus on what was wrong or what should be done about it. In Himachal Pradesh, the students studied the concrete impact of RUSA on their campuses, taking up issues that caused deep discontent amongst the students.

RUSA was opposed for several reasons. The draft claimed to 'improve access, equity, and quality in higher education through planned development of higher education at the state level'. There were a number of plans proposed in the draft related to building excellence in higher education, strategically increasing funds for institutions, providing institutional autonomy, etc. The objectives were projected so that the plan would appear as benefiting higher education. However, our detailed study on each of the clauses revealed an opposite and grim picture, which the government and the authorities were trying to hide.

The scheme, in reality, would have furthered the inequality in the system more than ever before. The number of seats proposed in each discipline in an institution was limited, and thus only a few students would get the opportunity to pursue higher education. Further, given the rural-urban divide in accessing educational facilities and success rates for students in the final examination process at the 10+2 level, there was a very high risk of a large number of students getting eliminated, particularly those from rural backgrounds, the economically deprived areas, and the Scheduled Caste (SC), Scheduled Tribe (ST) students. The way RUSA was designed would limit access, create more inequality, and decrease the gross enrollment ratio. HPU students issued a clause-by-clause analysis of RUSA, which showed how this plan was anti-student and exclusionary. They carefully identified the government's neoliberal agenda to rush RUSA through without developing the required infrastructure or strengthening the existing ones. It was a scheme to promote the public-private partnership that seemed inclusive on paper but, in reality, was an exclusionary project. Hence, the SFI-led agitation began, which mobilized students on these concrete issues, and for three long years, the students continued their struggle. The movement against RUSA had generated tremendous heat across the state; students of several colleges in the state went on strike, and the teaching faculty came along in support of the struggle. The movement against RUSA was a direct battle against the government's policy. The movement successfully forced the government to change several policies in the state, including a reversal to the annual from the semester system. The second instance of a determined struggle comes from the anti-fee hike movement by the students of Himachal Pradesh.

NOVEL PROTESTS AGAINST FEE-HIKE

Due to its low fee structure, HPU was one of the few universities in India where education was affordable for poor students. Such a structure was sustained due to democratic movements that had fought for the students' rights over many years. When the authority decided to increase the fees in 2014, HPU students fought back.

The students devised a novel way to protest; these unique campaigns led by the SFI-HPU campus unit frustrated the administration and pushed back their cunning efforts. The administration closed the hostels indefinitely through a dictatorial notice in reaction to the student protest over the fee hike. They thought they could break the students' spirit, but they failed. The SFI unit had decided that the students would not leave the campus. They would start their unique cooperative mess on campus and live on the campus itself. More than 400 students ate their dinner in the Arts block of the university under the open sky, a unique mess 'hall' without walls and a roof. After dinner, the students cleaned the open-air mess to sleep there. The following day, before classes began, the place was cleaned by the students before they went to their classes. There was tremendous support and empathy from other students and the general public for the protesting students. Many dayscholars decided to spend their nights on campus in solidarity with the ongoing struggle. This mess hall was run for four months.

There were ups and downs. The marks of the police lathis (batons) were visible on the bodies of the fighting comrades. The number of court cases registered against the students increased. The rustication of the student leaders from the university grew. The leadership of the movement was jailed and tortured. Despite the violence and harassment against these students, victory belonged to the students. They kept alive the dream that young people could enter the doors of higher educational institutions. This was not an isolated struggle. It was part of a process of continuous struggle, which, for now, ensures that the public sector educational system in Himachal Pradesh is alive and that the student movement is revitalized.

BAN ON STUDENTS' UNION ELECTIONS

The movements spreading across the state posed an immediate threat to the government and the university administration. The state, which operates on a neoliberal model, has no respect for any voice of resistance. We witnessed this on multiple occasions when the democratic rights of the students were being directly attacked and when the ruling government put a ban on the right to form associations and the right to strike. Against this backdrop, the VC started advocating for a ban on students' union elections, citing examples of violence on college and university campuses. On 26 August 2014, the HPU authority, in a meeting of the Executive Council, banned the students' union elections for one year on campus and the university's affiliated colleges. This was done as the authority felt the heat of the students' movement, which posed a challenge to the neoliberal policies of the government and the authoritarian rule of the administration. The existence of the students' union has been perceived as a threat regardless of who controls the government – the Bharatiya Janata Party (BJP) or Congress Party. Similar tactics of banning the students' union were adopted under the tenure of the Congress chief minister – the late Mr Virbhadra Singh – between 1986 to 1988 and 1994 to 1999.

The years 2013 and 2014 were particularly difficult for the students. They faced unprecedented attacks. Many SFI leaders were expelled from their respective colleges and universities for opposing the fee hike, RUSA, and the ban on the union election. Yet, they fought for their demands with collective spirit. So, what kept the students' movement in Himachal Pradesh so vibrant that it fought and won even when the movement faced a brutal crackdown by the State.

A FIGHT FOR BASIC ISSUES IS AN IDEOLOGICAL FIGHT

Education issues are at the core of the student movement in Himachal Pradesh. This may appear strange as the Himachal Pradesh student movement is known for its militant struggles on political and ideological issues. Students learn about larger political and ideological struggles, apart from their own. Focused study and organizing by activists around common and basic struggles reveal deeper political problems. The fire-brand student movement still has the responsibility to attend to the fundamental problems of campus life and experiences. Issues around how the broader policies of the economy impact a student's life on campus, how the communal policies divert their attention from the struggle for education, or how the small struggles over the library, the internet, mess food, and their teachers are the key issues which the administration blocks.

From our experience of various campuses, particularly where political and ideological debates are common, we found that in the thick of struggle on larger political and ideological issues, the leaders often ignore struggles around students' basic issues. This is contrary to our experience in Himachal Pradesh. In fact, it would not be wrong to state that when students' basic issues are ignored, exposing the students to the larger ideological and political struggles becomes more difficult. The campus struggles, which lack a focus on basic issues, often seem to adopt a top-down approach rather than agenda being evolved from the bottom up.

Since 2014, the BJP government has continuously attacked the idea of education and educational institutions. Students have had to defend democracy on their campuses and protect their democratic culture. The media highlighted the fights at Jawaharlal Nehru University (JNU), Univeristy of Hyderabad (UoH), Film and Television Institute of India (FTII), Indian Institute of Technology Madras (IIT-M), and other places since these were the flashpoints for the defence of campus democracy. Beneath this attack on campus democracy, however, is a much wider and less visible attack: the attack on the public sector educational system in India. There has been little concern by the media about this deeper assault on education.

To a certain extent, the student movement in such campuses failed to organize students on the issues of their campuses, which are the result of the neoliberal education policies. The impact of neoliberal policies is seen on a range of issues, including the decrease of PhD candidate positions in almost all universities, scholarships and fellowships cuts, the disregard for reservations, the continuing vacant faculty positions, and the lack of hostels.

It is comparatively easy to mobilize students on these issues since these directly impact them. If students are agitated on these issues, they cannot be divorced from the more profound political questions. A student movement needs to have a broad outlook and comprehensively understand the social and economic issues.

It is an integral part of the student movement to raise student voices against all injustice in society. Their prime responsibility is to struggle for social justice and against the exploitation of the marginalized sections of society, which demands a focus on campus and educational issues since it is on campus that the government is promoting social injustice and marginalization. Our experience in Himachal Pradesh shows that common issues should be the basis of the struggles. These can effectively link policy matters to broader political questions and successfully change the policy.

A DIALECTICAL APPROACH CAN CONFRONT RSS-BJP

The agenda of the current regime in India is apparent. BJP is committed to its agenda of – communalism, attacks on democratic institutions, attacks on rational thinking, and against any voice of dissent. Simultaneously, BJP is also hell-bent on pursuing neoliberal policies that are not only destroying our public education system, but are also changing the concept of education. These attacks on our educational institutions serve a twin purpose: to privatize education and to communalize education.

We have to understand the game plan of RSS-BJP, and must focus on educational issues and against communalization of education. We cannot imagine being a part of the societal struggle for social justice if we are not waging an uncompromised struggle on questions of social justice on our campuses. This is not a question of choosing one against the other. We have to dialectically link our struggle over the basic demands of the students and our struggle over education policy with the broader questions of communalism and neoliberalism. To combat the more significant challenge of communalism and authoritarianism, we need unity, which can be achieved for students when they are organized primarily around their demands for education and educational institutions. We have to mobilize students against these attacks by the authoritarian regime, but students' primary focus should be commercialization and saffronization of education along with the questions of social justice.

When students are mobilized around their fundamental issues, movements are built, and victories ensue. Consequently, the need arises to create an organizational structure for the students. This is very important for sustaining any struggle. Struggles cannot consistently be fought and won through spontaneity and without an organizational structure.

This structure is the foundation for sustaining any movement in any section of society; it also applies to the student movement. Students have to be organized into committees at every level since this allows the struggle to be democratic, unified, and strong. Students make their own decisions within the committees and evolve a sense of responsibility. Thus, the appearance of imposing decisions from the outside is eliminated. This is one area that is very strong in the Himachal student movement. The organized movement promotes collectivity.

ORGANIZED MOVEMENTS AND STRUCTURES ARE NECESSARY FOR SUSTAINED STRUGGLES

Neoliberalism seeks to create avenues for the profit maximization of finance capital, and it also creates a set of social and political values that help maintain the status quo. These values are based on 'individualism' and portray the current system where the success and failure of every individual depend solely on their efforts. This 'individualism' is perpetuated through various forms, including newspapers, films, and television. Thus, while inequalities and misery are continuously increasing, individuals are made to believe that their lack of effort is the cause for their condition. The overall result is to obstruct individuals from coming together, to realize that the system is the cause of their problems, and the need to work together to build resistance against the system.

Not only this, but these capitalist values portray the 'market' as the platform where individuals can realize their true 'freedom'. Even though this 'freedom to consume' is only for those who have the money to do so, people are made to believe that everyone can benefit from their individual initiative under capitalism. The belief that individuals can fulfil their aspirations to have a particular lifestyle or consume products of specific brands, isolates them into cocoons.

We can see the strong impact of these capitalist values among the students. Students are continuously facing this barrage of capitalist values. This results in the growth of a disbelief – that the status quo cannot be changed. Even more cynically, there grows a distrust in collective action. The impact can be seen everywhere, but the intensity is even more pronounced in the urban and metropolitan areas. The growing influence of the 'market' has undermined the organized student movement on various campuses, including some premier campuses. Capitalist values, such as individualism, have impacted the culture of campus politics. Arguments are made against the relevance of mass membership in student organizations; the emphasis is on spontaneous struggles and not on organized structure. The capitalist ideology makes individual freedom the top priority and considers individual efforts more important than collective efforts. While the attacks on education from the ruling classes are becoming more centralized, and there is an urgent need to build strong unity, these capitalist values are also becoming roadblocks to realizing collective strength.

This trend of individualism is not the only threat to the organized student movement. The same policies of the 'market' promote depoliticization in a new form. SFI's programme rightly identifies this depoliticization:[1]

[1] 'Programme', Students' Federation of India. http://sficec.org/organisation/programme

> Every demand for education, employment opportunities, and the right to work, and every slogan in defence of civil rights such as the right to speech, assembly, and association, and every protest against any injustice or oppression are invariably connected with the policies of the state, and thus assume a political character. In the face of this reality, it is hypocritical to subscribe to bankrupt slogans such as 'students should abstain from politics' and 'education should be apolitical'. The Students' Federation of India believes that such deceptive slogans have the political motivation of perpetuating political ignorance among the student community to conceal from them the harsh implications of the anti-people policies of the ruling classes, thus helping the conservative, exploitative social order to stay.

Today we are witnessing depoliticization in new and varied forms. Many small student groups with connections to NGOs and 'civil society organizations' have emerged over the last few years, particularly in the university centres. These groups have attracted some of the very brightest and most talented people. These organizations seek to disassociate the students' movement from the larger democratic movement of the country in the name of autonomy. They fight against the development of an organized democratic student movement, while they, themselves, are organized around specific anti-organization ideas. We must remember that these tendencies are not limited to our country. The experiences of major student movements over the last few years in Greece, Chile, Quebec, and elsewhere show that such tendencies have emerged everywhere. In fact, the ruling class promotes and aggravates such tendencies to prevent the creation of solid and organized movements.

What these groups are doing in the name of 'autonomy' is weakening the possibility of developing resistance against the policies of the ruling class. At a time when there is a far-right-wing government at the centre, and when there is a need for united actions, we must be aware of and guard against the harmful role of such groups. The student movement must discuss the challenge of depoliticization in all its forms at various levels and adopt appropriate plans of action to counter and check them. While doing so, we must not forget who are the main political enemies confronting the student movement. Unity and ideological struggle against such groups will have to go hand in hand with the struggle against the ruling class.

A REVOLUTION DOES NOT HAPPEN OVERNIGHT

There is yet another trend where groups of students are always ready for overnight revolution through radical actions. These groups don't believe in educating the masses of students but always insist on militant actions. Militancy, however, is measured not by force exerted at the barricades but by the depth of mass participation in movements. In many central institutions where these groups exist, working in the name of the Left – whether independent Left or true Left – they often bank on blockades and indefinite strikes, typically at the expense of building mass movements.

THE BATTLE OF IDEAS NEEDS TO BE ROOTED IN THE MASS MOVEMENTS

Educational institutions are the battlefield of ideas. It is the responsibility of the progressive student movement to lead the fight to push progressive ideas into the university. How should this struggle be conducted? Is it enough to raise slogans with these ideas, organize seminars and conferences, or should one organize militant struggles against the oppressor? If the latter, then how should these struggles be organized? How must a student organization analyze the struggle over ideas on campus? Is this struggle to be conducted at a theoretical and ideological level alone, or must it reflect the material conditions and policies on our campuses?

Our understanding is that this battle of ideas has to be in conjunction with the mass mobilization of students. Our idea of an egalitarian society – imagines equality for all and aims to end all exploitation – essentially means we are against all kinds of discrimination and against the policies that lead to discrimination and deprivation for the masses in general and students in particular. So, if we want to lead this struggle of ideas, then we have to wage a genuine battle against these policies. For example, if there is a fee hike on campuses that deprives students of their higher education, the struggle against the fee hike is the struggle for equality against the policies of the ruling class. When the government policies are shrinking the number of scholarships and fellowships for students from deprived sections, and there is an attack on reservations, the battle of ideas is really a struggle against these policies. When the ruling class's ideas teach the values of individualism and consumerism, the battle of ideas means mobilizing the students to create an organized student movement with structures and committees where they learn how to function collectively and how to create an egalitarian society.

It is the battle of ideas when students learn to fight for their cause through their own experiences; when they learn that the strength of the masses and their struggle can change the policies in favour of common students and challenge the ideas of the ruling class. It is our task to prepare students for sustained struggles, to teach them that the ideas of 'heroism', fighting for only radical actions – full of romanticism and devoid of basic organization where a few individuals become champions through their efforts alone – will not bring about the necessary change, because it isolates itself from the larger struggle of the masses. The battle of ideas does not happen in a vacuum but is realized in practice.

It is in this world that we have built our student movement.

On the one hand, globalization policies are erasing the boundaries for earning profits but are, on the other hand, confining people to individual cocoons. This effectively means that the policies affecting students might have social ramifications, but the ruling class's ideology makes the affected student unconcerned and essentially selfish.

Based on our rich experience, we can concretely analyze the prevailing situation on campuses in other parts of India and build movements based on the masses that are sustained and sharpened. This process will help us mobilize students against the anti-student policies and underlying neoliberal economics, the politics of the ruling class, and their ideology of exploitation.

Fight Back Against Right-wing Onslaughts: Some Experiences from Delhi University

Vikas Bhadauria

When your origins are rooted in resistance, you will always find yourself on the other side of power. This is true for Delhi University (DU), whose walls are a historical testimony to numerous student movements and their progressive legacy, beginning with the Indian Independence movement and continuing to the democratic struggles against the present regime. During the university's formative years in the 1920s, students joined the independence movement in large numbers and challenged the very founders of the varsity. They played a crucial role in the anti-imperialist Civil Disobedience and Quit India Movements.

In the post-independence era, students at DU coordinated and concretized a string of protests across the country. They actively participated in the aggressive and militant movement that became known as 'JP Andolan'.[1]

[1] During the 1970s, a student uprising was led by Jayprakash Narayan in Bihar, who called for a 'Total Revolution' against the 'misrule and corruption' by the state government. This uprising escalated, and it became a movement against the then Congress government under Prime Minister Indira Gandhi. Students from across various political affiliations joined the movement in large numbers.

The present-day anomalies in DU's student politics, which we will discuss, are not because students have become politically passive or that crucial support for democracy has waned on campus. Instead, it is a reflection of the policies that have crippled the democratic institutions and voices on the campus, carried out by the current dispensation that owes its existence to the once politically charged vibrant character of the university.

By their very nature, universities are centres of knowledge production, learning, and enlightenment. This involves learning about the inequalities in both educational institutions and society and then translating these learned theories and values into praxis and advocacy outside the classroom. To limit the students' right to activism on campus is to dismiss and defeat the very objective of higher learning. There is a fundamental relationship between classrooms and activism. The learned values of justice, equality, secularism, freedom, and democracy in the classrooms are made redundant if they are not materialized and fought for in our day-to-day lives. Education equips students with scientific inquiry and the art of critical thinking. Hence, it makes them important political actors in a modern democracy.

Since the university's inception, the progressive sections within DU have played a vital role in fighting and struggling against the various forms of injustice. From the Indian freedom struggle to building iconic progressive movements – recently concerning the rights of students and teachers – the students, the teaching faculty, and staff have together registered a direct fight against the authoritarian administration and the state. Ramjas college provided shelter to freedom fighters such as Chandra Shekhar Azad during the freedom struggle. Colleges, such as the Hindu, St. Stephen's, Zakir Hussain, and the Indraprastha College for Women, mobilized students and the masses for the Quit India Movement under the leadership of Mahatma Gandhi.

In current times, the progressive left sections at the university have built a larger network of solidarity and have been relentlessly agitating against the repressive Modi government and its henchman VC-led administration. The students have fearlessly fought against every attempt of the successive governments to introduce neoliberal reforms in the education sector and the communalization of the campus. Examples include the successful prolonged anti-FourYear Undergraduate Programme (FYUP) struggle in 2014 and the fight against the forceful imposition of the Credit-Based-Choice-System (CBCS) in 2015. In 2017, the students also registered massive protests against the Akhil Bharatiya Vidyarthi Parishad (ABVP) for attacking students and teachers of Ramjas College for organizing a seminar on the topic of 'Cultures of Protest'. In 2019, the students vehemently opposed and forced the university to remove the unauthorized installation, by the ABVP, of a bust of the ultra-right ideologue V.D. Savarkar. As exemplified in the latest series of protests against the unconstitutional Citizenship (Amendment) Act, 2019 (CAA) and National Register of Citizens (NRC), DU students have registered one of the largest mobilizations in the university's history.

RULING CLASS POLITICS AND THE APOLITICAL CAMPUSES

Like the rest of the universities in the country, the student movement at DU is facing an unprecedented double challenge: the aggressive attempts of privatization and the dismantling of the students' democratic rights. Once one of the most political campuses, DU is slowly becoming an abode for apolitical students – a manifestation of the government's concerted efforts to depoliticize the campus spaces and orchestrate organized violence to demonize students' activism.

The efforts of the ruling party and its allies on the campus to stifle dissent are not only carried out politically, but an overall discourse is being built that attempts to create two major divisions on campus: first, the manufactured division of the unbridled ideas of nationalism – 'nationalists' and 'anti-nationalists', which also equates to their idea of good and bad citizens and second, the division between classroom education and politics. Both these divisions, over time, actively encourage the students to keep a safe distance from any forms of political activity on campus, even those that affect them directly. This narrative not only helps in absolving the right-wing and its fringes but also supports the state's use of excessive violence against the students. This discourse of division among the student community has led to the militarization of the campus. Police, paramilitary personnel, and plain-clothed cops from the special cells can be found in every corner of the DU campus, surveilling and gathering information twenty-four hours a day.

The so-called division between classroom education and politics seeks to restrain the students within the confines of the classroom and educational institutions. This binary dictates their social role, wherein they are expected to only read 'textbooks' and gain 'knowledge' within the four walls of the college. Furthermore, another basic supposition is that if they study at a public institution funded by taxpayers' money, they are not permitted to indulge in any other activity outside their classrooms. Their freedom of expression is limited. The right to dissent ceases to exist for the students as it is meant only for full-time politicians. The effect of this binary is now apparent, with a larger section of students getting depoliticized with each passing year.

THE NEOLIBERAL REFORMS IMPACTING HIGHER EDUCATION

The higher education system has been subjected to a series of neoliberal reforms causing structural changes in the institutions and the very objectives of education. All of these neoliberal reforms, including the semester system, FYUP, CBCS, and now the National Education Policy, 2020 (NEP), are aimed at curtailing the responsibility of the State and transforming it from being a Welfare State to being a regulator of the economy whose duty would be solely to frame laws and create necessary policy to commodify the educational system and its entities.

When the dynamics of the market forces are allowed to act in the educational system freely, they mould students to serve the ever-changing requirements of the labour market. Without due deliberations with the stakeholders, the hasty introduction of neoliberal policies will ultimately result in a change in the traditional roles and relationship dynamics within the educational system. The new system wants the students to acquire the role of consumers and teachers to internalize the role of salespersons, thus driving the sales of 'products and services' offered by the institutions, which will, in turn, act as businesses. The FYUP was introduced to allow students to tailor their courses to remain competitive and to acquire 'skills' in place of 'knowledge'. This ostensibly was done by giving them mobility to move across colleges and universities to complete their major and to opt-out of courses even before completion when they felt trained and ready to serve the labour market requirements. When FYUP failed, CBCS was introduced to replace it. CBCS was a replication of FYUP; both systems were aimed at diluting the honours course to give room for marketable courses to provide academic freedom to students.

DU has been at the epicentre of all these attempts to reform the educational system. The effectiveness of policy changes and their implementation are analyzed to replicate the same design at other universities. It is very apparent from the changes in the study pattern during the last nine years that the government is under tremendous pressure from other developed countries and the World Bank to reorient the educational system to respond to the needs of capital and the 'free market'.

The introduction of the semester system in 2010 was the first step in the agenda of pushing higher education towards privatization and commercialization. The semester system's so-called purpose was to provide a 'flexible educational system' that allowed students mobility in academia. Still, it virtually curbed their mobility and participation in activities beyond the classroom, which enhances deeper learning, one of the many objectives of university education.

Before 2010, DU used to be a vibrant campus, giving students ample time to participate in extracurricular activities and various kinds of social and political endeavours. The current attempt to privatize every inch of the campus to cover up the crisis created by fund cuts and the withdrawal of government support has led to the shrinking of democratic spaces that were previously accessible to students and teachers.

The Arts Faculty lawns and Vivekananda Statue, which once were important protest sites at the university, have now become private spaces. Anyone, including those not even distantly related to the university, can hold a program inside the Arts Faculty if they can afford to pay the hefty fee. Thus, this privatization has precluded the students from accessing the campus space. The Students' Activity Centre above the Spic-Macay canteen was the space where student organizations, groups, and societies held their meetings. For several years, a bookstore that was a thriving hub known for its leftist literature and progressive writings was shut down unilaterally without citing any cause. This series of small encroachments on the students' rights went largely unnoticed.

The NEP 2020, whose goal is to change the educational system entirely to make it more exclusionary, goes even further than what other reforms sought to achieve. It not only seeks to privatize and commercialize the educational system but also aims for an extreme form of centralization. It proposes to set up a Rashtriya Shiksha Aayog – National Education Commission – that will be chaired by the Prime Minister and will be comprised of other Union Ministers and a small number of educationists on the board. Rashtriya Shiksha Aayog will be solely responsible for all decisions, both administrative and academic. This means it will leave no space for teacher or student representation on various bodies and committees of the university who are presently involved in collective consultations and deliberations. In a real sense, the students' role will be defined as merely a consumer of the educational system. Unfortunately, the NEP now recommends the four-year undergraduate degree program, five years after it was scrapped following intense protests by the students and teachers.

Soon, in pursuance of NEP, the government will enact a law to replace the University Grants Commission (UGC) and the All-India Council for Technical Education (AICTE) with the Higher Education Commission of India (HECI). One of the central functions of the HECI will be to encourage and grant autonomy to 'good' performing educational institutions according to the standards it lays out. The NEP mandates that the government is not only required to ease norms for setting up private universities but should proactively help private players in setting up new educational institutions. The objective is now apparent as to why the Ministry of Human Resource Development (MHRD) – now called the Ministry of Education (MoE) – awarded Reliance's Jio Institute with the Institution of Eminence (IoE) status in 2018 even before the institute was set up. Until now, the university exists only on paper. Despite this, its inclusion in the list of the Institutes of Eminence solidifies the government's support of the true objectives of the NEP. The tag of IoE is given to ten public and ten private universities, which ensures that they are given complete academic and administrative autonomy. Once the institutes are granted autonomy or – more accurately – are privatized, it is unclear how the mandated reservation policy will be adhered to in faculty appointments and admissions, furthering the exclusion of marginalized sections of society. The response of an RTI filed by Mulayam Singh on 2 November 2016 at DU revealed grim statistics in the appointment of teaching faculty members against the Unreserved/Scheduled Caste (SC)/ Scheduled Tribe (ST)/OBC

Name of the post	Unreserved	SC	ST	OBC	Total
Professor	294 (98%)	4 (1.3 %)	2 (0.66%)	-	300
Associate Professor	170 (90.9%)	15 (8.02%)	2 (1.06%)	-	187
Assistant Professor	161 (60.75%)	42 (15.84%)	22 (8.03%)	40 (15.09%)	265

categories in the departments of DU.

The under-representation of faculty members from marginalized sections continues with little or no visible change. According to the reservation policy in recruitment, 14 per cent for SCs, 7.5 per cent for STs, and 27 per cent for OBCs were to be reserved in the appointment of teaching faculty or other employees. However, from the above table, it is clear that the mandated reservations were not implemented. This is a reflection of the conservative attitude of the administration.

We have demonstrated the administration's attitude. Now, we will expose the attacks of the right-wing forces on the university.

THE RIGHT-WING ASSAULT ON DELHI UNIVERSITY

Academic freedom on campus has been under assault not only from the authoritarian state government but also from its right-wing allies like Akhil Bharatiya Vidyarthi Parishad (ABVP). The ceaseless attempts to curb academic discussions, alter syllabi and texts critical of the Hindutva politics, disrupt events, and stifle independent voices have become the norm.

ABVP has disrupted the university on multiple occasions. True to its fascistic ideology, it boasts each of those acts of vandalism with a sense of pride. The university and many colleges were forced to cancel events, including seminars, movie screenings, plays, and lectures, as these activities were branded as anti-national acts. In instances where a few colleges stood firm and refused to cancel the events, the ABVP resorted to vandalism and violence.

In August 2015, the ABVP-led Delhi University Students' Union (DUSU) disrupted the screening of *Muzaffarnagar Baaqi Hai*, directed by Nakul Singh Sawhney, at Kirori Mal College.

During the screening, even teachers were physically assaulted by the ABVP members.[2]

In the same year, the Shri Guru Tegh Bahadur Khalsa College's drama society's street play production of Ankur's *Welcome to the Machine* was disrupted by ABVP. The play portrays the use of violence by the Sangh and its affiliate organization to divide and polarize along religious lines.

In March 2016, the ABVP disrupted a play by a progressive theatre group called Sangwari, titled *JNU ka Sach* (Truth about JNU), calling it offensive and anti-national.[3] The ABVP was again caught up in fresh controversy within a few days. It brazenly indulged in hooliganism and disrupted a seminar on *Ambedkar on Caste and Social Justice* at Deshbandhu College, and forced the organizers to chant '*Bharat Mata Ki Jai*' (Victory for Mother India). Two months later, the ABVP again disrupted a seminar on *Annihilation of Caste* at the same College and demanded the organizers chant '*Bharat Mata ki Jai*'.

On 27 October 2016, the ABVP disrupted a public meeting, titled *Idea of a University*, organized by the All India Students' Association (AISA) at the Arts Faculty. They attacked the gathering of students and teachers with stones.

The new low in the ABVP's fear-mongering politics came on 21 February 2017, when ABVP disrupted a two-day seminar titled *Cultures of Protest* organized by Ramjas College's Literary Society and English Department. The ABVP not only disrupted the event but locked teachers and students inside and physically assaulted them with hockey sticks. They also threw stones and bricks at

[2] *Muzaffarnagar Baaqi Hai* is a documentary film released in early 2015. It documented the communal violence in two districts of Western Uttar Pradesh in 2013. The violence left around 100 dead and about 50,000 displaced. The victims were mostly Muslims.

[3] In 2016, the JNUSU President along with two students were put behind bars on allegation of raising 'anti-national' slogans. Using the national media, the BJP-led government vilified the university as being a 'hub of anti-national activities'. The play tried to portray the actual picture of the progressive nature of the university and its united resistance.

the conference room in the presence of heavy police deployment. Violent clashes followed outside the college premises the next day, which left hundreds of students injured, including faculty members.

Although prior protection was sought from the police at all the events, they did nothing to protect the students. The Delhi Police gave a free hand to the ABVP members to go on a rampage. Bharatiya Janata Party (BJP), with the help of the ABVP (the students' wing of the RSS) and their teachers' front in DU – National Democratic Teachers' Front (NDTF), has been attempting to rewrite and saffronize the curriculum of DU as well.

In July 2019, the ABVP coerced four departments of DU – English, Political Science, Sociology, and History – to alter the syllabi of undergraduate programs to advance its political interest towards a Hindu majoritarian state subverting academic freedom. The ABVP's assault on the syllabi cannot be seen in isolation. Instead, it works as a henchman for teachers associated with NDTF, an affiliate of Rashtriya Swayamsevak Sangh (RSS). NDTF marked up and objected to the syllabi of many disciplines in the humanities on non-academic grounds, calling them 'leftist' and 'propagandist'. As a result, papers on the Indian caste system, homosexuality in Hindu scriptures, and Gujarat riots, among other things, were removed, papers that exposed the hate politics of Sangh. After this, the ABVP resorted to vandalism and threatened the progressive teachers over the issue.

The ABVP has similarly objected to multiple syllabi in the past as well. In 2008, the ABVP, along with Vishva Hindu Parishad (VHP), protested against the inclusion of an essay by A.K Ramanujan titled *Three Hundred Ramayanas: Five Examples and Three Thoughts on Translation* in the history syllabus. The ABVP claimed it was anti-Hindu and that it portrayed Hindu gods and goddesses in a derogatory manner. Similarly, in 2010, Periyar's book, *Sacchi Ramayan,* was also dropped from the History syllabus by the academic council due to political pressure. For a decade, the BJP was not in power. During this period, the ABVP couldn't muster enough backing from State actors to bring about changes in other syllabi.

In 2017, NDTF and ABVP opposed the introduction of another book by Nandini Sundar, *The Burning Forest: India's War in Bastar,* in the sociology syllabus of DU. Not only forms of texts, art, and content that portrays the Sangh Parivar in a bad light come under assault, but violent attacks on the faculty members and students have also become a common occurrence at the university.

In 2018, DU's standing committee for academic affairs, under pressure from the Sangh affiliates, removed two books – *Subalterns and Sovereigns: An Anthropological History of Bastar* by sociologist Nandini Sundar and *Against Ecological Romanticism: Verrier Elwin and the Making of an Anti-modern Tribal Identity* by Jawaharlal Nehru University (JNU) Professor, Archana Prasad – on non-academic merits, claiming that the books were subversive and contaminated the mind of the students.

The coercive activities by the ABVP are directly aimed at shutting down every possible space for debate and discussion. Inadvertent censorship allows non-stakeholders to be active decision-makers and gives them a right to take offence. Under the political pressure and intimidation of the ABVP, the alteration of the syllabi violates academic freedom and allows voices who are not experts on the subjects to outweigh scholarly work and critical inquiry.

More than the assault, it is the complicity of the police and the university administration and their impunity that allows the ABVP members a free hand. This worries us more and raises serious questions on the present law and order situation on campus.

THE FIGHT-BACK AMID CHALLENGES

The DU student movement has undergone many challenges; many come from within the students' movement, but they also come from the state-controlled administration. One challenge that confronted the movement from within was on the issue of identity such as caste, gender, religion, region, etc.

On the one hand, the government is making concerted attempts to promote a business model of the educational system, which seeks to increase the managerial and financial control of the university; on the other side, the student movement is witnessing a high degree of fragmentation with the rise of identity politics. This fragmentation of the student movement across fault lines, taking the identity down to the individual level, has made the mobilization of the students and realization of a 'greater collective identity' a difficult task.

The degree to which particular students may feel moved to fight for a specific cause in a particular context may have more to do with a convergence of their other identities than with the mere fact that they are enrolled in a university. Towards the left side of the spectrum, identity politics has caused students to realize their identity. Adherence to personalized identities springing into spontaneous reactionary movements has replaced ideological commitments leading to political actions and mobilisation. Various organizations based on religion, caste, region, and gender with all kinds of ideologies, have forayed in DU. These attempts to tone down the collective identity and uphold personal identity have proved antithetical to the organized student movement as identity politics negates broader solidarity. This, however, is a challenge for the progressive movements to tackle. How to address the issues of identity that are questioning oppression based on gender, caste, and religion are part of the progressive political spectrum.

It's not that DU is an apolitical campus; the vast participation of students on many occasions has proven this wrong. Against the organized violence in Ramjas, some 10,000 students from across the colleges of DU marched in solidarity. The most distressing part was that this spontaneous mobilization of students dispersed, and we haven't witnessed such a robust mobilization since. The post-modern assault on student activism and the fear of being ridiculed for submitting one's individuality to the discipline of some organizations prevent students from joining the organized student movement.

THE ORGANIZED STUDENTS' MOVEMENT AND THE IMPACT OF SOCIAL MEDIA

In the information age, activism has taken many forms. The generation we are part of believes in 'slacktivism', which has harmed the organized student movement more than contributed materially. Social media activism in the context of student activism at DU has helped to inform and educate students on various issues but failed considerably to organize them or to inspire them to take their political advocacy to the mat to make a change. The organized student movement at DU has been reduced to spontaneous one-day outbursts of liberals. Having witnessed a series of attacks on the rights of its stakeholders and its academic character, DU hasn't been fully successful in fighting back, although there were attempts.

It's not that there wasn't sufficient political consciousness or effective dissemination of available information, but students, as well as activists, have failed to understand that there is more to be done beyond 'like, share, and comment'. The one-to-one mass contact of students through class-to-class campaigns for protests and public meetings has been replaced by social media posts and online posters, which isn't enough to make the change or intervention we require on a campus like the DU, as political awareness is decreasing at a rapid pace. Education without agitating and organizing and vice-versa defeat all intents and purposes of student activism or any form of activism.

The students' movement along with the teachers-staff associations, have been able to fight the neoliberal designs of the State to a great extent. They have effectively been able to force the State to roll back the FYUP that was discussed earlier in the essay. Whenever the right-wing attacked the students, all the progressive student organizations offered a formidable resistance. Progressive student organizations must continue to demonstrate that 'slacktivism' cannot achieve the necessary goals to maintain academic freedoms and a university system open to all, regardless of class, caste, religion or region.

Afterwords

The Disappearance of Najeeb Ahmed

Satarupa Chakraborty

An interview with Fatima Nafees[1]

India's premier university, the Jawaharlal Nehru University (JNU), located in the nation's capital, was in the news once again in late 2016. As is usual, in October that year, the country was preparing for a series of festivals. But JNU students, instead of celebrating, were on the streets protesting. An overwhelming number of people at the university were shocked and terrified by the mysterious disappearance of Najeeb Ahmed, a promising young student who had just enrolled in the university with his dream of pursuing a master's program in Biotechnology.

His disappearance was preceded by acts of violence by a group of students who belonged to a right-wing organization, Akhil Bharatiya Vidyarthi Parishad (ABVP), on the night between 14 and 15 October. The incident occurred amid the hostel's elections at JNU's Mahi-Mandvi hostel. A group of ABVP members were campaigning for their candidates and entered Najeeb's room. There were no eyewitnesses to what happened inside his room. However, many hostel residents, the security guards, the Jawaharlal Nehru University Students' Union (JNUSU) President, and the hostel wardens witnessed the violent attack on Najeeb

[1] Conducted on 17 November 2018 and updated in May 2022.

by the ABVP members on the day preceding his disappearance. Despite the gravity of the situation and intense communal slurs and threats hurled by the ABVP members, Najeeb is neither given any protection by the university administration nor any assurance of an impartial enquiry. Najeeb went missing from the university the next day, in broad daylight.

There was a massive uproar from the student community following the incident. The students' slogan – *Bring Back Najeeb* – reverberated around the university's administrative building, the local police station, and in the streets of Delhi. However, the JNU authorities allowed ABVP to run a rampant communal campaign on campus and let the perpetrators of violence to roam free throughout the campus. The police and the Central Bureau of Investigation (CBI) failed to find any trace of Najeeb.

The students protested continuously, demanding the government must take sufficient measures to find Najeeb. Fatima Nafees, Najeeb's mother, joined those protests and camped out in Delhi, seeking justice.

Satarupa Chakraborty from the Tricontinental Research, India spoke to Fatima Nafees to learn about her fight, seeking the truth about her son's whereabouts and her journey.

Can you tell us about your family, your children, and how you raised them?

My husband and I both are from Badaun. We have four children, three sons and a daughter. We have lived a simple life. Our family faced a lot of crises financially and otherwise. Despite our several ups and downs, we tried to provide as much support as possible for our children's education. We taught our children the value of money and using resources judiciously so that they learn not to waste them. We managed our lifestyle with few resources. At times, we could spend very little on food. Our children never went hungry, but neither did they get an abundance of exotic food. They lived on the minimal resources that we were able to provide. But we ensured that their education did not suffer. There were times when we did not have enough money to pay their fees. During those times, we borrowed from our relatives and paid them back when we could earn enough money. We sold off the few assets we owned and invested that money into our children's education.

Why did you consider their education so important? In your opinion, what value does higher education have?

I am not very well-educated, but I can read. My father was associated with newspaper work. During and since my childhood, whatever I could read in Urdu, I used to read, sometimes newspapers, sometimes books. I learned a lot of things by reading them. Education is crucial because it provides the vehicle for knowledge. I never wanted my children to discontinue their education due to any crisis. So, I first ensured Najeeb's education with the idea that if the eldest son studies, the younger ones will follow, and ultimately all of them could fulfil their own aims for pursuing an education. I am happy that they fulfilled my dream. My youngest child, and only daughter, has the dream of becoming a doctor, just like her eldest brother, Najeeb. My two other sons, Haseeb and Mujeeb, have earned both bachelor's and master's degrees in technology, and they are in the process of doing something good to serve their family and the country.

You mentioned that you invested first in Najeeb's education. What was Najeeb's journey in pursuing higher education?

Najeeb was the eldest. All my children continued to pursue higher education – they are students of science. Of all of them, however, Najeeb stood out when it came to his studies. He always showed great passion and sincerity towards his studies. Najeeb preferred to devote himself to his books rather than keeping himself busy with other things, which are of interest to most students at his age. Sometimes, he watched cricket matches, but most of his day was spent studying despite what others did around him – whether I was watching a TV serial or his peers were playing or doing other recreational things. He was never bothered or distracted from focusing on his books. He went to a private school and studied there until the eighth standard, where he topped the class. His passion for and love of doing well continued, which was also reflected in his results, and he did well in the twelfth standard too.

When his grandfather was admitted to the hospital, I saw the young students serving as doctors. Since then, I dreamt that Najeeb would become a doctor one day. He passionately started preparing for the medical entrance exam to fulfil my dream. In his first attempt, he missed getting a seat for the medical entrance exam by a thin margin of four marks. However, he got a seat to pursue other medical courses. Najeeb asked us to give him one more year to prepare for the medical entrance exam; he wanted to give it one last try. As he scored high marks, a coaching institute in Kanpur offered to coach him for a reduced price. He went to study there. Unfortunately, he fell ill within a couple of months, and we had to bring him back home. Later, after he recovered, he could no longer pursue the medical profession since, being the eldest son, he had to take on responsibilities in supporting the family. Completing his education took on even more importance. So, he dropped the idea of preparing for medical school and joined the bachelor's program at a college in Bareilly. He used to travel from Badaun to Bareilly daily. He finally earned his degree with high marks from college. Afterwards, he took several entrance exams and qualified for admission to many premier universities in our country, such as Jamia Hamdard University, JMI, AMU, and JNU. Najeeb had a dream to study at JNU. As he qualified for admission to JNU, he received greetings from friends and family as JNU is considered to be India's Oxford University. I was somewhat hesitant to send him to Delhi as he would be far from home. But getting admitted to JNU was his dream, so I did not hold him back. His admission to JNU was a matter of pride for people in our locality, as not many students from our town secured admission to such a reputable Indian university.

When did Najeeb join JNU? Was he happy at the university once he began?

Najeeb began attending JNU in July 2016. He was very pleased to be admitted there as he thought he had joined India's Oxford University. He seemed to have liked the campus very much. There were about thirty students in his class – most of whom were girls. He called me during the Rakhi festival and said, 'Ammi, one of my classmates tied a rakhi on me today'. He was pleased about that. From everything he shared with me after joining JNU, I always felt that he was in a good place where people cared for each other. JNU was, however, being defamed at the time my son was admitted. It was in the news regularly, and most of the Indian media portrayed it negatively. Once my son was at JNU, I realized how false those narratives were, as he used to tell me stories of how there was a great sense of love for each other, which was part of their campus life.

Did Najeeb tell you about any tension with students on campus? Did he tell you about any fights in his hostel on 14 October 2016?

Because of his nature, Najeeb was always admired by his friends and others around him. Since childhood, he had never gotten involved in any fight. He spent two and half months at JNU, and he never mentioned any negative things. He had been a resident of the Mahi-Mandvi hostel for only fifteen days when the incident occurred. Everything was new to him there. He hardly knew anyone in the hostel.

In the evening between 14 and 15 October, I was up until late as I could not sleep due to health issues. I got a call from Najeeb at around 2:00 am. I picked up the call immediately and asked him why he was calling so late. He said, 'Some students have beaten me up in the hostel. My roommate and a few other students have taken me to the Safdarjung hospital. Some students have filed a police complaint against me'. He did not explain further. Hearing about the hospital and the police complaint, I got scared and worried. I told him that I would start from Badaun immediately and be there by morning. I boarded the bus, which left Badaun at 4:00 am. It takes seven or eight hours to reach Delhi. In the morning, I spoke to him over the phone. It was 9 am. I asked him to go to the mess and have breakfast. He told me that breakfast time was over. I asked him to eat something and hung up the phone. Najeeb knew that I was travelling all the way from Badaun to meet him.

What did you see after reaching his hostel in JNU?

His broken chappal (sandals) was lying on the staircase. I rushed into his room. His roommate Qasim was in the room. I enquired about Najeeb, but Qasim could not tell me where Najeeb was. I waited in his room for some time, thinking that he might have gone to the washroom. His phone and wallet were still in the room, so clearly, he had not left the hostel. I got restless after some time. I asked Qasim and my son Mujeeb (who had accompanied me) to look for Najeeb. They could not find him. I was anxious; I knew very little about what had happened on the previous night. I started probing his roommate, and he finally told me there was a fight between Najeeb and some students belonging to the ABVP on the night of 14 October. I was shocked to learn this; my son was a first-semester student on campus. He had no affiliation with any student organization; how could he get involved in a fight with members of a student organization?

After waiting a few hours for my son's return, I broke down. I started crying; nothing made any sense to me. I kept asking, 'Where is Najeeb'? No one could tell me anything!

Some hostel residents who saved Najeeb the previous night came to his room and informed me that they saw Najeeb being beaten up by a group of students. Meanwhile, the students from

ABVP had already started spreading the lie that Najeeb had beaten them up. They claimed that Najeeb initiated the fight after seeing the *kalewa* (Hindu religious wrist band made of cotton thread) on their hands. What I did know was that some people wanted to frame my son. How could my boy – a boy who had gracefully accepted a rakhi from his classmate (who was a Hindu) – suddenly turn violent after seeing a kalewa on someone's wrist? He had never shown any intolerance towards others. It was unbelievable!

I asked the security personnel to request a vehicle from the administration to start looking for Najeeb. They made us wait, but they did not provide a vehicle. Having received no cooperation from the authorities, some of the hostel residents went out to search for Najeeb. But they could not find him anywhere.

When did you register your complaint with the police? What was your experience there?

We had to wait twenty-four hours to file a missing person's complaint. Along with the JNUSU members, my son Mujeeb and I went to register the complaint at the Vasant Kunj police station. The police did not allow anyone who had accompanied us to be inside the room. A few students who were eyewitnesses to the violence against Najeeb were also sent outside. The station house officer (SHO) told me, 'If you want your son back, write as I say'. I wanted my son back, but I was not aware of the conspiracy behind this attack. Three times my son, Mujeeb, repeated that the hostel residents identified those who assaulted Najeeb and that their names should be mentioned in the complaint. The police officer responded by threatening us not to write the attackers' names in the complaint if I wanted my son back in twenty-four hours.

What was the role of the JNU administration in the case? What has been your personal experience with the administration vis-à-vis Najeeb's case?

Our family has been surviving the constant pain of his

disappearance for the last several years. We could not come out of it. What is more distressing is the fact that the university authority has shown utter disinterest in and disregard for providing us with any support. Whether it is the case of Rohith Vemula or Najeeb, all we have received from the authorities is harassment and intimidation, which has added to our pain. The university administration was indifferent to what happened on the evening of 14 October. They treated us with utter disdain, as if we were the ones who had committed the crime. After Najeeb's disappearance, I wanted to meet with the JNU VC and other officials to discuss the matter and seek their help so that the process of finding Najeeb would be smoother and faster. The JNU authority did not meet with us even out of a sense of decency. When I almost forcibly entered the administrative building, they behaved with the utmost insensitivity. What was I asking for that they refused to provide? Was it not the responsibility of the university authorities to cooperate with us when within the confines of their university, an incident of group violence occurred and a student disappeared afterwards? Was it not the responsibility of the respective authorities to ensure proper measures after my son was mercilessly beaten by a group of students belonging to ABVP? All I asked for was a letter from the JNU administration to the Delhi Police confirming that the brawl took place at the Mahi-Mandvi hostel the night before Najeeb went missing and requesting that the Delhi Police do everything possible to find Najeeb. Instead of taking this responsibility, the JNU administration shied away from it and behaved irresponsibly. What should we take away from such acts? Should we not think that the university administration was involved in the entire conspiracy that led to my son's disappearance?

On Najeeb's birthday, 18 October 2018, a few JNU students and I gathered at the administrative building's stairs. The students were putting out candles. Suddenly, a group of security guards came, threatening us with disciplinary actions. I was angry and sad. This is a university; my child had a dream to attend this university. He withdrew his admission from Jamia Millia Islamia (JMI) to study at JNU. Today, at that same university, we were treated unconscionably, where even lighting candles for his birthday became a criminal act!

What were your demands from the government? What response did you receive?

We have held several protests in Delhi. We demonstrated at all public places where we could democratically raise our demands. A student went missing from a central university in broad daylight, but no one was held responsible. The administration, the ABVP members, the hostel wardens, the police – no one was questioned. The first investigation by the JNU Chief Proctor's office found nine ABVP students guilty of assaulting Najeeb. That report was later changed. In several pamphlets JNUSU highlighted all these facts in detail. But those criminals went free.

JNU protests, at that time, were so massive that the administration alone could not have been able to shield those ABVP members without some help from the powerful from outside. I was dragged away by a battalion of police during a protest in front of the India Gate. There were several incidents of lathi-charge and detention of the protestors. We were only demanding that the process of tracing Najeeb be accelerated and that the JNU administration and the perpetrators of violence be held accountable. The government did everything to save them and to punish us.

You have been leading protests demanding 'Justice for Najeeb' and 'Bring Back Najeeb' and playing an essential role in these protests. How have you been able to fight for so long? From where do you get the strength? How supportive were the JNU students and students outside JNU?

What I did, any mother would do. I have indeed been fighting for my son, and I am hopeful that he will be found one day! I shall continue the fight until he is found. But I am also fighting today for a larger cause. I am fighting so that no mother has to run from pillar to post searching for her child. I am fighting to stop any further incidents where a group of criminals has the courage and audacity to attack innocent victims.

Throughout this struggle, the JNU community played a crucial role. The students of JNU, JMI, Aligarh Muslim University (AMU), and many others have given me constant strength. I never felt that I was alone in the struggle. All progressive and democratic students' unions in Delhi and outside Delhi have extended their solidarity with the protests and become part of them. Whenever I called for a protest, these students have always supported me. Najeeb is my son; he called me *Ammi* – today, the entire fraternity of students call me *Ammi*. During this period, I developed a relationship with many students. They are all my children.

I shall not step back. As long as I am alive, this fight will continue until Najeeb is back.

What message do you want to give to ordinary people and the students of our country?

My first appeal to everyone is to remain united. I understand the pain of Radhika Vemula, Junaid's parents, and of all those families who lost their child or other loved ones. Nothing can end that pain. But I would urge everyone to stand by us today. I hope that what happened to Najeeb does not happen to anyone. I also appeal to young students to learn the lessons from the incident at JNU. I urge them to remain vigilant against such incidents occurring on any university campus. Finally, I appeal to everyone to fight until justice prevails.

'We Know the Value of Education and How it Can Uplift Society'

Pindiga Ambedkar

An interview with Radhika Vemula[1]

Educational institutions have continually witnessed students fighting for their rights. There are many issues around which the students agitate on Indian campuses. At the University of Hyderabad (UoH), the students have fought the unjust punishment meted out to five Ambedkar Students' Association (ASA) members. The struggles of ASA students are discussed in the essay by Kuldeep et al. and in an interview with Dontha Prashanth, one of the five students whom the university administration suspended. The students were fighting an administration controlled by the union government's Ministry of Human Resource Development (MHRD (now the Ministry of Education)). Rohith Vemula, unable to continue to fight the onslaught of the right-wing forces of the UoH administration, was institutionally murdered. He wrote searing letters against the institutional discrimination being faced by him and his fellow Dalit students, and in his Last Letter,[2] he wrote about what it meant to be a poor Dalit in the Indian caste

[1] Conducted on 25 November 2018 and updated in May 2022.

[2] Staff, 'My Birth is My Fatal Accident: Rohith Vemula's Searing Letter is an Indictment of Social Prejudices,' *The Wire*, 17 January 2017, https://thewire.in/caste/rohith-vemula-letter-a-powerful-indictment-of-social-prejudices.

society and the struggles one has to go through to survive in an educational institution.

His letter lit up protests across the country. Many university students and people from all walks of life across the globe stood in solidarity with the struggle of the suspended students of ASA. The shocking news of the death of her son, Rohith, reached Radhika Vemula as she awaited his return home, having prepared some of his favourite dishes. Learning that her son had succumbed to institutional murder, she, accompanied by her younger son, Raja, went to UoH to get his last glimpse. The government was so cruel that once the post-mortem was conducted, they cremated Rohith without the presence of extended family and friends. That is the level the State goes to deny dignity, even in death, to the untouchables of this country.

Radhika Vemula decided that she would continue to struggle for justice for her son and the other ASA students. She stayed put on the campus, demanding justice; she has since extended support to the students across the country for their just demands. In this interview with Pindiga Ambedkar of the Tricontinental Research, Radhika shares her story and what it meant to get her children educated as a single mother.

Could you tell us about your childhood and education?

I studied until the tenth standard (matriculation) in Kothapet, Guntur. My [adoptive] mother was a teacher. In April, I finished the tenth standard examination, and I got married in May. I failed the exam in the tenth standard. My [adoptive] parents didn't spend much on my education or on me. They used to say that there were boys in the family and other children who were younger and for whom they had to care. But there was an additional factor: I was an adopted child and not their own child, and my education was not given enough importance. After having two male children, they adopted me. They also had two daughters, the elder one was five years younger than me, and the younger one was eight years old when I got married. All of them were very young at that time. I was adopted for two primary reasons: first, my biological mother was weak, and she struggled to raise me; and second, being a girl, I could share the burden of the housework. My life has always been a struggle. From my childhood until my marriage, I faced a lot of hardships; and that continued even afterwards. During my marriage, my husband's grandfather made all the decisions. He found out that I was an adopted child and did not have any property rights. My marriage was a compromise. My husband was not aware of my details, and later when he found out, he became aggressive, so much so that I was treated almost like a slave.

How did you raise your children, and under what conditions? How did you educate them?

I was nineteen years old when I left my home. I never lost faith in my abilities. I knew how to work hard. I continued my work as a tailor. I knew that I might not get my children educated at big colleges, but I had immense faith that my children would study hard and get into government institutions for their studies. My mother paid for my children's school fees. Two of them studied in an English medium school; Raja attended a government school in Telugu medium.

I had three children – Neelima, my daughter, was the eldest; then my second child, Rohith; and finally, my youngest son, Raja. My daughter wanted to become a doctor or a district collector. She was very intelligent. I wanted my children to be highly educated. I was always worried about their future. We managed things well until suddenly I had a paralytic stroke, and it disrupted everything. Those were difficult times, as we were at my adoptive mother's home. With my deteriorated condition, our presence was seen as a burden. Sometimes, we were even asked to leave the house. Under those conditions, raising my children was a challenge. However, they did well in their examinations. Rohith stood second in school, with just one per cent mark less than the boy who stood first.

An acquaintance of mine, who used to work at the municipal school, was aware of our family conditions. She once asked me about my children, and I mentioned that Rohith would complete his tenth standard soon. She then told me about Andhra Pradesh Residential Junior College (APRJC). She said, 'If Rohith scores well, he will be accepted into APRJC'. The application fee was 300 rupees.

For ten days, I had to plead with my mother to pay for Rohith's APRJC application form. He applied to APRJC. He completed his tenth and was willing to study, but he did not have the required study materials. I showed him where the city library was so that he could access the study materials. Rohith did well on the exam and was invited to attend admissions counselling. Since my income was meagre, I submitted a government grant certificate to reduce the admission fee. Rohith was allotted a seat at the college in Kodigenahalli, Anantapur district, and he accepted it.

After his intermediate education, where did Rohith study for his undergraduate and master's degrees? How were his educational expenses met?

Rohith studied at the Hindu college in Guntur for his bachelor's degree. He wanted to study Microbiology. Rajshekhar Reddy, the then-Chief Minister, introduced a free reimbursement plan for students who wanted to attend the college. We were required to pay first, and then the fees would be reimbursed. My mother gave me the money for Rohith's admission, but not before creating a great deal of stress. We returned it to her after we received the reimbursement.

After finishing his bachelor's degree, he wanted to pursue a master's degree. At that time, coaching centres helped students prepare for the MSc entrance exam and provided the coaching free of charge. Rohith went for coaching. He attended the coaching centre for a month and then took the entrance examination, but he could not pass it on the first attempt. He returned to a coaching centre in Hyderabad, for which he had to pay around 30,000 rupees.

By then, I had begun sewing again and taking orders from a shop. It was going well. So, I contributed around 17,000 rupees, and my mother paid the remainder. Rohith prepared for the entrance examination and secured the third rank on the UoH MSc entrance examination, an all-India level test. He also secured seats at universities in Kerala and Pondicherry. Rohith eventually joined UoH. He considered UoH to be a very reputable university.

Rohith joined one of the best universities in India; what was your dream as he began university education? What did he want to become?

I was worried as Rohith was moving to Hyderabad. The Telangana movement was at its peak at that time; the police force was visible everywhere on the roads; There were several incidents of police beatings of students in the city. But, since he wanted to attend UoH, I accepted his decision. Rohith told me that if he attended UoH, he would easily get a good job. After his admission, I urged him to prepare for the UPSC examination. I wanted him to become a 'tall officer'. However, after completing his MSc, he was interested in pursuing a PhD; he wanted to become a scientist. I knew little about scientists, but I saw them talking on television during solar or lunar eclipses and how well they explained them to the people. So, with that idea of what scientists were, I thought it would be great if he became a scientist.

How did Rohith manage his education in Hyderabad amid the dire financial crisis in the family?

As he wanted to earn a PhD, he apprised me that it would take time for him to complete the courses. For some students, it took even seven or eight years. I immediately rejected that plan. However, he told me that his supervisor assured him that he could complete his PhD within four years. Given the family's financial condition and his professor's help, he was also looking for a job. But, since he had passed the all-India examination by the UGC, he earned the Junior Research Fellowship, which provided him with a scholarship of 25,000 rupees monthly.

Did Rohith send any money home from his fellowship?

For my children's education, I borrowed 40,000 rupees. The person from whom I borrowed the money only agreed to lend it to me when my mother co-signed the agreement. The loan, with interest, totalled 70,000 rupees. When Rohith got the fellowship, he would keep 5,000 rupees for himself and send 20,000 rupees home every month. Once, for almost nine months, he did not get his fellowship money. When he finally received the 2,25,000 rupees as a bulk transfer for the nine months, he sent the entire money home. I paid back the debt of 70,000 rupees.

Did Rohith share any incidents about the university with you?
Did you know Rohith and his four friends were suspended?
When did you learn about his death?

No, I was not aware of the suspensions. Every year, for the New Year, my children called me to wish me a Happy New Year. That year, Rohith did not call. I called him and asked, 'Nanna (my child) why didn't you call me?' Rohith, in an angry voice, replied, 'Why?'. I understood from his response that he was upset about something. I asked him, 'What happened?'. He said, 'Nothing happened, and everything is fine'. He simply said that he was busy as his examinations were coming up. Later, I found out the actual story.

After a few days, I called him again and asked whether he could come home for the Pongal (harvest) festival holidays as they were starting soon? Before bhogi (first) night, he asked me, 'Mummy aren't you watching television?'. I immediately panicked and asked him what was happening? He mentioned that there was a minor scuffle and that he, along with other students, was sitting in protest. I worried and told him to be careful and said, 'They will suspend you if you get involved. Make sure you pass all the examinations on time with good marks'.

I hung up the phone and asked Raja to turn on the television immediately. But I could not find anything on the news. So, I called up his friend Riyaz. Raja and Riyaz knew that Rohith had been suspended and that he was participating in the *dharna* (sit-in). Riyaz called Rohith after my call and informed him about our conversation. Rohith asked Riyaz to inform me that he would come on the following Sunday. He told Riyaz, 'Do not bring my mother to the university. But if I don't turn up on Sunday, on Monday, you can bring her to the university'.

I waited for him until Sunday evening, but Rohith did not come home. So, I called Vijay, his friend. He said that he would look for Rohith and call back. At around 4:30 pm, I got a call from someone who wanted to speak to Raja. I heard Raja cry out and then started calling people. Raja left home and said he would call me later. Later that evening, my daughter, Neelima, her husband, and her in-laws came to take me to the university. We reached the university around 2:00 am, where I learned about the incident. Rohith was dead! It was 17 January 2016.

Did anyone from the university administration – the VC or any other official – try to speak to you after the incident? What did you experience after reaching the university?

No one spoke to me. I reached the campus and witnessed a horrifying scene. It was like a movie – the police were beating students – water cannons arrived. I was so terrified. They had moved Rohith's dead body to a police van by then, and the police told me to sit in the same van. The students were sure that the police were going to harm me. They asked me not to sit in the van. Raja also asked me to stay in the *velivada* until the students arrived at a decision.

There was a huge media presence, but no one from the

administration was present. In shock, I asked the media, 'What was the reason for the suspension of my son?'. I questioned whether or not the authority had suspended him and why they did not inform me? I knew my son. Rohith was a brilliant student. I could not believe that he would have committed a mistake. I demanded that VC Appa Rao come out and give me an explanation.

The media started asking me continuously about my demands. I didn't even understand the concept of a 'demand'. Then I asked Raja, 'What does demand mean?' Raja said, 'Mummy, our first demand should be to revoke the suspension of the four students immediately; and the second demand should be that VC Appa Rao should give us an explanation about the incident'. Within two hours, the suspension was revoked.

The students informed me that a few eminent persons had come to the protest before my arrival and voiced their opinions against the suspension. They demanded that both the groups, the Akhil Bharatiya Vidyarthi Parishad (ABVP) members and the suspended students, sit down and resolve their differences. They pointed out that discriminatory action towards these students would jeopardize their lives.

While the student body and a handful of sensible people were making essential points, VC, Appa Rao, was saying, 'It is not up to me. A higher authority took this decision.' My question was: Why was it so difficult to revoke the suspension of the students before, and later how was it revoked immediately after my demand? Did the authorities wait for a bright young student to die? If they had revoked the suspension immediately, my son, Rohith, would be alive today.

Many people have called Rohith's death an institutional murder. What do you think?

He was murdered for sure. I think it was done because he was an educated Dalit.

Now there is a demand for legislation to end the caste-based discrimination in educational institutions and enact the Rohith Act; what do you think about it?

The Rohith Act should definitely be enacted. Before this incident, I did not know much about the universities or how strongly caste discrimination permeated our society. After Rohith's murder, I travelled to many universities, realizing that caste discrimination is rampant against the Dalits. I realized that Muslims and Dalits are being attacked everywhere in this country.

Before this incident, I never bothered to understand what was happening in society because I was deeply involved in earning a living and raising my children. Rohith's death made me see the reality of society. I had never heard of any student from dominant caste getting killed this way. I believe that now these (deprived) castes are improving their social status and getting a better education. Unfortunately, the people from the higher castes want to maintain the status quo and the existing hierarchy. Hence such incidents are occurring.

The upper castes are at the helm of all society's infrastructure – at the centre and in the states. At UoH, they punished the students because they wanted the Dalits to stop questioning the government, even though it is all citizens' constitutional right to question the government. The murder of Rohith was a message from the ruling party, which they wanted to send loud and clear: If Dalits raise their voices against them, they will face similar attacks. It's an aggressive and domineering way of maintaining their caste hierarchy.

After this incident, you mentioned that you travelled and campaigned across the country. You visited Delhi, Kerala, and many other states. How do we unite in our struggle? Do you see any avenues for building unity? What is your opinion on this?

Of course. We must unite, only then can we fight against our common enemy. There have been many attempts to bring about a unified, single platform. I absolutely encourage that initiative. Everyone – the Dalits, Muslims, and Other Backward Classes (OBCs) – should come together to fight against brahmanism. BCs think they are superior to us – however, it is not true – they are also oppressed. I saw certain things when I went to Delhi for the '*Chalo Delhi*' (Let's Go to Delhi) program. I was there for thirteen days, and I realized that after such a massive protest, in the end, we had to seek a politician's help. What occurs to me is that the Dalits need political power; we need to become political representatives. We must voice our opinions and stand up for improving our conditions. I mean true representation, not just being there in name only and acting like *chamchas* (stooges) of the upper caste. We should be able to stand in parliament and fearlessly voice our opinion. Only then can there be change.

What more do you think can be demanded to improve the life of the Dalits, minorities, and OBCs?

I am an ordinary person, and I can't think of such big issues by myself. I am not educated, but I can indeed say one thing – students should enter politics. Young blood needs to infuse our political movement. Most politicians are old and, at times, too soft in their views. Young people who can articulate the peoples' demands should enter politics; especially Dalit students, who are educated, should consider joining the direct political process.

According to you, to what extent is higher education important for Muslims, Dalits, and OBCs?

We need higher education because only through education can we understand the dynamics of society. Only with educated people can a country progress. Dr B.R. Ambedkar has clearly said that getting an education is of the utmost importance. For instance, Rohith knew many things and had a varied understanding of issues. That was possible only through higher education.

Rohith and others were protesting against the death penalty

given to someone who had already spent fourteen years in prison. The question of capital punishment is an important issue to debate. But the university responded by accusing all of them of being terrorists. The authorities believed that 'All Muslims are terrorists and those who support the Muslims are terrorists too'. To their uncritical minds, deep thoughts don't occur. I vaguely remember ACP Ramana saying, 'Amma, why does your son, Rohith, need higher education. This is where he will end up'. I replied by saying, 'Education is very significant to us. We are not just buying an education. My children worked hard, secured good ranks, and are studying. Being uneducated myself, I know the value of education and its impact. I don't know about society, but my aspirations for my children could only be fulfilled through higher education'.

What possibly could be the second reason for his suspension? His academic performance? He always passed every exam with flying colours. I think Rohith took the NET-JRF twice, and both times he passed easily. My children were studious individuals who went to the library, took good notes, studied hard, and passed the exams. It was a conspiracy to make my son a culprit by the VC and the government, who had a manuvadi mindset, killed Rohith. He would not have died otherwise.

Do you think the students should get fellowships, ensuring their dignity while studying? Do you think that the government should support education?

Yes, certainly. Not only this BJP-led government, but all previous governments have had no agenda for educating the Dalits and the Muslims. So, we should come together and create our own programme on how to educate the marginalized. In fact, the IAS and IPS officers from our community should mentor the students from downtrodden sections. We need a strong network and support from people to improve the education system.

That's true. But, by only using IAS and IPS, we cannot

ensure that all the students have access to education and are appropriately educated. But the government needs to take steps to make a more substantial impact, and if we, the Dalits, are part of that government, securing education as a right for the masses will be easier. What do you think? Education is commercialized now, and it has become highly unaffordable for the students belonging to the unprivileged sections of society. What are your views on this?

Of course! The government should take responsibility for educational institutions. Those living below the poverty line should have free education. Poor students and Dalits are bright and hardworking, but they do not have the resources to pursue education. At the same time, the wealthy and socially privileged students are well-educated and have a monopoly on education. For instance, those who have money buy seats in private medical colleges. The result is that their children, after completing their degree, fail to see themselves as doctors who should dedicate themselves to the treatment of their patients. Instead, they see their profession as merely a way to earn money. There is no social relevance in their education. They have only the minimum knowledge to carry out their jobs, whereas our children study rigorously and work hard. Since we are poor, we know the value of education and how it can uplift society. These children work hard, and they have a vision for changing society. They are highly knowledgeable children. We must have free education, and the government should provide it.

What is your vision for India?

I want every child to study and become an Ambedkar. Not like Ambedkar, but become an Ambedkar. If we're going to save our country, every child must be educated in every nook and cranny. We can protect ourselves and our country if all educated youths enter into politics and show that we can create a new life for everyone. Therefore, our children should get educated, enter politics, and become representatives to uplift our people. Whenever I go to any meeting, many people come just to talk to me, or they want to listen to me. They are interested. 'What will Amma say?' or 'What message will she give?'

This is what Rohith has given me – the value of my individuality and thoughts.

Acknowledgements

This book, *Students Won't be Quiet*, narrates the journey of student-led struggles throughout India in the last few years. It lays bare our refusal to cower in the face of the mighty State and their reactionary policies and how we drew inspiration from the breadth and depth of these struggles, covering key movements of our times. The book is a testimony to the unflinching bravery and the resilient collective struggles of the movement. It is a reference to guide us for the present-day struggles and teaches many lessons – preparing us to face the challenges of tomorrow.

We dedicate this book to the young student fighters of today and in the future.

It has been a long but persistent journey since the book was first conceptualized. In many ways, the authors and the respondents, through their writings and discussions, have shaped the book into what it has become. Perhaps, that's what a journey is all about, that things evolve in the process. We extend our gratitude to each contributor – the authors and the respondents who enriched this volume with their direct and lived experiences and impressions of the struggles.

This project of editing the volume gave us an opportunity to learn and re-learn a range of things. We are privileged to have our comrades and guides, Vijay Prashad and Srujana Bodapati, who not only have been extremely patient, but also have been an essential source of inspiration. LeftWord Books, especially Sudhanva Deshpande, have been very kind to allow us the time to slowly evolve this book. Without their support this project would have been incomplete.

A special thanks to Orijit Sen for designing the cover. His art has always stood with the downtrodden, and we are honoured to have his artwork become part of this book.

We are fortunate to have had Deborah Veneziale and Winnie Chauhan read the manuscript and enhance it through their editing. Deborah made essential contributions; her edits provoked us to think and modify many drafts, which was remarkable. Winnie patiently followed up the process and engaged in discussions in a way that made us feel at ease and overcame the pressure of submission time and again. Her meticulous reading and efficiency made it possible that this volume suffers from far fewer errors. We met these beautiful souls on this journey!

We extend our gratitude to the Tricontinental Research Team in India – Srujana, Subin, Srabani, Atul, Nitheesh, and Vikas. They contributed by offering support for transcription, verifying facts, and subsequent edits, connecting us to author(s)/respondent(s) *et al.* Prem has been of great help in getting us the necessary material.

In addition, we are grateful to several comrades who engaged with us in fruitful conversations and corroborated the facts and details of some of the historical events. We thank them for their input. We especially extend our gratitude to Suresh Garimella for reading the final draft of the manuscript, and drawing our attention to several minute details. We went to great lengths to ensure that the data and facts are accurate; if there are any mistakes, we are responsible for them.

The movements documented in this book speak of our collective strength, and how, when that strength is channelled to fight injustice and oppression, we shall be able to build an equal and just society. We must take up those challenges and fight to win.

Inqulab Zinabad!

Contributors

Abhinav Surya is currently pursuing a PhD in Economics at Center for Development Studies, Thiruvananthapuram. He graduated with BTech and MTech in Mechanical Engineering from IIT Madras (2017). He was formerly a Joint-Secretary of Free Software Movement, Karnataka, and formerly an active member of all Progressive Students' Organization at IIT Madras.

Aishe Ghosh is currently a Research Scholar at School of International Studies, Jawaharlal Nehru University. She is currently the President of the JNU Students' Union and Vice President of the Students' Federation of India Delhi State Committee.

Ameya Vivek Gore is an independent filmmaker, screenplay writer and editor, residing in Pune. He completed his education in film direction and screenplay writing from FTII in 2017. Ameya has made over 20 short films till date, engaging in fiction as well as non-fiction work.

Aravindhan Nagarajan is Assistant Professor at the Azim Premji University. His research areas include sustainability, climate change policy, and circular economy.

Dontha Prashanth is an assistant professor at Azim Premji University, Bangalore. He pursued PhD in Economics at the University of Hyderabad. Prashanth was active in student politics and served as the President of the HCU Students' Union. He also worked as the President of Ambedkar Students'

Association (ASA). Prashanth has published scholarly articles in different journals and books.

Fatima Nafees is the mother of missing JNU student, Najeeb Ahmed. Nafees has been fighting a hard legal battle confronting the state. Since the disappearance of her son Fatima Nafees has been taking part in movements and protests that seek to strengthen democracy and secularism.

Gaurav Gharde is a PhD researcher in Tyndall Centre for Climate Change research, at the University of Manchester. His research focuses on advancing the understanding of just transition in the power sector, with an emphasis on the Indian context.

Gitosri Sarkar is currently pursuing a PhD from Aliah University, Kolkata. She held the position of General Secretary of Arts Faculty Students' Union of Jadavpur University during 2014-2015. She also served as a Secretariat Member of the State Committee of Students' Federation of India (SFI), West Bengal.

Jishnu E. N. is a journalist based in Kerala. He completed post-graduation in Mass Communication from Pondicherry University. He was also the Secretary of the PU Students' Council during 2015-16.

Kadigalla Bhaskar is currently the District Secretary, CPI(M) of Ranga Reddy. Formerly he was the district President of CITU and Telangana state secretary of KVPS. Bhaskar was secretary of Students' Federation of India, undivided Andhra Pradesh. He became a whole timer of the movement soon after he finished his Engineering Diploma.

Kuldeep Singh Nagi was a former Students' Union President (2016-17) of University of Hyderabad. He was also the President of SFI HCU Unit during 2017-18. He completed his PhD in Economics titled 'Gender gap in educational performance among marginalized groups: A study of Andhra Pradesh and Telangana' from the School of Economics, University of Hyderabad. At present, he is working as a research associate at the Department of Economics, Indian Business School, Hyderabad. His area of specialization is Economics of Discrimination and Economics of Education.

Mineshi Mishra (BHU) is currently pursuing her PhD in Psychology from Banaras Hindu University. She completed both B.Sc., and M.Sc. in Psychology from BHU. She was a member of the Joint Action Committee during the 2017 movement at BHU for gender justice.

Pindiga Ambedkar works at Tricontinental Research. He completed his MA in Development Studies from TISS, Mumbai (2006-2008). He was the vice president of the TISS students' union during 2007-2008. He also did his MPhil in Sociology from CSSS, JNU(2009-2011). His research interests are Sociology of Education and Labour Issues. He is associated with Dalit Shoshan Mukti Manch, Delhi State.

Radhika Vemula is a single mother. She was a tailor. Since the institutional murder of her son, Rohith Vemula, she has been actively participating on issues and movements that impact students from marginalized backgrounds. She visited and addressed students' protests and meetings across India, and extended solidarity with students who are fighting to preserve the secular democratic fabric of the country.

Ranjith P.M. is an independent researcher who is currently working with the Office of the Minister for Public Works and Tourism, Government of Kerala. He is an invitee to the Central Executive Committee of the Democratic Youth Federation of India (DYFI). He holds a Master's degree in Women and Gender studies.

Sandeep Mahato is a doctoral candidate at the School of Habitat Studies, Tata Institute of Social Sciences, Mumbai. He works on Climate Change and Food Security.

Sangita Das is the joint secretary of Students' Federation of India, Assam State Committee. She is the co-convener of all-India Girls' Committee of SFI. She is the central secretariat member of SFI. Sangita holds Masters degrees in both Zoology and Sociology.

Satarupa Chakraborty is a researcher at Tricontinental Research. She is also a PhD candidate in the Center for Philosophy at JNU. Satarupa is currently a member of the state committee of All India Democratic Women's Association (AIDWA) Delhi. She was the general secretary of the Jawaharlal Nehru University Students' Union during 2016-2017. She completed her Masters from University of Hyderabad in 2012, and earned an MPhil degree in Philosophy from JNU in 2015.

Subhankar Chakraborty is a researcher and he is associated with the people's science movement in India. He is currently the General Secretary of Bharat Gyan Vigyan Samiti (BGVS), Karnataka. His primary research is in animal behaviour and population genetics. He has worked in several of the Bangalore based research institutions like IISc, NCBS and JNCASR.

Subin Dennis is an economist and activist, currently working as a researcher with Tricontinental Research. Hailing from Kerala, he holds M.A. and MPhil. degrees in economics from Jawaharlal Nehru University, New Delhi. He was active with the student movement, and served as the Delhi State Vice-President of the Students' Federation of India (SFI). Subin's writings in English and Malayalam on issues related to economy and politics appear in various periodicals and websites. He worked with the online news portal NewsClick before joining Tricontinental.

Suddhabrata Deb Roy is a PhD Candidate at the Department of Sociology, Gender Studies and Criminology at the University of Otago, New Zealand. He did his Masters from the University of Hyderabad. He mainly works on Marxist theory, analysis and politics. His work has appeared in journals like Capital and Class, TripleC, Journal of Graphic Novels and Comics, etc. His books include *Social Media and Capitalism* (Daraja Press, 2022) and *Mass Struggles and Leninism* (Phoneme Books, 2022). He is currently working on a book for Routledge on the impact of Covid 19 in India, along with his PhD.

Zuhail K.P. was the students' union president when the Rohit Vemula incident happened (2015-2016). He completed his PhD in physics from the University of Hyderabad and is currently working as an Assistant Professor of Physics at the University of Calicut.

Vikas Bhadauria is a Delhi-based journalist and activist. Vikas is a former president of the Students' Federation of India-Delhi State Committee. He currently works with NewsClick. His stories on law and public policy have appeared in The Leaflet, Live Law, and India Legal as well. He has an LLB degree and a Bachelor's degree in Science from the University of Delhi.

Vikram Singh is the joint secretary of All India Agricultural Workers' Union (AIAWU). He holds a PhD in Zoology from Himachal Pradesh University. He writes regularly on a range of issues concerning the rights of laborers, farmers, and students in various journals and news portals and newspapers in both Hindi and English. He was the general secretary of the Students' Federation of India between 2016 to 2018.